FOOTBALL IS LIFE

'freelance murderer' a send-off fit for a member of state. It was a national occasion and coverage was broadcast globally. He was survived by his wife Ceca and nine children.

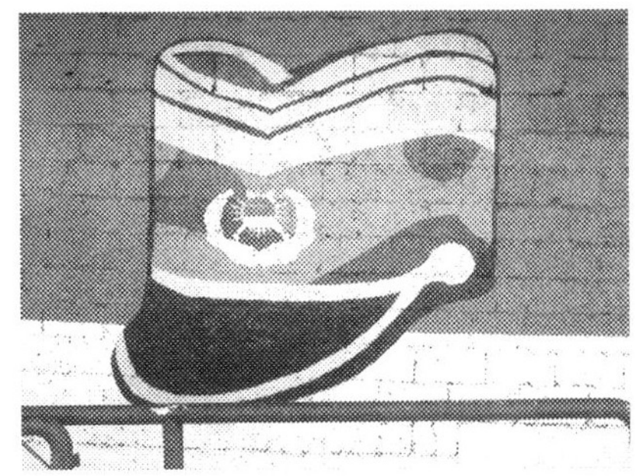

Arkan's grave and a tribute to him sprayed
on the wall of the Marakana Stadium

Despite a menacing glare from the ageing but able graveside security man, we took a few photographs, left Arkan in peace and took a taxi back to our hotel for a quick change of clothing before hitting the town.

I had no plans for a heavy night as it was now pouring down with rain and I still had a course of antibiotics to finish if I was to make a full recovery from the really virulent strain of man flu that had blighted my week. Rather than hit the town we headed for the Pietro Dell Oro Italian restaurant owned by Red Star legend Dejan Stankovic.

After being fed and watered and the night still young, we would have normally hit the city centre bars. However, the weather and my health had conspired against me and with a big day ahead, I ashamedly hit the sack before the clock struck midnight.

After a fitful night's sleep we were up and out by mid morning, taking in the sights of this bustling, cosmopolitan city. As we walked through Trg Republike (Republican Square) and up the pedestrianised boulevard of Kneza Mihailova, there was no sign of the previous evening's demonstration by Serbian nationalists protesting at the arrest of former Serb leader Radovan Karadzic for war crimes.

The 63-year-old war-crimes fugitive was arrested in July after spending almost thirteen years on the run. Former assistant US Secretary of State Richard Holbrooke, who brokered the 1995 Dayton accords that ended the four-year conflict, described Karadzic as the 'Osama Bin Laden of Europe'.

After the war, in April 1996, the Serbian Volunteer Guard was officially disbanded but with the threat of being reformed should the outbreak of war occur again. In March 1999, Arkan was indicted by the UN War Crimes Tribunal for atrocities committed during the Balkans civil war. It was a charge he vehemently denied. In response to the accusations, his prepared statement declared, 'I fought in the war in 1991 and 1992, Muslim soldiers were killed but my soldiers were killed too. I only killed enemy soldiers in a fair fight.'

The 1999 NATO bombing of the Federal Republic of Yugoslavia sent the rumour mill into overdrive. Western media reports alleged that Arkan's Tigers had been mobilised and sent to the new conflict in Kosovo. It was an accusation that Arkan denied, proclaiming that he would only fight NATO troops who were deployed on Yugoslav soil.

On 15 January 2000, Arkan was socialising with friends at the prestigious Intercontinental Hotel in central Belgrade when he was attacked by several armed assassins. In a highly organised premeditated attack, gunmen fired indiscriminately killing Arkan's bodyguard and his business associate. Arkan himself was shot in the face several times and died two hours later in hospital.

Three men were convicted of Arkan's murder. Dobrosav Gavric, aged 25, a former policeman and the man found guilty of pulling the trigger that claimed Arkan's life, received 20 years. Milan Djuricic and Dragan Nikolic, his accomplices, were sentenced to 15 years. Gavric, who was injured in the shooting, and his co-conspirator Djuricic were sentenced in their absence and remain at large. Five other defendants received lighter sentences ranging from three to nine years for their part in the gangland-esque execution.

Despite the convictions, family, friends and supporters of the Serb warlord were not convinced that the right people had been sentenced. Zeljko 'Arkan' Raznatovic was a fervent Serb nationalist. He lived a colourful life characterised by his gangster lifestyle and made numerous underworld enemies during his rise to prominence. Some think he was a victim of the establishment and believe that security forces acting upon the orders of Slobodan Milosevic assassinated him. Others suspected it was little more than a gangland hit by rival Mafiosi.

Forty-seven-year-old Arkan was buried at the Novo Groblje cemetery on 20 January 2000. Thousands of mourners attended the funeral, giving the man vilified by the world's press and once described as a

Football-related violence was on the increase in Serbia, especially in Belgrade, and fans were becoming increasingly more violent and difficult to control. Concerned by this, senior members of Slobodan Milosovic's Serbian administration were said to have approached Arkan to assume control of the Red Star supporters' club in the hope that he could pull the strings of the masses and rein them in.

He revelled in his new role as leader and his first task was to bring a halt to the infighting and unite the north stand. In 1989, the Delije (heroes/fighters) was born. Delije was the name given to Arkan's hard-core hooligans, many of whom matured to form the core of the notorious Tigers paramilitary group, also known as the Serbian Volunteer Guard.

Two of many Delije murals sprayed on the wall of Red Star's Marakana Stadium

Football hooligans from both the Delije and the Grobari were selected by Arkan and his henchmen and sent to private military training camps. It was here that Arkan turned the scourge of the terracing into an elite fighting machine that was at the forefront of military operations in the bloody civil war.

Arkan's Tigers were said to have been instrumental in the taking of the border town Vukovar, where an outraged anti-Milosovic Western media reported that around 250 men were removed from the sanctuary of their hospital refuge, transported to a nearby pig farm in Ovcara and systematically executed. Controversy followed this ruthless band of militia for the entirety of the civil war and their actions were condemned by political leaders throughout Europe and the rest of the world. But despite being widely accused of ethnic cleansing, barbarity and war profiteering, the Tigers were hailed back home as true Serb patriots.

his criminal behaviour was spiralling out of control, on his release from incarceration media reports suggest Zeljko's father used his influence to find him a position within the feared Yugoslav State Security Services (UBDA). But despite his father's best efforts to keep him on the straight and narrow, the gritty young Zeljko had other ideas.

In the early 1970s a youthful Raznatovic left Serbia and travelled to northern Europe, where he masterminded a series of daring bank raids. It was during this period that he picked up the *nom de guerre* Arkan. Fellow mobster and partner in crime Goran Vukovic once gloated, 'Of all of us, Arkan robbed the most banks; he walked into them like they were self-service stores – banks were his specialty as well as escapes from prison.'

However, Zeljko kept getting caught. The Belgians apprehended him in 1974 and convicted him of armed robbery. He was imprisoned for ten years but escaped after serving just over a third of his sentence. In 1979, he was arrested in Holland where he was convicted for his part in three more armed robberies and sentenced to seven years' imprisonment. But he escaped again, less than two years later.

In 1981, he was shot by German police during a bungled raid in Frankfurt. Ignorant of his criminal past and his capacity to escape custody, the Germans naively put him in the prison hospital under light guard. Needless to say, he escaped again soon afterwards.

Media reports claim Zeljko was also responsible for a daring courtroom rescue. Fellow gangster Carlo Fabianni absconded from the dock after a brazen Raznatovic burst into a Swedish court brandishing a couple of handguns, throwing one to his partner in crime in the dock whilst threatening the judge with the other, before making a speedy getaway.

The elusive Serb career criminal was understood to have passports in various nationalities and used at least forty aliases, including Arkan, the name by which he was later to gain worldwide notoriety. He returned to Belgrade quite a wealthy man but his criminal exploits in Europe and outstanding arrest warrants, including one by Interpol, meant that Arkan was a virtual prisoner in his own country.

On his return, with the help of some of Belgrade's most distasteful but influential characters, he set about building an empire that would make him one of the most powerful and feared underworld crime-lords in Serbia.

Football Is Life

Shaun Duffy

JANUS PUBLISHING COMPANY LTD
Cambridge, England

First published in Great Britain 2013
by Janus Publishing Company Ltd
The Studio
High Green
Great Shelford
Cambridge CB22 5EG

www.januspublishing.co.uk

British Library Cataloguing-in-Publication Data
A catalogue record for this book is available from the British Library

ISBN 978-1-85756-808-0

Cover Design: Brian Cannon – Microdot Creative

Printed and bound in the UK by PublishPoint
from KnowledgePoint Limited, Reading

What is a club in any case? Not the buildings or the directors or the people who are paid to represent it. It's not the television contracts, get-out clauses, marketing departments or executive boxes. It's the noise, the passion, the feeling of belonging, the pride in your city. It's a small boy clambering up stadium steps for the very first time, gripping his father's hand, gawping at that hallowed stretch of turf beneath him and, without being able to do a thing about it, falling in love.

Sir Bobby Robson (1933–2009)

Contents

Foreword	ix
Introduction Love Football, Hate Modern Football	xvii
Meet the Sopranos The Veciti Derby Partizan Belgrade v Red Star Belgrade	1
Total Football … Violence *De Klassieker* Ajax Amsterdam v Feyenoord Rotterdam	45
Rajmund and Remik R.I.P. The Wielkie Derby Ruch Chorzow v Gornik Zabrze	69
The Green Mile … and a Half O Classico Benfica v Sporting Lisbon	93
Desperately Seeking Dinamo The Marele Derby Dinamo Bucharest v Steaua Bucharest	113
Relentless The Gradski Derby FK Zeljeznicar v FK Sarajevo	137
No One Likes Us … We Don't Care A Derby Ujpest v Ferencvaros	173

Les Enfants Terribles
Le Classique
Paris Saint-Germain v Olympique de Marseille 199

A Pictorial Tribute to the Supporters ... because
Football without Fans is Nothing ... AMF 233

Afterword – a Brief Update 239

Bibliography 263

Foreword

The football bug has always been in my blood and is the primary reason behind my perpetual-travel lifestyle. Since my eighteenth birthday, I have been fortunate enough to have watched over 200 football matches outside the UK, taking in 162 cities in thirty-nine different countries. I have also enjoyed every single minute of it and without question, apart from family stuff, they have been the best years of my life.

I didn't want to write about the mainstream classicos as I found them to be a great disappointment. Most are little more than tourist traps devoid of any real atmosphere and represent much of what is wrong with the modern game.

The quality of football has never been in doubt in the super classicos. Barcelona and Real Madrid don't do mediocrity. This book, though, is not about quality football. It's all about going back to basics and experiencing proper old-school football cultures and the atmospheres generated by genuine grassroots supporters, in particular the Ultras, a much-maligned worldwide fan movement responsible for the birth of extreme fandom over sixty years ago. I wanted to immerse myself deeply into their fan culture. I wanted to experience fanaticism and danger. I wanted to understand the heated rivalry, hatred and passion of rival supporters whose lifelong obsession with their team knows no bounds.

In my world, fans are equally as important as the players we idolise. After all, we sign a lifelong contract with no get out clause It's a birthright; a sense of belonging. From the cradle to the grave, from one generation to another, in good times and in bad times, supporters are at the heart of everything a club achieves.

A supporter's obsession with their club has a bearing on almost every facet of their life. It can shape childhoods, destroy relationships and sabotage friendships. But football is a simple equation: Football = Life.

As my middle-aged memory bank had reached its overdraft limit, documenting past experiences was not an option. So it was on to pastures new and a search for the beautiful game that didn't yet fully incorporate the so despised 'modern football template' and its corporate mentality and where football is still an affordable commodity for its working-class communities.

This isn't a book about football viewed through rose-tinted spectacles. This is reality football, based on personal experience, interviews with supporters and hours of painstaking research. Nothing compares to the experience of a fierce-rivalry match, especially a cross-town derby, the most eagerly anticipated game on the fixture list.

Derbies and grudge matches are the pinnacle of football rivalry and provide thought-provoking writing material. There is something uniquely compelling about a tear-up between bitter rivals. The hostility stoked up at these habitually brutal encounters is a recipe for chaos, both on and off the field. These are games that can transform even the most reticent of supporters into a match-day villain. Football quite simply turns some of us into monsters that are barely recognisable within the confines of a stadium.

Football is tribal, generating an intense rivalry that can often descend into violence. This is a worldwide phenomenon that makes football a unique spectator sport. Some countries deal with fan violence well, others are lawless, making match days an unpleasant experience for the naive and faint hearted.

Football can also be a breeding ground for racism. Parts of Spain and much of Eastern Europe with its growing right-wing skinhead culture are plagued with the problem. But the hierarchy in the top echelons of the game choose to ignore it or pay it lip service. It is an accepted evil in many places and I witnessed this together with fan violence on many occasions during my travels.

Beyond the negatives are many positives. My travels gave me a fascinating insight into the multitude of different supporters' groups that bless the world's most watched sport.

To understand the traditions and the subcultures that exist within the game, you have to meet the supporters who have kept them alive throughout the decades and you have to comprehend the strength of their passion for football. In this book I have tried to encapsulate the history and tradition of eight matches that are less significant in terms of quality football, but fiercely chaotic and passionate in terms of fan rivalry. And where the clubs involved made a name for themselves before the global commercialisation of football kicked in. Nowadays, most of these clubs are famed for their mutual dislike of one another and erratic fan behaviour rather than their storied histories.

Football is Life is a pictorial travel memoir written from within the eye of the storm of extreme fandom. Terrace indiscretions are born of an explosive concoction of contrasting variables and football is the vehicle used to transport them. Geography (North v South), politics (Left v Right) and class (Rich v Poor) dominate UK, European and South American fan rivalry, whereas the Middle Eastern fan scene is plagued by complex, religiously (Christianity, Islam and Judaism) motivated outbreaks of violence that has led to many games being played out behind closed doors because of the risk of widespread sectarian violence. Religious fanaticism and military interference has decimated league structures in much of the increasingly volatile Middle East region, which has been blighted by prejudice and where violent disorder has in some cases resulted in the needless deaths of both players and supporters.

With the exception of the Old Firm derby in Scotland and the ingrained sectarian hatred in Northern Ireland, such religious complexities have never been an issue in the relative calm (in comparison) of the UK. In total contrast, British fan rivalries are, in the main, quite simply geographical or territorial, brought about by a boot-boy movement inspired by music and fashion. Punks and skinheads were the original terrace bovver boys before the mod revival in the late 1970s became the unlikely catalyst for the birth of the unruly football casuals and their designer label dress code. Consumed by hooliganism, UK stadia and the surrounding areas were often transformed into bloody battlegrounds as yobs waged war at every opportunity.

The European fan scene, one of extreme partisanship, became entrenched in gang warfare shortly after football violence reached its apex in the UK. The world's media christened the newly spawned 1980s European hooligan phenomenon the 'English disease' and blamed copycat outbreaks of gang violence on the behaviour of England's vast army of travelling supporters who wreaked havoc on away trips to European games.

Despite the hooligan problems, one thing that has remained constant in European football is fan support and the ungovernable emotion their religion (football) brings to the stadium. Through the prism of football, fans unleash a frenzy of aggression like no other fan culture in the world.

The most fanatical of the many fan groups that grace the European scene is the Ultra (fan) movement and contrary to popular belief, the origins of Ultra fan culture can be traced back to the former Yugoslavia in 1950. The hard-core supporters of Hajduk Split are believed to have formed the first Ultra group. Calling themselves Torcida Split, they still exist over sixty years later. It's a subculture that has spread worldwide, particularly in South America but more so in Italy, where the largest and most extreme Ultra groups are based.

Torcida Split, founded 28 October 1950 – two famous old school banners displayed at Hajduk Split games

Ultra mentality can be a somewhat complex and politically charged affair. Italy, in particular, has a sizeable contingent of powerful right-wing Ultra groups that have an unquenchable thirst for violence and have been responsible for much of the negative publicity geared towards the Ultra movement. For the vast majority of Ultras, however, violence is not a trademark of their mindset. They have a deep obsessive love of the game and in a football era dominated by wealth, it is remarkable just how much sway these fanatical supporters hold on their clubs. They are a very powerful, unofficial professional fan movement and their influence should not be underestimated. A passionate sport like football thrives on the energy these supporters bring to the game.

Ultras are loyal to their colours and their primary role in the stadium is to choreograph a tsunami of choral domination. They are extreme supporters who provide an intense energy and are famed for creating amazing *tifos* (Italian term for choreography), the official art form of the terraces. Spectacularly choreographed card displays, huge murals, pyrotechnics, smoke pots, firecrackers and streamers are all used in an effort to generate a cauldron of invincibility. And drums, together with the obligatory megaphone for the curva's capo, come as standard. Opposition teams are often greeted by a cacophony of noise and subjected to relentless orchestrated chanting for the whole ninety minutes. These are ingenious scenes that every football fan should witness at some point during their lifetime.

Some *tifos* take months to plan; the more important the game the more spectacular the show. Many of the groups have a base within the confines of their club and from there they can socialise and plan match-day choreography with military precision. *Tifos* can be expensive and to subsidise the cost of materials, the Ultra groups sell their own lines of unofficial club merchandise. Sales of t-shirts, hoodies, pin badges, scarves, calendars and fanzines all help bring in vital funding for terrace choreography. Even the clubs themselves are known to contribute towards costs.

Six decades of infamy, however, are now under threat. Cloaked in a poisonous blanket of illusion, weaving their modern football spell from deep in the shadows, the super-savvy business moguls with their nefarious hidden agendas are responsible for trying to sanitise the much loved Ultra-dominated cathedrals of noise. The Ultras' way of life is slowly being forced away from the terraces by these ruthless capitalist terrorists who want to eradicate all traces of traditional old-school support from thier modern stadia in their unforgiving pursuit of profiteering. Soaring admission prices and fan-unfriendly kick-off times dictated by a media powerbase that continues to maintain its iron grip on the game are having a detrimental effect on football-mad working-class communities. The maximisation of profits, reduction in competition, elitism and the once loyal players who are now primarily motivated by money have jeopardised the true spirit of the game.

But in a defiant defence of their sacred fan culture, the Ultra movement has recently ignited the 'Against Modern Football' campaign and actively protest and fight together in a unified stance against the global commercialisation of football that is leading to a gradual embourgeoisement of the beautiful game. As a result of the protestations, an age-old simmering feud between fans and security forces has been further exacerbated to breaking point. Many years of unwarranted police brutality towards the Ultras and a skewed justice system that is guilty of disproportionate, draconian sentencing, in some cases seeing football fans incarcerated for longer than paedophiles and rapists, has instilled a bitter 'us v them' mentality into the movement and resulted in a widely publicised hate campaign against law enforcement. ACAB (All Cops Are Bastards) banners are unveiled in stadia every weekend and ACAB graffiti can be seen sprayed across towns and cities throughout Europe, even more so in Eastern Europe where police repression is the most aggressive.

ACAB – All Cops are B******s

Hard-core football fans live life on the edge; it's an occupational hazard. But meeting these supporters and understanding their motives and beliefs, while not justifying the violence and skulduggery, it certainly helps put a perspective on the insanity of football rivalry.

A football atmosphere can be an exhilarating experience. But you have to accept that when staunchly loyal supporters deposit a lifetime of emotional investment into a team, it becomes pretty apparent that at some stage patience will sap. Tempers will become frayed. Rationality will go AWOL. And the outbreak of disorder becomes almost inevitable. No other sport is capable of bringing out – 'Mr Hyde' – like football and its temples of worship!

Fan-on-fan violence is a by-product of the game that has tainted our national sport for over a century. It's an inexplicable form of sadistic, gratuitous blood-lust generated by a dwindling number of the beautiful game's terrace faithful. A small minority choose to embrace it; the majority choose to shun it. But contrary to popular belief, despite the erratic exterior of the terrace rebel, football is life for all the cultured aficionados who devote their very existence to the weekend and their fix of football madness!

Let's not kid ourselves, football does have a dark and sinister side, it always has done and always will do. Football atheists, tabloid scribes and the game's detractors in the political arena, having never been a part of the match-day congregation, can never understand the mentality of football's extreme fan groups or the game's violence-prone subcultures that so often dominate the news headlines.

Whether supporters are Ultras, skinheads, casuals or politically motivated, to brand them all hooligans is little more than reactive tabloid journalism designed to grab the attention of the masses and damage the reputation of football's true disciples ... it's rank-and-file supporters!

Introduction

Love Football, Hate Modern Football

> Football is for the fans. It can be the greatest game in the world but if there are no people to watch it, it becomes nothing. The fans are the lifeblood of the game.
>
> Jock Stein CBE 1922–1985

The worst tragedy in the history of British football was to unwittingly become the catalyst for sweeping changes that would turn the modern game into a toxic monster. The 1989 Hillsborough disaster (JFT96) saw police incompetence play an unforgivable, pivotal role in the deaths of ninety-six men, women and children. Protected by an immoral Thatcher government and despite evidence to the contrary, Chief Superintendant Duckenfield and his police officers on duty have continually denied responsibility for their role in the needless tragedy. The truth will out.

Following the disaster, Lord Justice Taylor conducted a detailed, emotional enquiry and issued a 'final report' directed to formulating final and long-term objectives regarding the need for crowd control and safety at sports grounds. One of the key elements in that report was to enforce a policy of all-seated stadia in top-flight English football.

Saturday 15 August 1992 heralded the inception of an exciting new era in the 104-year history of the beautiful game. In hindsight, it was for me and my ilk the beginning of the end. Welcome to the newly formed English Premier League (EPL), where cash is king and a greed is good philosopy, is shamelessly promoted without fear of consequence.

The inaugural EPL was primarily created to generate much-needed financial support to help meet the rising costs of Lord Justice Taylor's radical, indeed groundbreaking, proposals. Money-spinning television revenue and sponsorship negotiations were key fundamentals to the funding of the recommendations that were set to transform English football beyond all recognition.

I, along with the rest of the lemming brigade, bought into this new format and looked forward to being a part of the exciting new transformation that was unleashed upon us in a blaze of publicity. Fast-forward twenty years and I, like the majority of supporters from my generation, have nothing but growing contempt for the agents, the self-obsessed badge-kissing mercenaries that take supporters for granted and, most of all, the asset-stripping vultures who burden our clubs with unmanageable debts.

Lord Triesman raised concerns about debt levels in the Premier League back in 2008. When declaring that debt posed a 'tangible danger' to the game, a swathe of indignation was thrust upon him by the Premier League illuminati who suggested the former FA chairman was a 'divisive figure'. Sports writer Oliver Holt condemned the frenzied campaign to blacken Triesman's character, rightly pointing to the downfall of Portsmouth and the monstrous debt at Manchester United, both clear examples of Triesman's concerns.

Like many others before me, football was my life from the moment I was conceived. Being a football supporter is a vocation; It's what we we're born to do. A family trait inherited from parents and grandparents and passed down through the generations to become a way of life. Football offers escapism that gives us a release from our everyday mundaneness. For ninety minutes we are at one with the team and the congregation, not knowing whether we are going to win, lose or draw. But it doesn't matter. Supporting your team runs much deeper than a result. It's about a unique emotional bond; an impenetrable bond that takes the art of supporting a team to the highest level of dedication.

Regrettably, the self-appointed parasites masquerading as custodians of our national sport have preyed upon the unconditional blind faith of loyal, working-class, football-mad families whose devotion is unwavering. No obstacle too big. No distance too far. No match day unacceptable. No kick-off time too early. No kick-off time too late. No ticket price too high!

The 1993 season saw lucrative television and sponsorship deals secured, guaranteeing significant long-term income. The football world was proclaimed to be teeming with promise and expectation. In 1996, almost thirty years after winning our one and only World Cup, England played host to the prestigious European Football Championships. Football had officially come home. This for me was the year that football became fashionable, accruing an influx of sycophantic Z-list celebrities and a posse of unimportant hangers-on.

I firmly believe that in a bid to re-invent the game's image and extract more revenue from a somewhat gullible British public, the FA, in cahoots with the satellite broadcasting companies they sold out to, set about dismantling the values and fraternal traditions of the great British working-class supporter, with the aim of manufacturing a new breed of football spectator; the consumer!

Suckered in by the euphoria of Euro 96, the fair-weather, suburban middle-Englanders targeted by the FA's spin doctors bought into the new look and helped transform OUR beloved game into the bourgeois product that it has become today. The prawn sandwich munchers flocked to the game in their droves and brought about a different crowd dynamic. The terrace revolution had started in earnest and quickly spread to the domestic scene.

What followed was the progressive alienation of the rank-and-file supporters whose no-frills dedication has served the sport well for over a century. They are without question the lifeblood of OUR game. Back in the day, supporters were a part of the entertainment on match day. Nowadays they just go to be entertained.

Few would dispute that atmospheres are not what they used to be. Long gone are the days of supporting your club with religious zeal. Atmospheres are much flatter and more sterile these days and the introduction of all-seated stadia has undoubtedly been a major contributing factor towards that. And gone are the halcyon days of old when match day was an affordable bonding session between like-minded individuals who got high on camaraderie that only football could conjure up. The concrete terraces where supporters stood side by side and brought stadia to life are sorely missed and all suggestions of a compromise are firmly rejected. Powerful images and compelling moments from the past are now consigned to the history books. The sadness of lifeless football stadia is something only a true fan can identify with.

It is blatantly evident that there is growing spectator discontent with the process of transformation in football. Match day is sadly no longer an affordable commodity for many working-class families, which in turn has led to a lost generation of fans, and because of this I have now developed a loathing of the modern game that has become almost immeasurable.

The reintroduction of traditional standing areas is still a very controversial and emotive issue. It just isn't going to happen. 'I wouldn't take the risks,' insisted former FA chairman Lord Triesman, when quizzed on the subject. The Premier League hierarchy lionised Triesman's stance by insisting that crowd safety would not be compromised and that reverting back to concrete terraces was not negotiable.

In March 1993, in response to the increase in football-related disorder, the introduction of all-seated stadia was mooted by the German Football Federation but they decided against it and chose instead to pursue the concept of regulated standing areas.

'Abolishing standing areas would make it considerably more difficult for socially disadvantaged football supporters to attend their team's matches,' declared the federation. 'Football, being a people's sport, should not banish the socially disadvantaged from its stadia, and it should not place its social function in doubt.'

Although the tragedy of the Hillsborough disaster certainly adds credence to the FA's stance, it doesn't stop me looking on with envy at our forward-thinking German counterparts, who have incorporated excellently designed safe standing areas into their world-class stadia. Sky TV money hasn't yet got a firm grip in the Fatherland, where football is still an affordable commodity for everybody to enjoy. Facilitating reasonably priced safe standing zones has helped to establish a special intensity on the terraces in Germany. It's a passion that is sadly lacking in top-flight football stadia in the UK.

The abhorrent sign of our times was highlighted by the infamous Roy Keane 'prawn sandwich brigade' rant after Manchester United's Champions League game against Dynamo Kiev on 8 November 2000.

'Sometimes you wonder, do they understand the game of football? ... We're 1–0 up, then there are one or two stray passes and they're getting on players' backs ... Away from home our fans are fantastic, I'd call them hard-core fans. But at home they have a few drinks and probably the prawn sandwiches and they don't realise what's going on, on the pitch. I don't think some of the people who come to Old Trafford can spell football, never mind understand it.'

Since the birth of the Premiership, there is no doubt that modern stadia are now safer places designed at great expense for comfort and security. Nobody would dispute that facilities have been vastly improved to accommodate a modern game-day experience. Nobody would dispute that the crowd violence and racism that characterised the 1970s and 1980s has, barring isolated incidents, been eradicated from British football stadia and nobody would dispute that the Premiership's unprecedented wealth has enriched our game by attracting a host of world-class foreign imports at the top of their profession.

Unfortunately the ills of old have been replaced with the ills of modern football and the expense that comes with it. We have to endure a generation of greedy agents representing tattooed, designer-watch-wearing teenagers, who change their flash cars more often than they change their socks. We have to endure overpaid, substandard foreign imports that are limiting the opportunity of our home-grown kids. We have to endure a new generation of players that cheat, sulk and dive their way through games without fear of meaningful retribution.

We have to endure an archaic FA that lacks cohesive vision and is a closed shop cut from the same cloth as the UEFA and FIFA mafiosi! Jobs for the boys where only yes men need apply! An organisation that has completely lost sight of what football means to supporters and has catastrophically failed us by allowing the game's finances to spiral out of control, leaving many clubs heading towards the precipice.

In the UK, our clubs have storied traditions but our once famous cultural institutions have now become costly playthings that enable Machiavellian billionaire oligarchs and business-savvy trillionaire oil barons to monopolise the game's wealth in their relentless, long-term pursuit of profiteering from the global commercialisation of our beautiful game.

Modern stadia and the tournaments and finals they host are geared towards corporate entertainment. Despite Lord Taylor warning against fans being priced out of the game, ticket prices have increased steadily above the rate of inflation every year since the launch of the Premier League. And kick-off times are aligned to be screened for prime-time viewing in Asia, as our rapacious cash-crazed custodians seek to expand our national sport globally in their efforts to maximise their profits. The beautiful game has turned ugly and is fast losing its status as a working-class sport for working-class people.

Drink and sex scandals dominate the headlines and drunken loutish behaviour has become the norm for some players who appear out of control and totally divorced from reality. Inordinate wealth at such a vulnerable age has alienated many young footballers from their working-class roots and is largely responsible for the ever widening gap developing between players and supporters. Add to this the overinflated ticket prices, the power of corporate sponsorship, the satellite TV domination of the fixture list and the demise of the 3pm Saturday afternoon kick-off. It's an unfolding tragedy of epic proportions. Our clubs have souls and those souls are not worth selling – not at any price. Football belongs to the people; it's the people's game. Football without fans is nothing!

There is for sure a mounting disdain for footballers like no other sportspeople. Money has corrupted our game and turned players into demigods. We have reached a point where the game's supporters have been gradually moulded into consumers. Mini cash cows being milked dry on demand! With each passing season, overinflated ticket prices are hiked up even further. The overpriced football kit market doesn't appear to have a saturation point and clever marketing strategies are being deployed in a bid to further exploit the nation's football-mad devotees.

Supporters are an integral part of the game, a fact the money-driven neophytes who now run the sport appear to dismiss with arrogance. To the suited and booted capitalists we are merely cash registers subsidising an exorbitant wage bill created by money-mad agents, whose only aim is to make themselves and their clients as rich as possible.

It's the undying passion of loyal supporters that has made the game what it is today. Our revered fan mentality brings our football temples to life, not corporate mentality.

With the English game now terminally infected by the 'corporate mafia', our footballing cathedrals sanitised by the 'prawn sandwich brigade' and a modern fan scene that has alienated many grassroots supporters, I had to travel away from the inhibited 'library like' English stadia in search of the rivalries that really justified the hype.

My journey begins in Belgrade ...

Meet the Sopranos

The Veciti Derby

Game: Partizan Belgrade 1 – 2 Red Star Belgrade
Venue: Partizan Stadion
Date: 5 May 2007
Attendance: 12,592

'Welcome to Belgrade,' beamed Rajko, as he greeted Michael and me outside our hotel reception. After a brief and slightly nervous introduction, he pointed to our transportation, a battered old Fiat Ugo parked opposite the hotel. 'Serbian Aston Martin', he joked, laughing out loud. Although Rajko spoke little English he had obviously mastered sarcasm, a typically British sense of humour.

Rajko is hard-core Partizan and very highly respected in the Gravedigger community. A proud, nationalistic Serb, Rajko was indoctrinated into the Partizan way of life from a very young age and was at the forefront of the 1980s terrace revolution that propelled the Grobari to legendary status.

Rajko's brother, Dragan, was our driver and his young English-speaking cousin, Alex, was our interpreter for the afternoon. We made a brief cigarette and petrol stop then headed to the customary derby-day watering hole on the outskirts of Belgrade.

We parked up outside a small, unassuming property in a quiet suburban street, but upon entry found it to be a homely little bar, frequented by a number of mature, dodgy-looking characters; *The*

Sopranos immediately sprang to mind. Rajko introduced us to bar owner and Tony Soprano lookalike Combe. He was head honcho and immediately arranged drinks for us. Combe, who also spoke very little English, introduced us to the rest of the group before seating us at the top table.

The smoky room, characteristic of an old-fashioned drinking den, was sparse in decoration and fitted out with only the basic amenities. A small but adequate bar area, a large freestanding fridge with a plentiful supply of cheap bottled beer and several long tables with enough chairs to seat a large family. Photographs of Radovan Karadzic and General Ratko Mladic, both war-crimes fugitives, hung proudly on the wall behind the bar. And a large mural depicting a thuggish looking Grobari skinhead posing proudly within the ruins of a brick wall was the scene-stealing focal point of this ultra-nationalistic bar.

Grobari 1970 mural

The majority of blokes in here, including the mural's artist, Zare, were founder members of the infamous Partizan 'Grobari 1970' fan group, strictly old-school and famous throughout the world. The names of the primary founder members of the group were written in Serbian Cyrillic beneath the skinhead mural on a roll of honour.

Organised fan groups first became apparent at the old JNA Stadium during the early 1950s and legendary Partizan supporter Voja Pancevac is credited with being one of the earliest terrace leaders on the JNA. The charismatic Pancevac, from Pancevo in Vojvodina, started life in the north stand but earned his iconic status on the south towards the end of the 1960s. He is widely accepted as Partizan's first capo.

The Partizan youth academy, which even today is rated as one of the best in the world, was responsible for producing the core of the team that won four league titles in five years between 1961 and 1965 and then went on to contest the 1966 European Cup Final against a formidable Real Madrid side. Their narrow 2–1 defeat at the Heysel Stadium in Brussels was seen as a huge achievement for the Eastern European underdogs and was greatly responsible for raising the club's profile. As a result of the most successful period in the club's history, there was a vast increase in their fan base and a new generation of Partizan supporters took up their place on the terraces at Humska Street.

The year 1970 is widely associated with the birth of one of the world's most formidable fan movements, the infamous Grobari. Meaning gravediggers or undertakers, the nickname originated during the late 1960s and was used by neighbouring Crvena Zvezda (meaning Red Star) supporters as a derogatory reference to the team's traditional black and white colours which were associated with the uniform of the local gravediggers. The stadium is situated on Humska (meaning tomb) Street and is also in close proximity to the nearby Topsider cemetery. But much to the annoyance of their rivals, rather than take umbrage at the term Grobari, Partizan supporters actually embraced the epithet and transformed it into a worldwide identity.

Grobari Jug, meaning Grobari South (south stand) is home to the diehard fanatics and self-proclaimed hooligans who express their devotion to the club in outrageous fashion. The Partizan hard core are responsible for some of the craziest shenanigans you're ever likely to see at a football match. They primarily focus on crowd noise with a deafening support that transforms the cathedral of death into a fortress on match days. The sense of overwhelming intimidation thrust upon visiting teams has been integral to the club's success throughout the years. Famed for their show-stealing choreographed designs, the terraces are often awash with black-and-white scarves, flags, banners and streamers, enhancing an atmosphere that really justifies the hype. And they use enough burning flares, firecrackers and smoke pots to transform the stadium into a rip-rooaarrriinng inferno of raw emotion.

Throughout the years, the silhouette of a sexton leaning on his shovel has become recognised worldwide as the universal symbol for the timeless Grobari fan movement that has now become a recognised brand name in itself.

The Grobari symbol for the notorious South Stand

Aleksandar, a young gravedigger from the Grobari Skojpe group based in Macedonia, tried to explain the mentality of the cult-like Grobari Jug. 'We have rules on the south,' said Alex. 'We are in many ways similar to an army.' The oldest and most respected group within the Grobari fan movement is Grobari 1970 and they are considered by many to be the General.

Then there are the three Colonels – Alcatraz, Juzni Front and Grobari Beograd. They are the command centre and responsible for almost everything that happens on the terraces. The Alcatraz firm are for sure the most dangerous group on the south. They use the name Alcatraz because most of the leaders in that group have been to prison.

The Juzni Front (*juzni* meaning south), formed in 1999, is a mixture of subgroups from all over Belgrade and along with Grobari Beograd, is a large fan group and very highly respected at the stadium.

These four groups are comprised from the many subgroups who are thought of as the infantry or foot soldiers. The most prominent subgroups are the 300-strong Niski Kartel, Erotica, Shadows, South Family, Headhunters, Grobari Krusevac, Grobari Dorcol, Grobari West Serbia, Grobari Skopje, Grobari Niksic, Grobari Zvezdara, Grobari Padinjak, Extreme Boys Crew, Brain Damage Firm and the very active and dangerous Young Boys.

There are also many Grobari members from different cities in Serbia and other parts of the former Yugoslavia, including Montenegro, Bosnia, Croatia and Macedonia. Each Grobari group and subgroup has their own banner at the stadium, some of which are many years old and have priceless sentimental value to the supporters.

Young Boys

Shadows

Alcatraz

Niski Kartel

South Guard

Grobari Krusevac

Extreme Boys Crew

Head Hunters Obrenovac

Although football is the religion of Sport Club Partizan, the Grobari support every team associated with this elite sporting institute. Like many sports societies in Eastern Europe, these diehard fans turn up and travel en masse to games involving the club's (men's and women's) basketball, handball, water polo and hockey teams. And wherever Grobari go, the infamous black-and-white mobocracy ensues!

Rajko and his friends in the bar are the core members of the Grobari 1970 fan group, named after the year Grobari was born. Most of these lads formed the nucleus of the famous Kaznena Ekspedicija (Penalty Expedition Crew aka Riot Squad) whose motto was *Do groba uz Partizan* – With Partizan to the grave.

In the early 1980s, the most prominent units of Gravediggers, Commando, Kop Crew and Old Guards, pioneered the formidable Kaznena Ekspedicija, the most dangerous group in the former Yugoslavia. The Riot Squad, a 500-strong mob of terrace revolutionaries, brought about a new crowd dynamic to the Yugoslav football scene and thrust the south stand into a prolonged era of violence and skulduggery. They were the country's first organised football firm and they travelled the length and breadth of the former Yugoslavia and beyond to support their team during a period of what can only be described as pure footballing madness.

They took inspiration from the English fan scene and created a new identity for themselves. And as in the UK, music, particularly punk rock, and fashion played a huge part in the popularisation of this newly spawned terrace subculture. They travelled to away games by train and brought chaos to every town or city that hosted them, often greeted by perplexed locals with sheer disbelief. Property was vandalised, trains were wrecked and police struggled to cope with this dark and violent underbelly.

Three of the most influential leaders of the riot squad era were Pampi, Trlaja and Zare. Pampi was a very unassuming guy whose terrace exploits in the 1980s secured him legendary status. He was tall, slim and wore glasses, quite geeky-looking really, but oozed charisma and according to those close to him, had psychopathic tendencies. He was afraid of nobody and respected by everyone.

Local hard man and keen bodybuilder Trlaja was a big, solid bloke and strong as an ox. He lived in the same neighbourhood as Pampi and they were inseparable as youngsters. Sadly, Trlaja is no longer with us after being shot dead in February 2000.

Zare is a terrace favourite, a real character and another Gravedigger who achieved iconic standing amongst his peers. Although not active like he was thirty years ago, Zare is a regular in Combe's bar and still held in the highest esteem by his lifelong friends.

One of the first serious incidents involving the Riot Squad occurred in Belgrade in September 1982. A frenzied Yugoslav media headlined with the story of the Riot Squad's attack on the Hajduk Split team coach.

A 300-strong mob of Partizan hooligans led by the 'usual suspects' rampaged through the centre of Belgrade destroying everything in their path. They were on their way to the Palas Hotel where the visiting Hajduk Split supporters were residing. On arrival, around two dozen older Riot Squad hools ran inside the hotel throwing tables and chairs and severely beating any Hajduk supporter who dared to stand and fight.

The second attack on the hotel took place shortly afterwards but this time coincided with the arrival of the Hajduk team bus. The Riot Squad took no prisoners and the bus became the focal point of a sustained onslaught of unremitting violence. Hooligans used bottles and stones to smash the bus windows and terrified players had to lie on the floor to avoid serious injury after an avalanche of missiles was thrown by the baying mob.

After the missiles came the gas bomb; after the gas bomb came the confrontation with Riot Squad hooligans armed with iron bars and sticks. Luckily for the players, the police arrived and dispersed the mob before further violence was inflicted upon them.

Pampi was a natural leader who worked tirelessly to ensure trips to away games were meticulously planned with military precision. The self-styled general and his trusty lieutenants led his troops into battle throughout the whole of the former Yugoslavia. Their initial clashes mainly consisted of street battles with local hoodlums as back in the 1980s Yugoslavia didn't have rival gangs of football hooligans.

But there was much more to Pampi than an obsession with football hooliganism. He revelled in the camaraderie and ensured the group's invasion of other cities and countries was both comical and eventful. His associates in the Ferry Union (similar to a student union in the UK) organised cheap train fares for all Partizan's away days and the storytellers from that era claim Pampi had a rare key to the buffet carriage, which would be rifled by his underlings ensuring a morale-boosting, plentiful supply of food and drink for his troops.

In September 1986, the Riot Squad was the first group allowed to travel outside the former Yugoslavia and made their hooligan debut in Germany at Partizan's UEFA Cup match with Borussia Moenchengladbach. They travelled to the game by bus and once out of the country, Pampi was said to have removed the driver and commandeered the vehicle for his own purposes.

The Gravediggers created many problems for the German *Polizei* as they embarked upon a new era of English-inspired football hooliganism. There were sporadic outbreaks of violence as the Riot Squad clashed with rival supporters and police before, during and after the game.

The security fencing around the Partizan section of the stadium was littered with an array of distinctive hand-painted banners. A union jack with Liverpool emblazoned across the middle was the centrepiece of a 1980s English-style display of support. It completely defined the path down which the Gravediggers had chosen to travel.

The Belgrade media wrote extensively about this trip and interviewed the traumatised drivers about their experience. 'We started with a new coach, we returned with a horse-drawn carriage,' grumbled one weary driver.

All those affiliated with the Kaznena Ekspedicija have only special memories of the 1980s. Their weekend Riot Squad escapades made them feel like brothers in arms and the trailblazing Undertakers Supporters Movement, an integral part of their everyday life, left an indelible and unique identity on a 1980s era that will live forever in the annals of Grobari folklore.

Litre bottles of Becks were the order of the day and Rajko's mates don't like to see you with an empty glass. Most of the lads in the bar spoke little English and I was initially concerned that the language barrier would prove to be a significant problem. Thankfully this wasn't the case. Football is a universal language and several of the Grobari lads spoke quite good English and helped with translation to the rest of the group, making for a very interesting afternoon.

Rajko introduced me to his lifelong friend Cegi. At around six foot two and built like the proverbial brick outhouse, Cegi was, let's say … big, with hands like baseball mits. Cegi is a terrace legend here in Belgrade; he has black-and-white blood running through his veins and is one of the most popular blokes on the south. He is old-school and like Rajko, was prominent in the Pampi era. I liked him; he is a top man, a gentleman and great company.

My conversation with Cegi was interrupted when a tall, portly, balding guy with a tanned, unshaven round face entered the bar and started to vent his anger at a bearded mature guy sitting at the opposite table to me. The bar went quiet and within seconds this lunatic pulled out an axe, raising it ready to strike his elder. Just as I thought Michael and I were about to witness the start of a good old-fashioned Serbian bloodbath, the angry roar turned to laughter. It turns out that the two of them were close friends acting out a private joke in their own spoof remake of Stephen King's *The Shining*. Here's Johnny! Indeed he was, but disguised as Pidja!

Pidja was the mad axe man. 'A little bit werrrr, a little bit weyyyyy, a little bit arrrrgggh' type of character with a magnetic personality. His bearded victim was terrace icon Zare. A wily old soul, in his mid fifties, Zare was a tough working-class bloke with three vices: football, drinking and smoking. He couldn't speak English but nevertheless greeted me with a warm smile and a firm handshake that 'Shake Hands', a character in Alan Bleasdale's *Boys from the Blackstuff*, would have been proud of. Zare was a good sort and really accommodating.

With at least five hours to kick-off, the bar was almost full to capacity and rocking. They are very vocal in this neck of the woods where drinking, eating and merriment is compulsory. The arrival of the PAOK contingent further livened up proceedings. The Gate 4 boys always receive a warm welcome from the black-and-white half of Belgrade. These two sets of supporters have a unique bond like no other in football.

The origins of their friendship can be traced back to a game between Partizan Belgrade and Dalmatia Split played in Thessaloniki in 1996. Hordes of PAOK supporters turned up to support Partizan for no other reason than that the team played in black and white, as do their own team, PAOK Salonica. Both teams also have a mutual hatred of their respective eternal rivals who coincidentally both play in red and white, Red Star Belgrade and Olympiacos Piraeus. Later in the year, the official Grobari fanzine, *Daj Gol*, paid tribute to the PAOK fans in recognition of their support.

In the years that followed the game in Thessaloniki, the hard-core Gate 4 boys from PAOK and the Undertakers from Partizan have made the seven-hour journey (by car) to each other's games on a regular basis and the friendship has grown to a point where PAOK and Partizan play friendly matches against each other as a gesture to their loyal supporters.

It is, however, a Union of European Basketball League (ULEB) basketball game between Red Star and PAOK in Belgrade that is widely credited with cementing a deep and everlasting kinship between the two extreme fan groups.

Around 30 PAOK supporters travelled to Belgrade by coach and were met on arrival by at least fifty Grobari. They partied hard all day, singing and chanting as football fans do. But five hours before kick-off, Serbian police officers tasked with supervising the supporters became unnerved and rapidly escorted both groups of fans to the stadium.

Red Star supporters entered the arena in huge numbers and began taunting and insulting their rivals. They also had many Olympiacos banners on show having formed a friendship with the red-and-white Athens outfit just to spite their noisy neighbours. Within moments of their arrival, hundreds of Red Star supporters stormed the visitors' section, pelting them with burning flares and broken seats.

Despite being heavily outnumbered, the combined mob of around 100 PAOK and Partizan supporters fought back ferociously and forced the Red Star hools to retreat back to their own sector. It was a vicious fight that transformed two supporters' groups with the same raw mentality into brothers in arms and galvanised a deep-seated respect for one another.

PAOK and Grobari alliance – Graffiti outside PAOK's infamous Toumba Stadium

Olympiacos and Red Star alliance – Graffiti outside Red Star's Marakana Stadium

The Greek contingent – Olympiacos Gate 7 boys at the Marakana

The barman decided to liven up proceedings by playing a tape of lively old-school Partizan songs. Cegi played choirmaster and the congregation didn't let him down, belting out one terrace classic after another.

> *Ooo partizane volimo te mi srcem svi,*
> *gde god ti da igras tu su tvoji Grobari,*
> *samo tebi verni samo tebi odani,*
> *o paokara,*
> *exo trela,*
> *me sto mjalo,*
> *obu kena pezis padata sa koluto,*
> *ja sena ta petano ke ja sena mono zo ...*
>
> (Inspired by the famous PAOK anthem 'O Paokara' and a song adopted by Liverpool supporters who sing 'Oh Campione.')

Shortly after our lively little sing-along, food arrived. Tray after tray of traditional Serbian fare was passed along until the tables were completely full. There was enough food to feed a small army. Thinking on, this was a small army!

All is not well at Partizan at present. Red Star won the league last year and a point in today's derby would give them back-to-back titles. Today's derby was different though. Rajko had informed me earlier that nobody in the bar would be going to this evening's game.

The Grobari had been boycotting games since their terrible start to the 2005 season which saw Partizan eliminated from the Champions League at the last qualifying stage by little-known Artmedia Bratislava. They also lost to Maccabi Petah-Tikva in the first round of the UEFA Cup several weeks later and went out of the Serbian National Cup to a third-division team. Poor domestic results followed, resulting in a well-organised protest from the Grobari that ultimately ended with a total boycott of all Partizan home games.

Club officials had been heavily criticised by the Grobari for selling the club's best players and accused of lining their own pockets with the proceeds rather than re-investing the profits back into the club. The supporters were very angry and would not return to the terraces until they forced the resignation of all those involved in this bitter debacle.

Serbia's two biggest clubs have totally dominated the domestic scene, winning forty-three league titles between them, Red Star on twenty-four and Partizan on nineteen. The Serbian premier league is considered to be little more than an annual duel between the two Belgrade heavyweights, confirming the league's status as a perennial duopoly.

The former Yugoslavia had a great footballing tradition and produced many talented players over the years. Players like Safet Susic, Dragan Stojković, Predrag Mijatović and Zvonimir Boban were fantastic talents and revered throughout the world.

However, since the brutal 1991–95 civil war and the break-up of the football leagues in the former Yugoslavia, there has been a severe deterioration in the standard of football at every level and this once proud footballing nation has struggled to compete on the world stage. Following independence, Serbia, Slovenia, Slovakia, Macedonia and Bosnia-Herzegovena all struggled to qualify for the major tournaments. Only Croatia performed on the world stage but I suspect their success will be short-lived once the golden generation passed their sell-by date.

On the domestic front, Serbian and Croatian teams are considered little more than cannon fodder by Europe's elite and like all the other less affluent footballing nations, are only in European competitions to make up the numbers. Any flourishing talent is cherry-picked by the top clubs and with promises of untold wealth are whisked away to ply their trade on foreign soil.

There has been a call for the Croatian and Serbian leagues to unite in order to increase competition and improve the quality of the standard of football. But given the justifiable unremitting animosity between the two countries, those calls are likely to fall upon deaf ears.

Kick-off time was almost upon us. Despite the boycott, Michael and I insisted on going to the game. Rajko agreed to chaperone us to the stadium and organised a lift with his brother Dragan, a fervent Red Star supporter. We said our goodbyes and left the Sopranos in pursuit of oblivion and judging by the amount of alcohol they had consumed, amongst other things, their arrival was imminent!

It was only a fifteen-minute journey and match traffic brought chaos to the normally quiet neighbourhoods around the vicinity of the stadium. Motorists parked on the pavement, double-parked and generally abandoned their vehicles wherever they liked. I don't know about the legalities of parking in Belgrade but vehicles parked anywhere on match day, no matter how inconsiderate or dangerous.

Rajko's brother dropped us off in a congested street just across the way from the stadium and with only forty-five minutes to kick-off we headed straight for the ticket office.

The heavy police presence at today's game became quite apparent upon leaving the car. Hundreds of riot police with shields formed a protective ring around the stadium and specialist riot units were deployed strategically on street corners and access areas. Helicopters whirred overhead, police on horseback were here in numbers and military-style security vehicles performed reconnaissance duties in and around the wooded areas leading up to the ground.

Despite the boycott by the Grobari, it was blatantly obvious that the police were taking no chances. Eight thousand Red Star supporters were expected to make the short journey across the park where confrontation is accepted as almost inevitable at the Balkan's most volatile fixture. There is an overt hatred that exists between these two Serbian superpowers. Widely recognised as one of the world's most violent derbies, it is an event characterised by the violent clashes between rival supporters and police. It's a game that goes well beyond the pale of rivalry because, at its apex, this wasn't just a football fixture, it was localised civil war!

Partizan Football Club was founded on 4 October 1945 as part of the Partizan Yugoslav Sports Association and was widely accepted as the army club due to its military funding from the Yugoslavian National Army. Nowadays, the 'Partizan Family' has twenty-five clubs in as many sports (men's and women's), including basketball, handball, water polo etc. Although football takes precedence, the Grobari also have a great appreciation for basketball, Serbia's second most popular pastime.

The Grobari pride themselves on their passion for sport and their ability to generate an incredibly unique and febrile atmosphere. Their assiduous devotion has been popularised, mythologised and misrepresented. Partizan is a religion and their piety quite often spills over into widespread crowd disorder, reinforcing an international notoriety achieved after three decades of chaos on the terraces.

Take for instance last year's (June 2006) basketball game between Partizan and Red Star. Police officers finally lost patience and turned viciously on to the Delije after being constantly abused and bombarded with bags filled with urine. But as much as the two sets of supporters hate each other, they also have a mutual disdain for law enforcement. In a rare display of unity, the Grobari attacked the police with violent intent in what appeared to be a show of solidarity between the two rival hooligan groups.

However, as the battle with the police intensified, the inevitable happened as hostilities between the two adversaries promptly resumed and a full-scale riot erupted as rival fans and police fought toe to toe with each other resulting in twenty-seven people, including nine police officers, being injured and thirty suspected hooligans arrested, according to Belgrade's B92 Radio coverage. Riot police are said to have fired live rounds into the air and used teargas to disperse fans both inside and outside the hall. Welcome to the dark side of Belgrade!

With no queue at the ticket office and only a token gesture home support expected, tickets were plentiful and Rajko acquired three seated together in the east stand.

There was a stadium ban on alcohol but we had consumed enough prematch beer to stay drunk for the whole of the weekend. What goes in has to come out, so once I was through the turnstile I headed directly to the nearest WC. As I came down the stairs the stench of urine hit me; there was no escape. It was so pungent I could almost taste it. The toilets were antiquated and the urine-soaked floor squelched and splashed as I made my way to the beloved urinal slab. Football stadiums just wouldn't be the same without them.

Like most inebriated supporters, I have never perfected the art of eluding the splashback zone and nearly always end up sharing urine spatter with the fans either side of me. Luckily, on this occasion the WC was empty and I had only myself to blame for my pee-sodden trainers. With the deed done I darted for the exit, making my way up three flights of stairs in one breath.

I caught up with the others and we made our way to our seats situated on the halfway line opposite the dugout. To the left of me was the south stand, home of the fiercely loyal and notoriously ruthless Grobari fan movement. The Undertakers have a unique identity and on derby day they transform the stadium into a cauldron of frenzied over-exuberance. Today it was deserted, just a mass of empty blue and yellow seats and an apathetic graveyard silence! I could see the disappointment in Rajko's face and he was almost apologetic as he gestured with his outstretched arms towards the south stand.

The boycott takes its toll – an empty south stand falls silent on derby day

In contrast, the 8,000 Red Star supporters behind the goal to my right had come here in a jubilant mood hoping their team would get the point that would see them clinch their twenty-fifth title in the backyard of their hated rivals.

The calm before the storm – Red star fans awaiting kick-off

Party time in the north stand

The Partizan Stadium itself could hardly be described as an impressive construction. None of the seated area in this oval-shaped structure is covered, leaving spectators open to Mother Nature's almost unforgiving elements on a cold and rainy winter's day.

Formerly known as the JNA (Jugoslavian National Army) Stadium, it was built in 1951 and back in the good old days when top-flight football stadia could boast terracing, had a record attendance of 55,000. This football, track and field stadium was refurbished in 1998 and made into a 33,000 capacity all-seated stadium in order to comply with the new UEFA legislation, enabling them to compete in European competition.

Stadium Partizan

GROBARI – Welcome to the Cathedral of Death

The token gesture 2,000 or so home supporters who attended the game tried in vain to give their side a good reception as they came on to the field. But try as they may, they were completely drowned out by a chorus of deafening boos and jeers from the mocking Red Star supporters or Cyganis (gypsies) as they are affectionately known by their hated Partizan counterparts.

Without the crazy support from the south stand and with a juvenile first-team squad it was always going to be an uphill battle for Partizan. However, the form book is tossed aside on derby day and even under difficult circumstances, today was no different. Partizan started the brighter of the two teams, having the lion's share of the possession.

That was until Asprogenis, the Partizan keeper, had a misunderstanding with defender Obradovic. In a completely empty Partizan penalty area, Asprogenis managed to flick the ball over the oncoming defender's head, straight into the path of Red Star midfielder Burzanovic who didn't look a gift horse in the mouth! Let the party commence. Red Star fans were jubilant and lit up the whole north stand with red flares, which is mandatory in these parts.

Red Star supporters celebrate the opening goal

Despite the early setback Partizan continued to dominate and pressed forward in search of an equaliser. The half-time whistle couldn't come quickly enough for the visitors.

The teams came out for the second half and with Red Star only forty-five minutes from their second league title in succession, celebrations in the north stand had already begun. Red distress flares lit up the early evening sky and supporters danced on the terracing in unison.

The Delije light up the north stand

Only five minutes after the break, 24-year-old Partizan defender Rukavina gave the sparse home crowd something to cheer about. He drove home a superb long-range effort from the edge of the box to deservedly level the scores. Undeterred however, Red Star supporters carried on with the party safe in the knowledge that if the scores remained level, the title would be theirs.

As Partizan upped their game, fate dealt them a cruel blow. An innocuous-looking challenge from Smiljanic on Milijas resulted in referee Mihajlo Jeknic awarding a dubious-looking penalty to Red Star. Milijas duly dispatched the 66th-minute penalty leaving Red Star to celebrate their twenty-fifth league title.

As we approached the end of an entertaining game, hundreds of riot police formed a human barricade in front of the north stand ensuring no pitch invasion by celebrating Red Star supporters. And although no fan confrontation occurred, police patience was tried on numerous occasions as visiting fans continually pelted them with red distress flares.

Riot police await the final whistle

The final whistle sparked joyous celebrations of delirium amongst the red-and-white half of Belgrade. Their victorious team made their way to the north stand, arms aloft, singing and dancing in front of their loyal fans. Half-naked men hung precariously over security fencing, chanting incessantly to their heroes and hoping to catch the players' shirts as they were thrown appreciatively into the crowd.

Red Star may have won another battle but Partizan supporters never lose focus and always believe they are winning a war that will last for eternity. The few home fans left in the stadium applauded the home team for their efforts; this young team had played with dignity and passion, the minimum requirement from the Grobari Jug. These scenes were obviously too much for Rajko so we left the stadium and headed to our meeting point.

With 8,000 Red Star supporters still in the ground celebrating their title success, the area outside the stadium wasn't as congested as it would normally be. Blue flashing lights lit up the night sky and police sirens could be heard in the distance. Armoured vehicles drove up and down and police units still patrolled every street corner.

Off the field, the boycott maintained by the Grobari had ensured the 130th Belgrade derby was a tame affair and not the usual violent encounter it is famed for.

The football hooliganism phenomenon in Serbia dates back to the 1980s. The Delije (pronounced Deli-er) are the hard-core supporters of Red Star Belgrade and have a reputation for being one of the most feared, best-organised and best-choreographed supporters groups in the world.

Formed in 1989 after the amalgamation of the other main supporters' groups (Ultras, Red Devils and Zulu Warriors etc.) in the north stand, the founder members of the Delije, like the Grobari, in their pomp, were a pathological band of brothers who thrived on football-related violence and were feared throughout Serbia and beyond.

Red Star supporters modelled their crowd dynamics on the Italian Ultra scene, often using pyrotechnics to choreograph the terraces at matches.

In contrast, the Grobari movement was inspired by English supporters from the 1970s and 1980s era. They were, indeed still are and always will be, very passionate with an unquestioning loyalty to the team. They bask in their fanaticism and choral power. Win, lose or draw it's a devotion that never wavers.

They love a local hero here at the Temple Of Football. Achievements can help make a legend, but it's what people say and do that determines their status in life. Even in death, the much loved Dragan Mance retains a demigod-like status amongst Partizan followers. His 25-yard half-volley against QPR in the first leg of the UEFA Cup quarter final tie is considered to be the best goal ever scored by a Partizan player.

Born in Belgrade on 26 September 1962, Mance started his career with FK Galenika Zemun, but shortly after making his first-team debut aged just 17, the talented youngster signed for his beloved Partizan

Belgrade. In the 1982–83 season, his fifteen goals in thirty games helped Partizan lift the Yugoslav title, his one and only honour with the club. He scored 174 goals in 279 appearances and was famous for celebrating every goal by sliding on his knees towards the home fans. It's an iconic goal celebration still used by many of the world's best footballers today.

The charismatic 22-year-old was the darling of the Belgrade media where he was looked upon as the Serbian equivalent of James Dean, with a movie-star lifestyle ahead of him. Nobody could envisage the tragedy that was to unfold on the fateful Sunday morning of 3 September 1985.

Mance left home in his new sports car for a 10 a.m. training session but never arrived. On the way to the training ground a young child walked out in front of Mance's car and he had to swerve to avoid killing the child. In doing so he crashed into a pole at high speed and lost his own life. Many questions remain unanswered about this tragic loss of life, but in death, the legend of Dragan Mance lives forever and his memory is sure to be passed on from one generation of Grobari to the next. Fans still to this day sing a song in his honour:

> *'Otis'o si Dragane, ostala je tuga, uvek ce te voleti Grobari sa Juga.'*
>
> 'You're gone, Dragan, only sorrow remains, Gravediggers from the south end will love you forever.'

In a letter published in the *PUP* football fanzine, lifelong Partizan fan 11-year-old Igor Todorovic describes his feelings at the news of Mance's death:

> It was not until I turned 11 years old, the second day of school. 11 a.m., I was in the bathroom, getting ready for the afternoon shift. The telephone rings. Mama occurs. A few minutes later I go into the room. Mom sat on my bed, her eyes filled with tears. I looked into it. I see that something was wrong. Facing the wall above the bed, looking at the posters. The entire wall of our single room is in black and white. Poster to posters, pictures, flags, scarves, and in the middle instead of icons Mance on his knees. Mama looked at me, she want to tell me something, but no power. Aborting dead silence and wonder just who called while I was in the bathroom. She managed to come together and says, 'Dad

called from work ... on the radio reported that he died, Dragan Mance!' We raise our heads to the wall. I watch him on his knees, I close my eyes and open them again, everything was blurry, tears shed ... My mother comforts, but no effect. She turned and called the school and classroom manager that I will not come to school. When asked the reason for my absence, simply said, 'God people, Mance died!' On Thursday, from head to toe dressed in favourite colours and went to school cried. All friends comforts. I still me. Teacher, otherwise Herzegovian, fan of Velez, hugged me and said I could go home and not come to school before Monday. I stayed because it's much easier to be in the company, but all day I'm sitting in the room next to the poster. At the moment geography teacher, seeing me in tears, approached me and said condolences. Along the way he asked me what was my deceased Mance. 'Idol,' I replied at first. I still cannot believe that Mance meant to me so much, but here and now, 25 years later, it took me two hours to write these few lines, because the tears are not allowed to do it fast.

Dragan Mance – A gift from God and posthumously christened September's Child by sections of the Belgrade media. He was born in September, signed for Partizan in September, scored his last goal in September and died in September. R.I.P.

Dragan Mance
26 September 1962 –
03 September 1985

Every old-school football temple has at least one sector designed for spitting out ear-piercing noise levels, and the south stand in the Partizan Stadium fits the bill perfectly. Holding more than 10,000 fanatical Gravediggers, this section amplifies noise and strikes fear into the opposition and their supporters like no other stadium in the world. Combine this with the other 15,000 ear-splitting devotees in the east and west sectors and the stadium becomes a compacted, open-air, hate-fuelled bear pit of delirium.

Simon Stainrod was interviewed shortly after Partizan had overturned a 6–2 first leg defeat in London with a 4–0 win at the JNA, to send QPR crashing out of the 1984–85 UEFA Cup. The shell-shocked Hoops striker gave a post-match interview to the Belgrade media and put into perspective the effects of having to endure ninety minutes of relentless Grobari hospitality, and here is a rough translation of that interview:

> Stainrod: Even today it looks like a nightmare, Partizan players just ran over us! They played fantastic, unrepeatable!
>
> Belgrade journalist: Why your team played so bad?
>
> Stainrod: We were scared from Belgrade audience, when we went to the pitch to warm up 30 minutes before the match, loud song and we had to avoid coins, lighters, papers ... I looked towards our younger players and I saw fear. None of us have ever played in that kind of atmosphere, I don't believe that any other club in Europe have similar crowd!

The perfect example of Grobari devotion was realised during a domestic league game way back in the 1975–76 season. Partizan Belgrade played Hadjuk Split in a league match at the JNA Stadium, unaware that their support that day would be written into Grobari folklore and justify their reputation as one of the greatest supporters' movements in the world.

The 1–6 defeat against Hajduk did not dampen the enthusiasm of the Grobari Jug, nor did it subdue the spirit within. Amazingly, each goal scored against Partizan only succeeded in making each and every home supporter more frenzied and more vociferous in their mission to get their team back into the game, even though they were quite clearly chasing a lost cause.

Dusan Sredic, a well-known journalist from that era, describes this amazing show of unity in his own colourful way and here is a rough translation of his words:

> Spring 1976.
> Partizan–Hajduk, the game that decides.
> South, never prettier before.
> It begins.
> First miss … Second …
> Misses that are promising.
> Oh, no!
> Visitors are up!
> The first 'bomb' strikes the soul of the fan.
> Then second … and third …
> Let them leave. Where?
> That's the way to love Partizan.
> And then – song!
> Hoarse, husky … never prettier, never more clear.
> The song that is a guardian of black and white.
> The song that guards the soul.
> Next three bombs just slipped down the soul.
> To forgiveness.
> Goooaall!! Gooaal!! South celebrating. We want second, we want second.
> End.
> 1–6.
> Applause.
> Yes, the applause of the winners.
> From South, Partizan's South.
> To be seen, heard and remembered.

At the final whistle, a tidal wave of emotion engulfed the players as supporters rose to their feet and gave a rousing standing ovation to the home team. It was the game that fused the crowd and the team together, characterising the unique bond between the players and their fiercely dedicated supporters. It's a union that will never be broken because the fans live their lives through their idols who don the sacred black-and-white colours every time they take to the field. For the Humska Street faithful, Partizan is life!

The two neighbouring Belgrade giants and their respective fan bases have a deeply ingrained hatred of one another with no sign of a cessation of hostilities on the horizon. Not now, not ever! The infused violence between the Delije and Grobari fan movements has always been the focal point of the Veciti (Eternal) derby. The atmosphere between the two is toxic, with enough blood shed down the years to saturate the local haematology ward.

The animosity that exists between the supporters is born out of a strange mix of disdain, malice, misfortune and even respect. When these types of emotions exist between two clubs' devotees, what should be a celebratory match between same-city rivals, instead becomes an epic tussle between the righteous on the light side ... *Cheer* ... and the resident evil on the dark side ... *Boo* ... Of course, which side is which depends upon with whom your allegiance lies. Partizan, the people's club, or Red Star, a club immersed in celebritydom and scandal!

Serious clashes between rival hooligans from Red Star and Partizan date back to the 1970s but became more prominent in the 1980s and 1990s resulting in the fatalities of supporters from both clubs. After the passing of Tito and his generation of leaders in the 1980s, Serbia saw a resurgence of militant nationalism and with Communism on the brink of collapse, a crisis loomed large in Yugoslavia.

Both the Grobari and Delije fan movements were exposed as a mouthpiece for Serbian nationalism, specifically in the late 1980s and early 1990s. With public anxiety rising throughout the whole of the former Republic and interethnic rivalry gaining momentum, Serbia was a powder keg waiting to explode.

On 13 May 1990, football hooliganism attained a level never seen before as inescapable ethnic and religious tensions reached the point of no return. Led by the infamous Balkan crime-lord Arkan (more about him later), a 3,000-strong ultra-nationalist Delije contingent arrived in Zagreb for a Yugoslav league match against Dinamo Zagreb. Violent clashes with Dinamo's Bad Blue Boys broke out shortly after the arrival of the Serbs but nothing could have prepared the authorities for the appallingly violent scenes that were to unfold in the stadium.

The Serb 'army' residing in the south of the stadium hurled acidic invective in the direction of their Croat counterparts in the north stand. They taunted the home section with chants like 'Zagreb is Serbian', before indiscriminately attacking surrounding Croats with stones, broken seats and bottles. The police stood idly by, preferring instead to concentrate on containing the home sectors.

Thousands of hate-filled Dinamo fans, apoplectic with fury, broke down the north stand fences protecting the players from fans on the terraces and fought with hundreds of Serb-controlled riot police, whilst the Delije continued to systematically tear the Maksimir Stadium apart before swarming on to the pitch and clashing with rival supporters and security forces. Players had to quite literally run for their lives, quickly seeking refuge in the relative safety of the dressing room. The game was abandoned after only ten minutes as thousands of hooligans, high on rage, fought pitched battles throughout the evening.

Police helicopters airlifted Red Star players out of the stadium in extremis, while Dinamo captain Zvonimir Boban secured hero status after infamously kung-fu kicking a Yugoslav police officer who was attacking a home fan. Boban was suspended by the Yugoslav FA and subsequently missed the 1990 World Cup Finals in Italy.

Serb and Croat football hooligans have been fighting each other for decades but the unprecedented scenes in and around Dinamo's Maksimir Stadium on that fateful evening escalated to the point of infinite danger. It's a match that will always be remembered by many residents of the former Yugoslavia as the game that started a war!

Inter-club rivalries were temporarily suspended as hooligans from the Grobari and Delije united to fight side by side as Serbian Nationalist Slobodan Milosevic led them into the bloody Serb–Croat war of 1991–95. Many of the older Undertakers I had met earlier fought in that long and gruelling conflict, experiencing the horrors of the front line at very close quarters and ultimately surviving the bloodiest Balkan conflict ever.

However, with the civil war still raging and showing no signs of abating, hostilities resumed in the derby of 1993 and it was business as usual. Hooligans fought pitched battles that led to over 100 people requiring hospital treatment.

Trouble between these well-organised hooligan factions is all too familiar. Rioting is a vocation here in Belgrade and every derby between Partizan and Red Star requires a full call-up of police reserves. Unfortunately, the enhanced police presence does little to quell the conflict between supporters.

In the October derby of 1999 a young 17-year-old Red Star fan was killed inside the Partizan Stadium after being shot in the chest by a propelled flare launched from the south stand. Serious disorder broke out immediately afterwards leading to scores of arrests and many injured fans seeking hospital treatment.

Back at the meeting point, the lack of home support, the obligatory title celebrations and an area awash with law enforcement meant it was all quiet on the western front for a change. Red Star fans were still in the stadium celebrating their title success but Dragan had made a special effort to leave the party early and get us back to the pub.

We were back at the bar in no time and the defeat to Red Star didn't appear to have dampened the spirits of Combe and the rest of the boys. The drunkest men in Serbia were in a buoyant mood and the prematch party had immediately morphed into a post-match party. So when in Rome and all that ... 'A bottle of Becks for me and a Tueborg for Michael please, Rajko?' Destination, oblivion!

The lads had considered taking us to a Partizan basketball game due to be played at the 7,000 capacity Pionir Hall, in nearby Palilula. However, due to our hosts' overindulgence, it was quite clearly a non-starter. Our barman put on some more old-school Partizan music and we had a little hand-clapping, foot-stomping party of our own.

Time was getting on and Michael and I decided to head into the centre for a night on the town. Rajko agreed to accompany us but not before the lads tried to persuade us to stay into the early hours. It was an offer that we had to politely decline, for sanity's sake if nothing else.

I was probably as drunk as I have ever been in my life! One by one, each of the Grobari boys wished us well and demanded we return for a game at the Marakana, home of rivals Red Star. After meeting the number-one Serbian hospitality machine that is the Grobari, it would have been rude not to!

The bitter dispute between club officials and supporters was now in the midst of an explosive endgame and if not resolved could result in dire consequences for all concerned. The clock was ticking and time waits for no fan. The stubborn stance taken by the board and the boycott by the Grobari was slowly squeezing the life out of the club. Failure to overcome their differences would be to the team's detriment and I feared for the future of this great sporting institution should this stand-off continue beyond the end of the season.

17 Months Later ...
Game: Red Star Belgrade 0 – 2 Partizan Belgrade
Venue: Marakana
Date: 5 October 2008
Attendance: 18,000

It's derby eve all over again on a cold, rainy Belgrade afternoon and how rapidly things change in football. Since my last visit to the capital, the Grobaris' game of brinksmanship with the board has finally paid dividends. Out went club director Nenad Bjekovic and club secretary Zarko Zecevic, resulting in the Grobari ending their boycott and bringing the south stand back to life again, just in time for the start of the 2007–08 season.

In return, the players duly delivered their twentieth league title and completed the domestic double after winning the cup just a few weeks earlier. The feel-good factor was back in earnest and the Grobari were firing on all cylinders!

I arrived at my hotel around midday and for around 40 euros you get a working lift and not much else. Brian arrived the night before and was itching to get out and see the city after spending much of the evening flitting between his bedroom and the clip joint located on the second floor.

After a quick swill and change of clothes we headed into town to the unofficial Grobari shop. Run by supporters for the supporters, it was only a small store, hidden away in a little shopping arcade under the subway in the centre of town. It was well stocked with official Grobari merchandise but it was the unendorsed Gravedigger t-shirts that were the order of the day for the pair of us.

Next port of call was Belgrade's Novo Groblje cemetery, resting place of the infamous Serbian warlord Arkan. It was only a short taxi ride from the centre and our driver dropped us off in front of the main visitors' entrance. This labyrinthine necropolis is a testament to the past two centuries of Serbian history and a number of generations have been buried here. The cemetery is the final resting place of many statesmen, politicians, scientists and artists.

Finding Arkan's grave wasn't going to be easy. It was late afternoon, the skies were grey, light was fading fast and the cemetery had thousands of plots spread over a vast area. The guy in the cemetery office wasn't interested in our plight and rather arrogantly sent us on our way with nothing more than an ill-tempered grunt, a groan and an ignorant shrug of the shoulders.

Next stop was the cemetery chapel where a number of priests had gathered at the entrance. Brian wandered over to see if he could obtain directions but he returned empty handed. I suspected it was more to do with his dulcet Scouse dialect rather than the priests' command of the English language. 'Ee ya, lad, wers Arkan bereed?' isn't the smartest way to endear yourself to a Serbian man of the cloth!

I felt a more subtle approach was the way forward. 'Excuse me, can you help us please?' I asked in my finest northern tone. 'We are looking for Arkan's grave.' 'Arkan,' he replied. 'Mmm, yes,' and with that he took a moment to gather his thoughts before overcoming the language barrier to provide me with directions. I thanked the priest for his help and we set off for our appointment with Serbia's most famous warlord.

Just a few metres from the chapel was a stunning monument dedicated to the soldiers who lost their lives defending Serbia's capital during the First World War. It's called Belgrade Defenders 1914–1918. This eye-catching sculpture, a Serbian soldier towering above a fallen German eagle, is one of the main focal points of this incredibly well-maintained cemetery.

The priest had instructed me to turn right at the monument and head for aisle 92 where he assured me that I would locate Arkan's grave somewhere in that vicinity. After spending a few moments admiring the monument and reading the inscriptions, we continued on our way.

We reached aisle 92 and just to the right of us we could see a large black marble headstone that stood out from the rest. I suspected this was the grave we were looking for and decided to take a closer look. There was a gold plated bust in military regalia and the inscription on the headstone was in Serbian Cyrillic. It read: АРКАН 1952–2000.

Zeljko Raznatovic, aka Arkan, was a charismatic figure and many aspects of his life still remain shrouded in mystery. The son of a Yugoslav Air Force officer, Raznatovic was born in the Slovenian town of Brezice on 17 April 1952. In 1969, aged just 17, teenage delinquent Zeljko served a 3-year prison sentence for street robbery. Worried that

Karadzic supporters had since held weekly protest marches in the city centre and in the first weeks after his arrest the demonstrations often degenerated into serious outbreaks of violence with both Grobari and Delije members openly accused of being the ringleaders.

At the bottom end of Kneza Mihailova is the remains of the historic Kalemegdan Castle. The Serbs have afforded plenty of hostilities over the years and this hilltop retreat has seen more than its fair share of action. Strategically placed where the Danube and Sava rivers meet, the views to the north-west are extraordinary, reinforcing the castle's standing as Belgrade's premier tourist attraction.

As noon approached I received a text from Rajko giving me the address of the Grobari 1970 bar. We hailed a cab outside the rail station, gave our driver my phone and instructed him to drive to the location in the text.

Given our cabbie's demeanour and his constant reference to his A–Z, I wasn't exactly filled with confidence that we would reach our destination at any point this side of kick-off time. My suspicions were confirmed shortly afterwards as we drove up and down the same street several times, stopping at every opportunity to ask for directions.

Brian was becoming increasingly agitated by our man's incompetence and the fact that the meter had clocked up around 500 Dinar (£5.00). The thought of paying one Dinar over the odds was just too much for Britain's tightest man and was the green light for a volley of relentless Scouse abuse. Fortunately, the driver couldn't understand a word he was saying.

I felt so sorry for this poor cabbie; he was genuinely lost and now had to cope with Brian turning bandit and chewing his ears off for the duration of the journey. It was now in his own interests to get us to the bar before tinnitus set in.

Lady Luck must have taken a shine to him though because we arrived at our destination within moments of Brian's last verbal assault. I paid the 600-dinar fare but gave him 1000 dinar for the abuse he took and we made our way up the steps and into the bar. As we walked in I was immediately greeted like a long-lost friend by Combe, Belgrade's most hospitable landlord. He shook my hand and gave me three kisses to my cheeks, a traditional Serbian greeting. I introduced him to Brian and he took us to the bar and ordered up two beers for us before taking us over to Rajko's table.

Rajko hadn't changed at all and despite his best efforts neither had his limited English vocabulary. 'Hello, Shon (Shaun), how are you, my friend?' asked Rajko. 'I'm good, how are you?' I replied. Rajko looked at me with a grimace; he was hung over (again) after overindulgence at a wedding he had been to the night before and was feeling pretty delicate. I introduced him to Brian who offered to buy him a drink but Rajko declined, pointing to a sore head and dodgy stomach.

With the boycott a distant memory, the Grobari were at full strength for today's derby and the bar was packed with a mixture of youth and old-school from the many different supporters' groups. I spoke to Davor, one of the main young faces of the 300-strong Niski Kartel firm from Nis, some 200 kilometres south of Belgrade. He was an interesting young man and told me many different tales about fights with rival Delije boys on the long journeys into Belgrade for derby matches. He was only in his early twenties but was already battle hardened with an intense hatred of the eternal enemy.

'Fighting between Delije and Grobari is normal,' said Davor. 'We fight at football, basketball and also in the local bars and discotheques.' Like oil and water they perfectly repel and inevitably these violent clashes end with fatalities.

Aleksandar Panic was the last Partizan supporter to be killed when he was stabbed to death in an organised fight after rival Grobari and Delije hooligans fought a pitched battle in a Belgrade park back in July 2006. Unfortunately, this is not an unusual occurrence and Aleksandar is just one of many young boys who have lost their life on the hooligan battlefield.

Until recently, Serbia's endless connection with football-related violence was blatantly swept under the carpet by the endemically corrupt authorities who adopted a 'see no evil, hear no evil' approach. Serious outbreaks of disorder have blighted the sport for three decades and with the exception of the archaic hands-on approach, wade in first and ask questions later, there was no apparent strategy to combat the hooligan problem.

However, all that changed after the carnage at the Marakana in December 2007, when Red Star supporters rioted at the home game against Hajduk Kula. Twenty-year-old Red Star supporter Uros Misic was sentenced to ten years' imprisonment after being convicted of the attempted murder of plain-clothes policeman Nebojsa Trajkovic. The plain-clothes police officer suffered life-threatening injuries in what the judge described as a 'lynching'.

Misic inflicted serious burns upon the traumatised and viciously beaten police officer using a blazing distress flare, forcing the officer to discharge several warning shots into the air. 'It was a barbaric, brutal and monstrous attack on a policeman on duty,' Judge Velimir Lazovic said after the courts passed the guilty verdict. 'The assault was also completely unprovoked and it had to be qualified as attempted murder because Trajkovic was fighting for his life out there,' he vented.

These horrific scenes prompted the capital's governing bodies to pass new zero tolerance laws allowing judges to pass stiff sentences down to football hooligans.

Needless to say, the ten-year sentence passed down to young Misic was met with disdain by Red Star supporters. In fact, the whole Serbian footballing community was appalled with what they described as a draconian sentence. The Delije recognised that Misic's crime could not go unpunished but they were adamant that his jail term was excessive and did not fit the crime. They vowed to explore all avenues in an attempt to fight for a reduction in sentence on his behalf.

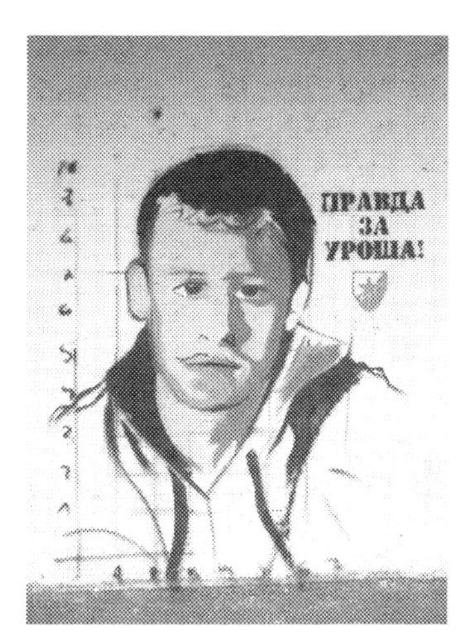

Justice for Uros graffiti sprayed on the walls outside the Marakana Stadium

There was a protest expected at today's derby but anyone thinking of stepping out of line was under no illusion about the consequences of being convicted of football-related disorder in Serbia. New legislation would compel police to bring hooligans before the courts where they could expect to receive harsh sentences in excess of five years' imprisonment.

Rajko informed me that police surveillance units had turned up outside the bar and were busy filming activity in the area. This was a first for the boys in the Grobari 1970 bar and confirmed the authorities' intention of cracking down on the criminal activities of known faces at football. Not that anyone was perturbed by the impromptu police visit; it was business as usual for this bunch of wise guys.

It was almost 4 p.m. and we had time for a couple of team photographs before around forty of us left for the game by car. Brian, Aleksandar and I jumped into a car with one of Rajko's mates. He spoke good English and was really into the (Oi) punk music scene, especially the Cockney Rejects. So it was no surprise when he cranked up the volume for track 15 of the C.R. Punk Singles Collection, the timeless Cockney Rejects classic 'War on the Terraces', before setting off in a ten-car convoy.

GO!
It's all gone quiet over there
The seats, and the stands are bare,
But you remember not long ago,
All the times that we battled there.
The sun, it shines right on the gutter
And you remember that he was there,
And you should know, weren't too long ago,
That you grabbed him by his hair.

War on the terraces
War on the terraces
It was war on the terraces
War on the terraces

The local pub, it stands silent
Opening time will be soon
Remember the pints we sank
We sunk, they told us just what to do
Do you remember those wagons
They took us straight down the nick

And when you think back to it
Don't make you feel like a prick

War on the terraces
War on the terraces
It was war on the terraces
War on the terraces

So you look out on the terrace
And a smile it breaks your face
Cos soon the younger generation
Will be here to take your place

War on the terraces
War on the terraces
It was war on the terraces
War on the terraces

'War on the Terraces' lyrics by the Cockney Rejects

Barely two minutes into the CD and our car shuddered and slowly but surely ground to a halt. Our driver turned to face us in the back and with an embarrassed look on his face uttered those immortal words, 'We are out of petrol! It isn't a problem though,' he said, 'the others will take you and I will get a lift to the gas station.' Within moments the panic was over and we were all picked up by another car and on our way to the game again.

We drove to the south of the stadium, parked up and joined the hordes of supporters making their way to the game. Distinguishable black attire was the dress code and Aleksandar warned us that confrontation was a distinct possibility if rival Red Star supporters had infiltrated our access to the ground.

As we approached the stadium I spotted a large casual-looking mob loitering with intent outside the visitors' section. Around 300 in number and all dressed in black, they were hard-core Grobari and the large police presence corralling them appeared anxious to clear the concourse and usher the risk element through the turnstiles and into the stadium.

Rajko sorted the tickets out but was still half a dozen short and needed to work fast to avoid disappointment. After a little jiggery pokery, a few dodgy handshakes and some sleight of hand that David Blaine would have been proud of, everyone was in. Kick-off was imminent so we made our way deep into the south stand and stood in the seated area reserved for the 5,000 or so Grobari that had made the short journey across the park.

Known colloquially as the 'Marakana' after the famous football cathedral in Rio de Janeiro, and situated just 500 metres across the divide from Partizan's 'cathedral of death', this grand old stadium bears testament to a rich and proud history. This venue played host to the 1973 European Cup final between Ajax and Juventus when the Dutch ran out 1–0 winners in front of a crowd of 91,564.

Back in the days when stadia featured terracing, the Marakana could hold up to 100,000 supporters. The official record stands at 96,070 for a European Cup Winners' Cup semi-final clash between Red Star Belgrade and Ferencvaros (2–2) in April 1975, but such lofty attendances are confined to the past, with crowds for league matches now as low as 3,000, and for safety reasons the capacity has been reduced to a moderate 52,000.

On the very rare occasions when the stadium is sold out, the hype associated with the Marakana is certainly justified. Even though it has a running track, this iconic old-school arena is architecturally a noisy stadium, capable of transforming itself into a zealous hotbed of energy. The din spewed out by the Delije thrives on the stadium's superb acoustical characteristics that direct crowd noise on to the pitch. The Marakana really packs a punch and can rock with the best of them on the big occasion and those occasions don't come much grander than the perennial Belgrade derby.

The iconic Marakana Stadium – a view from the south stand

Reigning league champions Partizan were going into today's game unbeaten and on the back of six straight wins. In stark contrast, Red Star, European Champions less than twenty years ago, had been a shadow of their former selves. They'd had a dreadful start to the season, managing two wins, two draws and two losses, and were languishing in mid table. Add this to the club's dire financial situation and it pointed to troubled times ahead.

A giant mural outside the Marakana depicting
Red Star Belgrade's 1991 European Cup triumph

The Grobari were in fine voice and as the teams were introduced, you can't imagine the level of invective hurled at the home team. Every Serbian curse was spewed out in a barrage of pure hatred. 'Cygani, cygani, cygani,' was the cry as the Grobari unfurled a huge flag just before the game kicked off.

I was later told that the flag actually belonged to Red Star supporters and was stolen in a prematch altercation after fans clashed in the city centre earlier in the day. The stealing of a rival fan or fan groups paraphernalia is commonplace in Eastern Europe and widely considered to be a game of one-upmanship, similar to the taking of a rival firm's pub or home sector, as English hooligans used to thrive upon back in the day.

Red Star supporters stood in silence with their backs to the pitch for the first few minutes of the game, in protest at the ten-year jail sentence handed down to Red Star fan Uros Misic for his attack on the undercover police officer. I didn't witness a great deal of sympathy from the Gravediggers as they began to jump up and down in unison, chanting relentlessly at their lifeless counterparts.

Partizan opened the game the brighter of the two teams and had two great goal-scoring opportunities in the first ten minutes, both judged offside by referee Mazic. On twenty-four minutes, Red Star's Milijas threatened the Partizan goal with a long-range free kick but was thwarted by the crossbar, a lucky escape for the Undertakers. This gave Red Star fresh impetus as they upped their game and started to dominate proceedings in a thoroughly entertaining first half.

I stood with Davor for the whole of the opening forty-five minutes and listened intently as he reminisced about the derby days of the 1980s and 1990s. 'Red Star has always been the glamour club of Yugoslavia,' he frowned. 'They have been forever supported by the rich and famous, looking down on everyone else. Their image is completely media driven and often portrayed as representing everything good about the former Yugoslavia. In comparison, Partizan is associated with negativity but we are proud of our heritage and we are not for change.'

Davor pointed to the north stand, home of the Delije, and told me that during the 1980s a handful of the top Grobari boys, the 'usual suspects', used to regularly go in there on big European nights and goad Red Star supporters without reprisal. The fear factor the Grobari held over their neighbours was immense and some say the inferiority complex remains to this day.

Lots of the Grobari were big players within the criminal fraternity back in the day and those who crossed them would be dealt with accordingly. The impromptu visits by the Grobari only came to an end when Arkan formed the Delije and united the north stand.

The criminal element that did business together during the week couldn't let their working relationship be affected by terrace conflict. And contrary to popular belief some of the very same Grobari boys were recruited by Arkan to fight with him during the Balkan conflict.

I moved over to the left side of the south stand for the second half and sat with Rajko and the boys. This game needed a goal and within ten minutes of the restart we got one. Partizan's Diarra latched on to a defence-splitting pass from Portuguese midfielder Almani Moreira and slid a low shot past the helpless Red Star keeper, Sasa Stamenkovic.

The south stand exploded into a paroxysm of unrestricted, frenzied exhuberance and the 8,000 strong army from across the park, who were beside themselves with joy, leapt into the air en masse. The stadium shook for three long, lingering mimutes. The noise was deafening. I found myself bear-hugging complete strangers as fans around me were overcome with unbridled emotion. Others jumped on top of each other as they clambered to the bottom of the stand. Fans scaled the security fences, faces contorted with a mixture of happiness and derision. Seats were ripped out and smoke bombs let off, and luminous flares lit up the early evening sky as the 5,000-strong away following celebrated Grobari style.

Shortly afterwards, Partizan playmaker Moreira and Red Star defender Ibrahima Gueye were sent off after exchanging blows in an ugly exchange. Milijas hit the post with a superb free kick as Red Star threw caution to the wind and attacked with great gusto. However, deep into injury time fate delivered a cruel blow as Partizan hit Red Star with a perfect counter attack. Substitute Milos Bogunovic raced clear and delivered a perfect low cross for Juca to sweep home from close range and clinch a seventh consecutive victory for Partizan.

Cue the Grobari and one of the most frenetic goal celebrations I have ever been a part of. It was completely off the scale. Once again, supporters hurled themselves on top of one another, flares were lit, seats were thrown and the roar that lingered after the goal was immense. At the final whistle, Red Star players trooped off with heavy legs and bowed heads. The tank looked suspiciously low on fuel and the players, body language suggested they were in for a long, arduous season.

In contrast, Partizan players danced their way over to the joyous celebrations in the south stand. Shirts and shorts were thrown to the black-and-white faithful as near naked players celebrated yet another victory over their illustrious neighbours.

As the celebrations continued, overexuberance set in and some fans thought it would be a good time to burn the flag that was stolen from Red Star supporters earlier in the day. As the flames gathered momentum, so did the fire. Some of the fans wasted no time in ripping seats out to add to the mini inferno. Very quickly, the smoke became dense and acrid, almost like soot. We had to move back to avoid choking. Security didn't appear to be concerned though as they looked on with no sense of urgency. Their heads were shaking in disbelief as the seating area at the rear of the goal was completely engulfed in flames.

Rajko rounded up our posse and we headed back to the cars for the short drive back to our watering hole and a night of celebration.

The bar was buzzing and I anticipated yet another marathon drinking session with the Grobari. Antibiotics prevented me from full participation but that didn't stop Brian's overindulgence in the night's offerings.

Fast-forward two hours and the excesses of the day were clearly having a profound effect on Brian as he networked his way through the bar. Those dulcet Scouse tones were getting thicker with every drink. Some of the lads could barely speak English so understanding Brian's consonant crunching Scouse dialect would be nigh on impossible.

People's champion Brian struck up conversation with probably just about the most fluent English-speaking lad in the bar and he introduced me almost immediately to 31-year-old ex-Partizan 'nightmare' Zoran. He was a tall, handy-looking bloke with an athletic build and casually dressed but without the chav. And for sure, he was probably the most wrecked bloke this side of Belgrade. Nevertheless, we got along swimmingly and he proceeded to give us an insight into life with the Grobari.

Zoran started life on the south stand as a young boy but quickly worked his way up the ranks to become one of the main young faces in the notorious Alcatraz firm, the most feared subgroup on the south. Even a short spell in prison didn't deter him from a life of violence and mischief on the terraces. He was now married with two children and although still in touch with his pals, the crazy days of the past were now only a memory for him as he pursued work that would provide a decent standard of living for him and his family.

Zoran had been working in the UK for most of the year and was now awaiting the return of his visa application which was due at any time. He had been working long 13-hour days during the week and worked as a London doorman at the weekends to further boost his income.

Football was his life back in his younger days and nothing else mattered to him. He was fearless, respected and loved the buzz that only life on the terraces can bring. Thinking back to those crazy times with Alcatraz, he recalled a game in Georgia in the early 1990s. 'Only around a dozen Grobari travelled to this game,' said Zoran. 'Georgia was a very dangerous place back then; residents were under curfew and armed forces were policing the streets. We travelled with the team and stayed in a really nice hotel, better than the team hotel. We had free drinks, women and whatever else we fancied, all at the expense of the club. I was just a young guy at the time and loved every minute of it. Back in the old days, the club used to pay for all the top boys to travel to away games, even in Europe.

'Leaving the hotel was not an option due to the unrest in the city so we entertained ourselves,' he said, with a nod and a wink. 'The following evening we were escorted to the stadium along with the team. Shortly after kick-off we were attacked by locals; within moments we were surrounded, outnumbered by at least ten to one. There was no hiding place. We literally fought for our lives until the police rescued us. After the game we were escorted by police to the Partizan changing rooms and put on the same coach as the players, before being swiftly escorted by armed guard all the way to the airport, minus our belongings.'

Zoran's reminiscing was enthralling but time was getting on and we needed to head back into the city centre. Zoran was going that way and kindly offered us a lift and a quick tour of some of the city centre pubs. It was time to say our goodbyes to Rajko, Combe, Zare, Cegi and the rest of the boys. These wise guys were the most hospitable band of outlaws I have ever had the pleasure of hanging out with. They have an old school mentality and despite their much publicised indiscretions that portray them as 'wrong 'uns', all have a genuine love for their football club. Partizan is in their DNA: cut them in half and they will bleed black-and-white blood. They were perfect hosts and treated me like family. When you make friends with the Grobari, you have a friend for life, and I have. Make them your enemy and you really could end up sleeping with the fishes!

Ziveli, pronounced 'zjee-ve-lee' (cheers).

Feyenoord play their home games at the 51,000 capacity Feyenoord Stadium, known by all as *De Kuip* (The Tub). It is located in the Feyenoord district of Rotterdam and is famous for the intimidating atmosphere created by the fanatical home supporters. The fans are held in such high esteem at this club that the number 12 shirt is never given to a player. It is specifically reserved for the fans in honour of their unconditional loyal support.

Stadion Feijenoord
aka 'De Kuip'

Rotterdam is the industrial heart of the Netherlands and a global centre for trade. It's a resolute port city that is home to over one million inhabitants from 162 countries. On 14 May 1940, Rotterdam suffered a devastating aerial bombardment by the ruthless German Luftwaffe. The resulting firestorm claimed the lives of over 900 innocent Dutch civilians and made in excess of 80,000 people homeless. Approximately one square mile of the city centre was razed to the ground.

At the end of the Second World War, a doggedly determined Rotterdam workforce commenced reconstruction of the historic city centre, and now, over sixty years later, a new, modern port city has evolved from the carnage of war. Rotterdammers are immensely proud of their working-class origins and although the post-war regeneration of the city centre has established Rotterdam as a business city, the physical demands of the port ensure a high dependency on manual labour.

Rotterdam poet and Feyenoord supporter Jules Deeder once said: 'Holland's money is earned in Rotterdam, divided in The Hague and flushed down the toilet in Amsterdam.'

Amsterdam is home to AFC Ajax Amsterdam (named after the Greek warrior) and their perceived bourgeois congregation. Considered arrogant and smug by many Dutch fans, they often stand accused of portraying a superiority complex to match their team's unrivalled heritage. They retort by accusing Feyenoord fans of having second-city syndrome and say their hatred of Ajax is purely based on jealousy.

The iconic Dutch club was formed in 1900, eight years prior to bitter rivals Feyenoord. Their devastatingly fluid playing style has made them famous throughout the world and they are without question Holland's most successful football club. Amsterdammers have been brought up on a diet of *totaal voetbal* and have witnessed their club churn out a host of footballing legends like no other club in the world.

Hendrik Johannes Cruijff (Johan Cruyff) was Ajax and Holland's greatest ever player and boasts a CV like nobody else in world football:

Ajax
1 x Intercontinental Cup (1972)
3 x European Cups (1971, '72, '73)
2 x European Super Cups (1972, '73)
8 x Dutch Championships (1966, '67, '68, '70, '72, '73, '82, '83)
4 x Dutch Cups (1967, '71, '72, '83)

FC Barcelona
1 x Spanish Championship (1974)
1 x Spanish Cup (1978)

Feyenoord
1 x Dutch Championship (1984)
1 x Dutch Cup (1984)

As a manager Cruyff won the European Cup Winners' Cup (1987) and two Dutch Cups (1986, '87) with Ajax and the European Cup (1992), European Cup Winners' Cup (1989), four Spanish Championships (1991, '92, '92, '94) and the Spanish Super Cup with Barcelona.

Honours
3 x European Footballer of the Year (1971, '73, '74)
1 x IFFHS (International Federation of Football History and Statistics) European Player of the Century
1 x World Cup Player of the Tournament (1974)

A product of the Ajax youth system, born-and-bred Amsterdammer Cruyff embarked upon an illustrious football career at the tender age of 17. Mr Ajax was the complete footballer, the most gifted individual of his generation and heir apparent to Pele as the greatest player in world football.

Cruyff was a maverick forward with unparalleled vision, lightning-quick pace and extraordinary ball control with both feet. He was the heartbeat of the great Ajax team of the 1960s and 1970s and instrumental in everything they achieved.

Sports writer David Miller lauded Cruyff as the greatest because of his extraordinary leadership qualities that enabled him to bring out the best in his teammates. Miller dubbed him 'Pythagoras in boots' for the intricacy and accuracy of his passes and wrote: 'Few have been able to extract, both physically and mentally, such mesmeric control on a match from one penalty area to another.'

Of course, Cruyff wasn't the only exceptional talent of that era. Piet Keizer was a brilliant winger and the architect of many of Cruyff's goals. Keizer also enjoys iconic status at Ajax and committed the whole of his 15-year playing career to the Amsterdam club. Technically gifted midfielder Johan Neeskens was another a key performer in 'that' famous Ajax team.

Cruyff's Ajax succeeded Feyenoord as European Champions in 1971 and went on to become one of only three clubs (with Real Madrid and Bayern Munich) to retain the trophy three times in succession, between 1971 and 1973. Several months after Ajax's European Cup triumph over Juventus in Belgrade, Cruyff joined his mentor Rinus Michels at Barcelona. He was signed for a world record fee of over £900,000 and a year later helped Barca to win their first league title since 1960.

Munich's Olympiastadion was the venue for the 1974 FIFA World Cup final and Rinus Michel's total footballing Netherlands team were overwhelming favourites to win the competition. Cruyff, by now widely regarded as the best player in the world, shone like a beacon throughout the competition and the final against host nation West Germany was considered to be nothing more than a formality by the game's leading experts. 'On the day of the 1974 final even West Germany expected Holland to win. They were a better team,' declared Uli Hoeness afterwards. Winner of the Germans' equalising penalty, Bernd Holzenbein summed up the fear in the German team. 'In the tunnel, we planned to look them in the eye, to show them we were as big as they were. They had the feeling they were invincible; you could see it in their eyes. Their attitude to us was, "How many goals do you want to lose by today, boys?" While we waited to go on to the pitch I tried to look them in the eye, but I couldn't do it. They made us feel small.' Despite taking an early first-minute lead courtesy of a Johan Neeskens penalty, Gerd Muller's late-first-half strike was enough to seal an unexpected 2–1 victory for the hosts. Cruyff was named player of the tournament and the German World Cup finals was Cruyff's one and only appearance at FIFA's showpiece event. He retired from international football in 1977.

After short spells in America and Spain, Cruyff returned to Ajax to a hero's welcome and the second coming of the great man helped the club win back-to-back titles and a domestic double.

In 1984, the final season of a long and prolific playing career, Cruyff did the unthinkable and after a minor spat over a new playing contract committed the cardinal sin of signing for arch rivals Feyenoord. His unexpected arrival was the catalyst to a mini Feyenoord revival and he helped lead the Rotterdam club to a domestic league and cup double, their first league title for 10 years. He was also voted Dutch footballer of the year.

Despite the ugly rivalry between the two clubs, Cruyff played an integral part in the history of both of them and enjoys cult status amongst both sets of supporters.

The overwhelming majority of the Ajax success story unfolded at the old 19,000 capacity Stadion de Meer located in the Watergraafsmeer neighbourhood of the city.

Stadion de Meer

Ajax's fans loved de Meer; it was their spiritual home for over sixty eventful years. The team revelled in the intensity generated by their aggressive and hostile supporters. The notorious F-Side in particular had a fearsome reputation that terrified visiting teams and their fans. Sadly, a minority acquired an unhealthy fixation with fire crackers and other incendiary devices, often throwing them at visiting players and their supporters.

With football heading into an innovative new era of cash-rich globalisation and all-seated stadia, Ajax quite simply had to take advantage of their standing among Europe's elite and buy into the concept of modern football. The team's extraordinary success and increased fan base forced the club to depart their beloved de Meer and heartbroken fans had to bid a painful and tearful goodbye to the place where many Ajax legends had showcased their skills to a global audience.

They also left behind the infamous Ajax youth academy where so many precocious talents where harnessed and unleashed upon the world of football. Cruyff, Keizer, Neeskins, Van Basten, Rijkaard, Bergkamp, Davids, Seedorf, Kluivert and the de Boer twins were all graduates of this world-famous talent factory.

The Ajax focus on youth development now continues at De Toekmost (The Future) football academy, a state-of-the-art training facility custom built almost adjacent to the Amsterdam Arena. With an intake of up to 200 students aged between 7 and 19 years, the future of the next generation of Ajax superstars is in safe hands.

Ajax started a new chapter in their coveted history when in August 1996, they moved into the newly built 51,000 capacity Amsterdam Arena. Along with De Kuip, it is the only other UEFA five-star-rated stadium in the Netherlands.

Amsterdam Arena

This flagship stadium personifies the commercialisation of football and football stadia. Seen then as a prototype for innovative multi-use stadia, the arena is the focal point of a modern commercial village, designed to incorporate a shopping mall, a concert hall, a theatre and a cinema. A special feature of the arena is a state-of-the-art retractable roof, providing a fully enclosed all-weather facility.

Ajax is not a Jewish club but Amsterdam has a sizeable Jewish community and was home to 80,000 Jews prior to the Second World War. According to Simon Kuper (author of Ajax, The Dutch, The War), 'The great Ajax teams of the 60s were built on the support of the rich and driven survivors of Jewish Amsterdam.' Kuper recalls the pre-war Jewish–Ajax alliance that saw wealthy members of the Jewish community mingle freely on match days with affluent, middle-class locals.

In other parts of the Netherlands, it is widely perceived that a large percentage of Ajax supporters are not Jewish and have no idea what Jewish religion is about. However, the fact remains that it is a significant part of Ajax culture. The Star of David is synonymous with Ajax supporters and can be seen on t-shirts, hats and scarves. Many banners and flags also carry this most famous of Jewish symbols. Back in 2003, in a celebration of their Jewishness, Ajax fans unfurled a giant Star of David banner in the lower tier of the south stand just before the start of the Ajax v Valencia Champions League game.

Yet despite this pro-Jewish stance by the supporters, the club made a bid to distance themselves from their image as a Jewish football team. Ajax chairperson John Jaakke's New Year's speech once declared, 'Ajax is being presented as a Jewish club and some of our supporters have taken to calling themselves Jews as an honorary nickname. I want to state for the record that Ajax wants to shed this image and will do what is necessary to achieve this.' Club spokesman Simon Keizer also added, 'There is no historical basis for the club's Jewish image. It might be due to the fact that in the 1960s there were several players of Jewish descent' (source: AFP).

Reading between the lines, it is becoming apparent that the general consensus amongst club officials is that Ajax supporters calling themselves Jews is stoking up rampant anti-Semitic fervour amongst fans at other clubs. One thing is for sure, the Jewishness of Ajax Football Club and its supporters is a very contentious issue at present and is best left to debate by those far more qualified on this subject than me.

Tell people you are going to Amsterdam and there's every chance you'll get a nod and a wink from your mates and a death stare from 'er indoors. Hardly suprising really, because this is sin city, home to hashish coffee shops and sex traders. Despite its raunchy reputation, Amsterdam has something to offer for everyone. Most of it looks like a seventeenth-century metropolis, but Amsterdam is progressive and relaxed unlike any other city in the world.

Thanks to Amsterdam's unique blend of traditional and contemporary, the city is now a burgeoning tourist destination, a desirable place to live and a premier hot-spot for business. Its narrow streets lined with retail outlets, coffee shops, themed bars, a diverse nightlife, a red-light district and cultural venues assure a lively and modern scene for its inhabitants and tourists.

We left our hotel and headed for Amsterdam Centraal Station. As we walked through the red-light area it was hard to imagine that barely six hours ago this place was a hive of activity. With its neon lighting, flesh-filled windows and thumping music blaring out loud, Amsterdam was alive and kicking. Stag parties, hen parties, birthday parties and just about anybody needing an excuse to get rotten drunk, high and laid was here the night before. Several hours later you would barely recognise the place; no neon lights, no noise, no party people and no sex traders. It was just a quiet winter's morning awash with small groups of tourists meandering about the cobbled streets quietly killing time.

With Dave's hip playing up again, the ten-minute walk to the station descended into a twenty-minute chore but our timing was impeccable. The train was in and on time. It was only three stops to Duivendrecht and took approximately fifteen minutes.

We tagged on to the noisy red-and-white army departing our carriage and made the short walk to the stadium. As the arena came into view, so did the welcoming committee. Around fifty black-clad, baton-wielding robocops stood between us and the no-man's-land segregating home supporters and the arrival of the visitors' specially commissioned train.

The futuristic-looking arena had the appearance of a giant UFO and although almost 12 years old, this stylish 140 million-euro structure still had the look of an ultra-modern football stadium fit for the Ajax experience.

After collecting our match tickets from the ticket office we parted company and Dave headed off to the nearest bar to lubricate his troublesome hip. Given that I was still feeling the effects of the night before, I opted to clear my head with a walk around the revolutionary Ajax complex.

It was just over two hours before kick-off and the area around the stadium was frantic with activity. Replica shirts, hats, scarves and Israeli flags dominated the souvenir stalls littered across the concourse and there was no shortage of places to get a drink. Indoors or outdoors, it was the punter's choice. Drinking in the vicinity of the arena appeared to be compulsory, with thousands of Ajax supporters enjoying a beverage or two around the stadium before the game.

As I walked around the north side of the stadium I noticed a markedly heavier police presence. With the police helicopter hovering above and mounted police strategically placed, I sensed I was heading for the section that was reserved for the away supporters. As I got closer I could see the railway station in the background complete with the covered walkway that enabled the police to escort away fans directly from the train and into the stadium, immediately nullifying the risk of fan violence.

The same system is in operation at Feyenoord's De Kuip stadium. It's a safe and unique method of crowd control. Since its introduction, it has all but eradicated outbreaks of hooliganism between rival factions around the stadium.

Lawlessness has blighted Dutch football for many years. Organised thugs wreaking bloody havoc on a grand scale turned Holland into Europe's most troubled footballing nation. The S.C.F. (Sport Club Feyenoord) of Feyenoord and the F-Side from Ajax were two of the most active hooligan gangs whose notoriety dragged the game into the gutter and provided the sport of football with a negative image in the Netherlands.

Feyenoord's first explosive encounter with hooliganism occurred in Rotterdam at the second leg of the 1974 UEFA Cup final against Tottenham Hotspur. The sporadic outbreaks of crowd violence before, during and after the game resulted in over fifty Spurs hooligans being arrested and up to 150 supporters, mostly Feyenoord, being injured.

The S.C.F. hooligan group were established shortly afterwards and further enhanced their infamy with their frequent violent escapades throughout Europe. They gained worldwide notoriety and Feyenoord Football Club became synonymous with football hooliganism – the English disease! It's a reputation the club has been saddled with and has been unable to shed to this very day.

Their rivalry with the Ajax F-Side (named after the block in which they used to stand at the old de Meer Stadium – Vak F) is well documented and there have been many serious clashes. In 1989 the S.C.F. attacked Ajax supporters with two homemade nail bombs, injuring nineteen supporters, nine of them seriously. The de Meer stadium was transformed into a bloodthirsty war zone that day and it's a miracle that nobody suffered loss of life. The unprecedented media coverage helped to amplify the issue of football hooliganism and perhaps proved to be a major contributing factor in the long battle against football-related disorder in the Netherlands.

Ajax F-side in their new home at the Amsterdam Arena

In September 1989, Ajax became the first Dutch team to be banned from European competition after trouble broke out at the UEFA Cup match between Ajax and Austria Vienna at the old de Meer stadium. Missiles, including an iron bar, were thrown at the Austrian keeper resulting in a one-year ban from European competition. In fact, the whole of the 1980s saw a huge increase in hooliganism outside the stadium. The upsurge in violence saw shops being looted and innocent passers-by being attacked and robbed. Hooligans also caused havoc on the public transport system, sometimes causing thousands of pounds worth of damage to trains and trams.

Dutch football was making headlines for all the wrong reasons. It wasn't possible for ordinary supporters to attend matches without fear of being attacked by the lunatic fringe. The Ajax v Feyenoord games in particular were spiralling wildly out of control. The hatred between the two sets of supporters had literally exploded and the authorities, both footballing and political, had to take action. There was much-needed government-sponsored research on football hooliganism and this indicated a need for a preventative approach to the problem.

In addition to the Dutch fan projects established in 1986, the decision was taken to introduce all-seated stadia in the Netherlands, with a strong emphasis on CCTV being installed in and around the stadium area. Although this proved to be a major success in preventing outbreaks of violence within the confines of the stadium, it did little to prevent rival supporters clashing elsewhere. These new measures simply forced the hooligans away from the stadia and into the public domain. Fights became more organised with rival hooligan gangs arranging premeditated fights away from the prying eyes of the police and security services.

The 1990s saw hooligans become more organised to escape the watchful eye of a more experienced and better-equipped Dutch police force. As in the UK, the use of mobile phones kept the risk element one step ahead of the law as rival factions sought confrontation at unlikely times in secret locations.

On 23 March 1997, hundreds of rival Ajax and Feyenoord hooligans descended on the small town of Beverwijk in a prearranged brawl prior to Feyenoord's game with AZ Alkmaar. Extremely violent clashes ended with a leading Ajax F-Side member, 35-year-old Carlo Picornie, losing his life. He was beaten and stabbed to death by rival Feyenoord hooligans.

Gang members were reportedly armed with baseball bats, hammers, truncheons and knives as they fought a pitched battle on waste ground just off the A9 motorway, approximately 20 miles from Amsterdam. It is suspected that dozens of other supporters were injured or wounded but precise details could not be released as fans fled the scene in their cars before police arrived at the scene.

This was a well-organised tear-up by rival supporters who used mobile phones to outwit police. Dutch police admitted they knew there was going to be an outbreak of disorder but were powerless to act as the hooligans only decided on their combat zone at the last minute. 'We would have needed airborne troops to get between them,' a local police chief told Dutch radio. Feyenoord's chairman, Jorien van den Henrik, said it was 'a black day for Dutch football'.

Fifty-five people were arrested within days of the incident and many more afterwards. Extensive police investigations led to eight Feyenoord hooligans being jailed for their part in the killing of Carlo Picornie, who has the unenviable distinction of being the first person to die in football-related violence in the Netherlands. As a mark of respect to Carlo, the Ajax F-Side leave his seat empty at every Ajax home game and maintain to this very day that the 'battle of Beverwijk' was not a fair fight. This savagery was probably the worst of a litany of violent encounters between the two marauding groups of hooligans locked in a noxious game of one-upmanship.

Despite the tragic events at Beverwijk and prolonged efforts by the Dutch government to stop the escalation of football hooliganism in Holland, Ajax and Feyenoord supporters continued to wage war with each other showing nothing but contempt for the local police and government. The clubs' hate-filled feud has simmered for decades. There is bitterness, suspicion, extremism, insularity and a cultural chasm. Add paranoia to the mix and it becomes a cauldron of revulsion.

After the 1998 Dutch Super Cup final between Ajax and PSV played at Feyenoord Stadium, Ajax supporters set fire to the ground and clashed with police around the stadium. The following year saw eighty Feyenoord fans arrested after violence soured title-winning celebrations in Rotterdam city centre. Over 150 Feyenoord hooligans attacked police with missiles and other weapons and caused damage to property as well as looting shops.

Police were forced to discharge live rounds to restore order but this resulted in four fans being shot. It is estimated that rioting fans caused damage to property to a value in excess of six figures. Four months later another twenty-seven Feyenoord supporters were arrested for smashing up their train on the way back to Rotterdam after their match with Ajax.

On 15 April 2004, the never-ending culture of hatred between Ajax and Feyenoord football thugs reached a humiliating public nadir. Scores of Ajax hooligans invaded the pitch after a reserve team game between Ajax and Feyenoord played at the Ajax De Toekomst sports complex. They attacked the Feyenoord reserve team on the way back to the changing rooms.

It was a violent, frenzied and unprovoked attack in which a number of young Feyenoord players suffered injuries; Gerard de Nooijer, Danko Lazovic and Robin van Persie were punched in the face and treated for minor injuries. Jorge Ancuna, however, was beaten so badly he required hospital treatment for face, head, neck and rib injuries. He also suffered from concussion and complained of liver pain. Dutch media also confirmed that the Feyenoord reserve team coach was threatened with a knife.

Ajax were acutely embarrassed by this incident and vowed to swiftly identify and prosecute anybody remotely involved in this deeply unnerving affair. The most notorious band of Ajax supporters, the F-Side, took the extraordinary step of issuing a public statement, confirming their unequivocal disapproval of the carnage at De Toekomst:

> The F-Side strongly disapproves of the incidents after the game between Young Ajax and Young Feyenoord. The F-Side feels strongly about the code that players are left alone, both around matches and as individuals. Unfortunately and apparently this code is no longer respected by other factions. The F-Side regrets this. Breaking this code is inappropriate and causes damage to innocent persons. This should not have happened. We will, if possible, approach the persons involved in order to bring our viewpoint across.
>
> Feyenoord players have unjustly become the victims of the hatred between factions of the respective clubs' supporters. It has been the other way round on several occasions in the past. This hatred was stirred up by Feyenoord and the Rotterdam city council last Sunday. However, this does not legitimize this kind of excesses.
>
> The F-Side

F-Side Forever – a permanent F-Side mural in front of the south stand

Only 12 months after the De Toekomst debacle both sets of supporters brought shame on their clubs once again. Prior to the Feyenoord v Ajax game in Rotterdam, rival hooligans fought pitched battles outside the stadium. Both sets of fans attacked police before clashing with each other, resulting in a host of injuries amongst supporters and police officers. The level of hatred appeared to be getting worse and this was yet another sorry chapter that tainted the reputation of the two giants of Dutch football.

Given the history between these two bitter rivals, it becomes clear and easy to understand why *De Klassieker* is classified as the mother of all high-risk games. They don't share the same city but the fans genuinely hate each other. It's a strange hatred, almost unique. The authorities have spent a fortune on policing these intense affairs and no stone has been left unturned in the search for a solution to the unacceptable outbreaks of violence between the rival hooligan groups attached to both these great clubs with storied histories.

As I continued my walk around the arena, I spotted a large colourless contingent of Ajax supporters loitering in the vicinity of the north stand. They were drinking, eating and making small talk. Whilst most fans probably congregated here for the right reasons, I did suspect others had a more sinister motive for being there.

With the arrival of the Feyenoord fans almost imminent, the police presence increased and armoured vehicles formed a barrier across the concrete concourse. As the first of two specially commissioned trains carrying 1,600 visiting supporters arrived, crowd numbers visibly swelled, the mood turned from agitated to aggressive and the welcoming committee surged forward towards the police line in a futile attempt to harangue the visitors protected by military police, guard dogs, armoured vehicles and the safety of the football special. Drinks were thrown, insults hurled and firecrackers set off but the police refused to be drawn into confrontation.

Due to the violent nature of this fixture, no independent travel to the game is allowed. Visiting Feyenoord fans can only attend the Ajax game if they purchase a combi (combined match and travel ticket). Supporters travel from Rotterdam direct to the Amsterdam Arena on two heavily policed football specials. The visitors are escorted from the train and taken through the covered tubular walkway into the safety of the arena. At this point, both sets of fans hurl bile and vitriol up and down at each other safe in the knowledge that height, distance and no-nonsense policing keeps them apart.

Ajax supporters often taunt their rivals about the German bombardment of Rotterdam back in May 1940, whereas the Legion takes great pleasure in yelling anti-Semitic slogans, pouring scorn on the Ajax Jewish connection and the holocaust. Hissing sounds can often be heard, making reference to the Nazi death camps that the Jewish community were dispatched to during the war.

The intensity of the 'verbal exchanges' is usually the catalyst for clashes with the local robocops. It's not uncommon for supporters to throw missiles and firecrackers and let off smoke bombs as I had witnessed earlier. Although the riot police are deployed to keep order, they apparently have a notorious reputation for being overly aggressive and disproportionate in their actions. However, on this occasion it was a very low-key affair and I witnessed none of the shenanigans that normally mar this high-octane fixture.

I called Dave and arranged to meet him outside entrance *Zuid G*. We arrived at the meeting point at pretty much the same time only to find quite a sizeable queue had formed. With the start of the game almost upon us, I feared we would miss the kick-off.

Panic began to creep in as there didn't appear to be any way forward. We had become immersed in a static, colourful heaving mass of bodies. Raucous noise and song filled the early-afternoon air and I sensed a fever pitch of anticipation that intensified with every slow step forward. Thankfully, our apprehension was unexpectedly short-lived. Although the Dutch have a significant appetite for beer, they are a patient and orderly lot and despite my early fears, access to the stadium was quite smooth and relatively quick given the circumstances.

We used the escalator to get to the first floor and walked up several flights of stairs to get to our section. We found Block 406 and asked the steward to find our seats. My contact had come up trumps again, two seats right on the half-way line. Perfect.

With only five minutes to kick-off time the stadium was almost full to capacity. The whole arena was on its feet and the expectant home support charged up the atmosphere with their incessant singing and chanting. High up in the north stand, the token 1,600 Feyenoord contingent tried to make themselves heard but each time they burst into song they were mercilessly drowned out by a chorus of boos and whistles from the venomous home supporters.

Feyenoord have been the long-suffering bridesmaids of Dutch football, forever in the shadow of their illustrious rivals. Ajax have been crowned Dutch champions a record twenty-nine times, over double the number residing in their Rotterdam rivals' trophy cabinet. However, Feyenoord have not been without success themselves, accruing fourteen league titles, ten Dutch Cups, two UEFA Cups and contrary to popular belief, Feyenoord were Holland's first ever European Champions, beating Celtic 2–1 in extra time at the San Siro in 1970.

Together with the 1969–70 European Cup, the great Feyenoord team of the 1960s claimed four Eredivisie titles, including two league and cup doubles. Mercurial winger and Feyenoorders' all-time favourite player Coenraad 'Coen' Moulijn was the inspiration behind much of the 'club from the south's' success.

Born and raised in Rotterdam, the legendary number 10 played all but the first of his 18 years at his hometown club. Despite making only thirty-eight international appearances, Johan Cruyff named Coen in his all-time favourite Dutch national team, labelling him an 'exceptionally talented footballer, a typical product of the Dutch school'.

In 1961, Barcelona travelled to Rotterdam to discuss a transfer for the left winger but were promptly chased out of town and Mr Feyenoord signed an eight-year deal with the club that would make him financially sound for the rest of his life. Iconic old-school players like him, Hans Kraay (1960–68), Frans Bouwmeester (1960–66), Hans Venneker (1964–67 and the only Feyenoord player to score five goals in a single match against Ajax), Wim Jansen (1965–80) and Joop Van Daele (1967–76) were responsible for sowing the seeds that made Feyenoord the historic club it is today.

Feyenoord hosted the 2002 UEFA Cup final and went on to win it for the second time, beating Borrussia Dortmund 3–2 in the final on home soil.

Shortly before 12.30 p.m., the two teams of players entered the arena to the delight of both sets of supporters. They were greeted with rapturous applause and some well-organised Ajax tifosi. A huge red-and-white flag was unfurled in the north stand; it covered both tiers and was said to be the largest flag ever seen at an Eredivisie match. The rest of the stadium held up coloured cards, choreographed to spell out the name Ajax in the traditional red-and-white club colours. I was now looking forward to an enthralling ninety minutes of total football.

The north stand unveiling their colours

Ajax choreography (*tifosi*)

Sitting in this fantastic arena, surrounded by tailor-made fascia boards and drop-down banners reminding everyone of their illustrious past, you couldn't help but cast your mind back to the Ajax glory days of Rinus Michels and his concept of total football. Quite simply, the total football philosophy, believed by many experts in the game to be the single most tactical innovation in football history, is the ability of players to naturally interchange positions, effortlessly and efficiently, on demand. Adaptability is the key fundamental and is schooled into Ajax players from childhood. It's about being aware of space, creating space and utilising space. Attacking and defending as a single unit. Brilliant and jaw-droppingly entertaining when executed. The great Johan Cruyff once said, 'Simple football is the most beautiful. But playing simple football is the hardest thing.'

Rinus Michels created the great Ajax teams that so dominated Dutch football in the late 1960s and then also went on to conquer Europe in the early 1970s. He will always be remembered as the man who gave the world total football. He was named FIFA's coach of the century in 1999 and became affectionately known as the father of Dutch football. Under his guidance, world-class players like Johan Cruyff, Piet Keizer, Johan Neeskens and Rudi Kroll emerged and propelled both Ajax and Holland to footballing superpowerdom.

However, despite Michels' unprecedented success, in an interview with the BBC's Howard Booth, Ajax expert and Dutch author Menno Pot actually credits the emergence of total football at Ajax to little-known Englishman Jack Reynolds. 'Everything this club is about and everything this club is known for was invented and introduced by Jack Reynolds.'

Born in Bury on 23 September 1881, Reynolds was little more than a journeyman footballer who achieved modest success in his short and disappointing playing career. At the tender age of 30, he cut his managerial teeth at Swiss side St Gallen, before taking charge at Ajax in the first of two successful spells in his twenty-seven-year association with the Amsterdam club.

Reynolds is credited with revolutionising the way football was played, preferring skill over physical power. According to Menno Pot, Reynolds wasn't just a coach or a manager; he was the boss of a whole club and was responsible for introducing professional training methods and professional training facilities into an average amateur club, as Ajax was back then.

He transformed Ajax by focusing on youth development and introducing wing play, an offensive footballing concept never seen before in Dutch football. Whilst the acclaimed Reynolds success was indeed praiseworthy, lifting the Dutch cup in 1917 and winning eight league titles, his *pièce de résistance* was the development of a system that changed Ajax forever. Jack Reynolds retired from football management in 1947 and died 15 years later aged 81. He is remembered as one of the greatest managers Ajax ever had and his total football philosophy, adopted and perfected by Rinus Michels, continues to this day. The club honoured his memory by naming the VIP area in the Amsterdam Arena the Jack Reynolds Lobby and is also home to the commemorative plaque that used to adorn the stand named after him at the old De Meer stadium.

Jack Reynolds 1881–1962.

The home team started the match brightly, playing their usual high-tempo pass-and-move game, and it took only eight minutes before it paid dividends. Ajax defender John Heitinga scored with a neat left-foot shot from twelve yards out. The arena erupted into a red and white sea of embraces as fans around us exploded into life, hugging each other intimately and dancing around madly. With barely ten minutes on the clock, the crowd already sensed a home victory.

Ajax playmaker Gabri looked the real deal and was the chief tormentor of Feyenoord. When he had the ball Ajax always looked dangerous and right on the stroke of half-time, goal machine Huntelaar connected with a perfect right-wing cross from Gabri and headed the home side into a comfortable 2–0 lead. The ecstatic Ajax supporters celebrated wildly in the stands, taunting their anxious Rotterdam counterparts mercilessly.

The visitors' section high up in the north stand had no response and to be honest their team had really let them down in a very one-sided first half. A team that is famed for its grit and determination was completely outplayed, out-thought and, more alarmingly, outfought.

Dave volunteered to go down for the half-time refreshments whilst I relaxed and soaked up the occasion. I managed to scrounge a spare team-sheet from one of the Dutch journalists sitting in front of me. As I looked at today's official Ajax line-up, it suddenly dawned on me how far Ajax had fallen from grace.

Only thirteen years earlier, they were crowned Champions of Europe for a fourth time when Louis Van Gaal's underdogs beat hot favourites AC Milan 1–0 in Vienna, and the national team was composed almost entirely of Ajax players. The following season they were runners-up to Juventus, losing 4–2 on penalties in Rome. The team consisted of many great players such as Edgar Davids, Marco van Basten, Jari Litmanen and Clarence Seedorf, the only man to win three European Cups with three different teams (Ajax, Real Madrid and AC Milan). All were household names and famous throughout the world. Nowadays, only Jan Klaas Huntelaar is anything like a household name and more alarmingly the illustrious Ajax status has diminished to that of feeder club.

However unfortunate, this has now become a frequent occurrence, not just at Ajax but within Dutch football itself. The Eredevisie (Dutch League) doesn't generate anywhere near the income of Europe's other top leagues and the financial gap is getting bigger every year. Unable to offer the same footballing gravitas as the top clubs, Dutch teams are resigned to losing their star players, many of whom they have nurtured from an early age. Nearly all of the national team ply their trade in other leagues where they can earn exorbitant amounts of money. It is an endemic crisis that plagues the lower echelons of European football.

The second half started much like the first had ended, with Ajax a constant attacking threat and Feyenoord offering little in the form of resistance. The game was in danger of freefalling into little more than a training session for the home team and the lack of energy from the visitors had sucked the life out of the capacity crowd.

Midway through the second half, the Vak 10 boys attempted to ignite the stadium into life again. Founded in 2001, Vak 10 are based in Block 410 in the second tier of the arena, hence the name Vak 10 Boys (Block 410 Boys). This fan group was formed to generate a good atmosphere in the north side of the stadium. They are a lively, vocal young group who like to sing for the whole ninety minutes. They have an Italian Ultra mentality and love to bring their block to life using flags, banners, luminous flares, firecrackers and smoke pots.

A carelessly discarded distress flare caused a plume of viscous black smoke that threatened to engulf the whole of Block 10 to the left of me. Flames quickly swallowed around half a dozen plastic seats and the mood shifted from jovial to one of concern and apprehension. Fans 'rubber necked' from either side of the affected sector and for a fleeting moment the biggest game in Holland became something of a sideshow. Stadium security appeared to have been caught napping, but although slow to respond, the fire was thankfully contained and completely extinguished within seconds of their arrival.

After our brief flirtation with danger, it was back to the game. Ajax were pressing forward with intent and once again it was Gabri who impressed. He was providing plenty of ammunition for his rampaging teammates but a rather fortuitous Feyenoord defence somehow managed to hold out. I did however sense it was only a matter of time before Ajax further increased their lead against this very feeble Rotterdam outfit. A Feyenoord performance of this calibre served no purpose other than to further enhance the well-documented, insufferable Ajax superiority complex. When two styles go to war, attacking football should always prevail and rightly win the day.

Shortly before the end, a great move from new signing Lindgren gifted Huntelaar his second and Ajax's third and final goal of the game. The whole stadium erupted into song and taunted the visiting supporters with a perfect English rendition of the Monty Python classic, 'Always Look on the Bright Side of Life'.

The F-Side to my right and the Vak 10 Boys to my left sang with renewed vigour and breathed life into a capacity crowd that had been eerily subdued for most of the second period. There was a real buzz about the place now as there should be when two great rivals clash.

The final whistle was imminent and it was party time for the boys in red and white. Two minutes later and the 'fat lady' called time. All

49,000 Ajax supporters were on their feet, whistling, cheering and clapping, whilst down below the players basked in the glory of their second victory of the season against their bitter rivals. The artists had beaten the pragmatists!

Meanwhile, over in the visitors' sector there wasn't much to cheer about for the weary Feyenoord faithful. They had just watched their team totally outplayed in one of the most one-sided classicos in recent years. Subdued and disappointed, special non-stop trains would be waiting to take them on the sixty-minute alcohol-free journey back to Rotterdam.

Dave and I left the arena amongst jubilant Ajax fans heading for the nearest bar to celebrate their victory and with a glut of small beer stands and outlets serving alcohol, they hadn't got far to walk. Ajax had played well but most importantly, they entertained. They may not reach the heady heights of the past and they may not win the league title this year but victory against the *kakkerlakken* (cockroaches) makes Amsterdammers very happy. Silverware can wait, for now!

Between them, these clubs have dispensed with the services of over 20 managers in the last decade and both have suffered major upheaval behind the scenes. The expectation at both clubs is high, especially at four times European Champions Ajax where success is not only expected but demanded. In reality, Ajax, although big in stature, can no longer be considered a top European side and in the current climate both clubs will always struggle against Europe's wealthier clubs and that must hurt.

As for the chaos this fixture normally brings, we saw none of it today. Not a punch thrown in anger. There was no crowd disorder, no acts of drunkenness, no prejudice, no police brutality and no wanton vandalism. It was a decent game of football, played in the right spirit in a very modern stadium.

Violence at football is widely acknowledged as a serious problem by the Dutch authorities. They firmly believe that despite the introduction of all-seated stadia, CCTV surveillance, better stewarding and increased intelligence, hooliganism still poses a major threat. I am certain that the Dutch, as in England, do as much as is humanly possible to prevent outbreaks of violence at football. Sometimes, circumstances are beyond the control of football clubs and the authorities employed to keep order.

For Dave and me though, the night was still young and it was back to the chaotic tendencies of the centre and one last look at the forbidden fruit before heading back to Blighty.

Rajmund and Remik R.I.P.

The Wielkie Derby

Game: Ruch Chorzow 3 – 2 Gornik Zabrze
Venue: Slaski Stadion
Date: 2 March 2008
Attendance: 41,000

Poland and Ukraine easily overcame opposition from Italy and the collaboration of Croatia and Hungary to be chosen as host countries in their joint bid for the 2012 UEFA Championships, sparking scenes of happiness and celebration not seen since the end of the Communist era in 1989. The four Polish host cities of Gdansk, Poznan, Warsaw and Wroclaw, together with Krakow and Chorzow who are on the reserve list, partied all night long.

Since that historic evening back in April 2007, Poland has successfully attracted approximately 140 billion euros' worth of investment, most of which has come in the form of EU grants. It has effectively become the largest construction site in Europe and there is much to do in order to avoid the ignominy of losing the finals as many of its detractors predict. In order for them to succeed, which of course they will, they must conquer a significant shortfall in labour, caused primarily by Poles taking advantage of new legislation that simplifies access to the employment market and migrating to EU member states in search of the 'promised land' and a better quality of life.

Having had the experience of watching football in Poland on several occasions over the course of the past three decades, I can safely say that although the Poles are not renowned for producing the best football, their fans are passionate about the beautiful game at every level. The atmosphere they create is unique. Polish supporters, with a rich football heritage and their extraordinary fan culture, see themselves as part of the match-day experience, not just spectators, making Poland worthy suitors for jointly hosting the prestigious Euro 2012 event.

Attendances, although widely accepted as some of the lowest in Europe, have steadily increased in numbers over the past three seasons, with statistics confirming the average attendance is set to reach over 7,000 for the first time in recent years. This would constitute an almost forty per cent increase in the average gate since 2005.

Despite the growing optimism, Polish football is struggling to deal with the latest unshakable allegations of corruption levelled against its teams. Widzew Lodz and Zaglebie Lubin will both be relegated to the second tier this year for their part in one of a number of exceptionally damaging corruption scandals. Both clubs admitted to their participation in match fixing by bribing referees, according to the unofficial report by Przeglad Sportowy. They were accused of rigging the results in twenty-one games between them during 2004–2005. Over sixty football organisations' officials have also been detained on charges of fixing matches.

Combine this with the glut of ramshackle stadia in Poland, a chronic lack of funding and an uncontrollable hooligan epidemic that the authorities maintain will resolve itself, and it comes as no real surprise that this football-mad nation has become an easy target for the finger-wagging Euro 2012 doubters.

Regardless of the black cloud threatening to pour scorn on the integrity of the Polish league, the Ekstraklasa (Polish Premier division) remains ultra competitive and unpredictable. Ten different clubs have claimed the Ekstraklasa title in the last two decades. Despite the shortage of real quality players, the overabundance of high-profile games in the competition has ensured a distribution of success like no other league in Europe, making football an attractive and exciting proposition to the game's disciples.

Rivalry matches are a Polish specialism and the Silesian region harbours one of the most prolific grudge matches in the country. The great Silesian derby, colloquially known as the Wielkie derby, is contested by Ruch Chorzow and Gornik Zabrze, Poland's two most successful teams. They were the Polish heavyweights of the 1960s, '70s and '80s era and before the end of the Communist regime, games between the two eternal enemies attracted in excess of 100,000 supporters. They completely monopolised the Polish league, amassing a record total of twenty-eight titles between them.

Although records show fourteen titles each, Ruch fans insist they would have a record fifteenth title but for the disruption caused by World War Two when Ruch were leading the title race. Gornik can proudly boast the only ever European final appearance by a Polish team. They contested the 1970 European Cup Winners' Cup final against Manchester City. A 68th-minute goal from Stanislaw Oslislo set up a grandstand finish to the game but despite a valiant effort they couldn't find the elusive equaliser and Manchester City hung on for a famous 2–1 victory, played out in appalling weather conditions in front of 8,000 fans at the Prater Stadium in Vienna.

Silesia is a sprawling working-class union comprised of fourteen cities. It is one of the most industrialised regions of Poland, quite comparable to the Ruhr district in Germany. It's an area dominated by working-class communities and is famous for its mines, steelworks, football and of course deprivation. The Silesian region was rich in mineral resources, and during its peak could boast in excess of sixty working mines, nineteen steelworks and over a dozen large power plants. Tragically, the economy in Silesia has flat-lined. The majority of the mines and foundries, the Silesian population's primary source of income, are now obsolete having been decommissioned, leaving a once thriving province with a spiralling unemployment issue.

Back in the days before World War Two there were many Germans in the Silesia region and it was split into two in 1921 with a Polish–German borderline. Chorzow was on the Polish side and Zabrze was on the German side. Zabrze, one of Poland's oldest mining settlements, was badly damaged during World War Two and was transferred back to Poland in 1945.

Ruch Chorzow Football Club was formed in 1920 by the Polish citizens of Silesia as an opposition to the glut of German clubs in the region. Starting out under the name Ruch Hajduki, the club was one of the founder members of the Polish league in 1927 and went on to claim five league titles in the six years between 1933 and 1938. Ruch's most celebrated footballer was perhaps the catalyst to the team's monopoly of Polish football only 13 years after their formation.

Controversially, Silesian-German Ernst 'Ezi' Wilimowski will always be credited with helping establish Ruch as the earliest dominant force in Polish football. He signed for Ruch in 1933 aged just 17 and went on to score a phenomenal 112 goals in 86 games, including a record ten goals in the 12–1 defeat of Union Touring Lodz. Ezi was also the first player to score four goals in a single World Cup game in Poland's 6–5 defeat to Brazil in the 1938 World Cup finals and by the outbreak of war he had scored a prolific twenty-one goals in twenty-two international matches.

After the division of Poland, Wilimowski switched his allegiance and became a bona fide German citizen. He continued his football career whilst Poland was under Nazi occupation and represented Germany at international level. The Silesians never forgave him for his treachery and after the war the Polish government forbade him from returning to Poland, labelling him a traitor. Sadly, Wilimowski died in Germany in 1997 and despite an invitation from Ruch Chorzow to celebrate their seventy-fifth anniversary in 1995, he never did return to Poland after his enforced exile.

The name Ruch, meaning 'movement', is believed to be a tribute to the Silesian insurgent movements that fought for Silesian independence from the Fatherland during the 1919–1921 uprisings. In the aftermath of the bloody conflict, the German city of Kattowitz became the Polish city of Katowice and the eternally grateful inhabitants of the region's capital paid tribute to the heroes who fought by erecting Poland's largest memorial, the Silesian Uprising Monument, which can be found in downtown Katowice.

The outbreak of the Second World War saw the Nazis roll into town and promptly shut down Ruch, replacing it with their own football team, Bismarckhutter SV 99. The original club, however, was reborn shortly after the end of the war in 1945 and after the merger of the Hajduki Wielkie and Chorzow, the club assumed the current name Ruch Chorzow. And regardless of a number of other 'mandatory' Eastern European name changes during the Communist era, despite what it says in the history books, the club will always be remembered as Ruch Chorzow – the team of the steelworkers.

Throughout the German occupation of Poland, the city of Zabrze, considered as the 'most Polish of cities' by Charles De Gaulle, was called Hindenburg and was only renamed Zabrze when the borders were altered after the end of the Second World War. Several years later, in 1948, FK Gornik Zabrze was formed. The club was an amalgamation of four minor clubs (Zjednoczenie, Concordia, Pogon and Skra) that merged together with the intention of developing a formidable football club to represent the city of Zabrze. The name Gornik means miner and the club is nicknamed the team of the miners.

The team spent their formative years in the lower leagues before eventually gaining promotion to the first division for the first time in 1955. Ironically, their first opponents in the top flight were arch rivals Ruch Chorzow, whom they successfully defeated 3–1 in front of 25,000 supporters.

They won their first league title in 1957 before going on to dominate the 1960s, winning five consecutive league titles between 1963 and 1967. Their 1967 title triumph saw the team elevated into the 1967–68 European Cup competition. After fantastic victories over Swedish champions Djurgardens and Soviet champions Dinamo Kiev, Gornik were paired against Manchester United at the quarter-final stage. They lost the first leg 2–0 at Old Trafford but over 100,000 fans celebrated a famous 1–0 home victory. Despite elimination, Gornik remained the only team to defeat Manchester United in their inaugural European Cup-winning season.

The Polish league's most prolific goal scorer, Ernest Pohl, was instrumental in Gornik's success during his 12-year (1956–67) association with the club. He scored a record 186 top-flight goals in a 14-year career. In 2004, Gornik renamed their dilapidated 17,000 capacity ground the Ernest Pohl Stadium in his honour, it having originally being constructed in 1934 as the Adolf Hitler Stadium.

Although both clubs are staunchly working class and their fans share similar backgrounds, one very important word separates the two sets of supporters. Patriotism! Gornik's fans are exceptionally pro-Polish and the Patrioci (Patriots) flag is a prominent feature at all their games. The overwhelming majority of Ruch fans, however, declare themselves Silesian and their cause is publicly supported by the many banners draped around their stadium emblazoned with pro-Silesian slogans – '*TO MY NAROD SLASKI*' (It's us – the Silesian nation), '*DZIS KOSOVO*

JUTRO SLASK' (Today Kosovo, Silesia tomorrow). Pro-Silesian chanting is also a prominent feature at Ruch games – '*POLSKA, POLSKA BEZ SLASKA*' (Poland, Poland without Silesia), '*CHUJ Z WASZYM POLSKIM – JESTESMY NARODEM SLASKIMI*' (F*** your Polish – we are the Silesian nation).

Ruch fans are somewhat isolated and claim to have no friends in the Upper Silesian region. The youth of Ruch insist they have grown up in a 'they hate us, we hate them' environment that has been further exacerbated by the plethora of local rivalry within the Upper Silesian district and can make match day an unpleasant and dangerous experience. Gornik Zabrze, GKS Katowice, GKS Tychy, GKS Jastrzebie, Piast Gliwice and Polonia Bytom are all considered enemies of Ruch and are responsible for instigating a complex network of alliances who engage in violent activities against Ruch supporters at every opportunity.

In a region characterised by such a hostile rivalry, simply wearing the wrong colours in the wrong part of town can lead to dire consequences. Serious assaults are commonplace and rival supporters will steal your colours (scarf, shirt, hat etc.) to burn at the next derby against your team.

The burning of rival supporters' flags, scarves and shirts at games is a European phenomenon exercised by all hooligan groups in Poland. Each burning item symbolises a rival supporter being attacked, beaten and relieved of personal and sometimes irreplaceable club regalia. The public destruction of the enemy's colours signifies a small victory for the perpetrators responsible for the thefts.

Back in the 1960s and 1970s, although a great rivalry existed between Ruch and Gornik, it was always about matters on the pitch. It was a proper sporting rivalry consumed in banter and joviality. Violence was not a feature and segregation was unheard of.

Despite the lack of success in recent times, both teams still remain well supported, although the huge crowds of yesteryear are long gone. Today, these two fallen giants muster an average combined match-day attendance of approximately 8,000. Ruch have a large fan base throughout the whole of Silesia, even in Katowice, the capital of Upper Silesia. Although the area is monopolised by fans of local side GKS Katowice, the city is still widely regarded as a Ruch stronghold, especially in the older districts.

Gornik fans mostly come from Zabrze, with only a minority based in other areas. Ruda Slaska, a district in the heart of Upper Silesia, is one of the few cities with a shared allegiance between the two Slaski rivals, albeit a very volatile one. In a hooligan terms, Ruch, which has the best firm in the whole region, are considered the strongest.

We arrived in Kracow mid afternoon the day before the main event and made plans to go to the Wisla Kracow v Widzew Lodz game at Stadion Wisly. Our taxi driver had warned us that Windstorm Emma was on her way into town with heavy rain and up to 140-kmh winds expected. Not the best weather to socialise and watch football but hey, this is Poland, a connoisseur of extreme weather conditions.

After checking into our city-centre hotel, we headed straight into town. Unfortunately, our taxi driver's prediction proved to be correct. The rain was relentless so we took shelter in an American theme bar. We had a few beers and a decent meal before heading for the game. In spite of the inclement weather conditions, a decent-sized crowd was still expected for this unassuming televised fixture.

The game kicked off with hardly any away fans present. Seven hundred Widzew Lodz fans were expected at the game but only a fraction of that number actually made it on to the terracing. We found out later that the police had stopped the majority of the Widzew Lodz fans travelling. Apparently, this happens quite often in Poland. If the police think there is any hint of fans travelling to cause disorder they can pretty much use whatever measures they feel are appropriate, however disproportionate.

Wisla went 1–0 up just before half-time in a game almost as drab as the weather. The second half began in much the same fashion as the first and with conditions rapidly deteriorating we decided to call it a day and headed back to the hotel for a change of clothing.

After a quick shower we headed towards Market Square where we stumbled upon the Irish Mbassy Sports Bar on Embassy Street, the largest Irish bar in Poland and home to four floors, a myriad of plasma sports screens, good food and cheap beer. Home at last and a heavy night on the ale whilst watching Atletico Madrid destroy Barcelona 4–2 in a high-quality game of football, before turning in just after midnight, unwisely hammered, knowing we had an early-morning train to catch.

* * *

'Two single tickets to Katowice please,' I asked politely. The lady behind the glass screen glared at me with a menacing expression, paused for a second, then hit me with an almighty verbal assault in accelerated Polish. Well at least that's what it sounded like. I do try to speak a little of the native tongue in most places I visit but unfortunately for me Poland is not one of them. I have never been able to come to terms with a language that has more exceptions than rules. The complex mishmash of consonants and vowels splashed upon every signpost is a tourist's nightmare and the spoken word sounds like someone is about to throw up. Luckily for me, the young student behind me could speak English and volunteered to be my translator or I may have never got out of the station.

Apparently, the ticket attendants in Poland are known locally as *Panis* and they are renowned for their immense dislike of foreigners. This particular *Pani* had a brown bobbed haircut and looked hard and almost masculine in appearance, reminding me of the infamous Colonel Rosa Klebb of James Bond fame.

Klebb featured in *From Russia With Love* and was a villainous character who poisoned her foe by means of a venom-tipped dart hidden in her shoe. A fate I did not want to succumb to, so I thanked my new-found friend for his help and darted, no pun intended, to the platform, followed very closely by a very tired, half asleep and, in the guise of Rowley Birkin QC (*The Fast Show*), a very, very drunk Dave.

Dave and I boarded the old-fashioned-looking train and as the hangover had kicked in we claimed the first two vacant seats available. Train travel in Poland is strictly old-school, straight from the scene of a black-and-white movie. The carriage was worn but clean and comfortable with plenty of leg room. So comfortable in fact that within minutes of departing Kracow Glowny, Dave was sound asleep, leaving me to endure a two-hour journey devoid of conversation with only my ipod for company. I got myself comfortable and drifted off into a semi-conscious state with just Roger Daltrey for company.

Only four tracks into the *McVicar* album and my slumber was disturbed with a tap on the shoulder. The ticket inspector had arrived. He was a large brute of a man with a bald head and a doorman's demeanour. Surprisingly though, he was English-speaking. He apologised for waking me and merely clipped our tickets and scurried away down the narrow corridor and into the adjacent carriage. Try as I might, I could not drift away again and became agitated with my efforts to relax. Dave didn't help matters with his constant snoring; he was obviously suffering from the excesses of the night before but oblivious to the torture he was inflicting upon me.

We were just over forty minutes from Katowice and Dave was still fast asleep. As I gazed through the window the countryside appeared endlessly flat and nondescript, engulfed in a monochrome blandness where villages looked medieval and inhospitable. Poland looks soulless during the winter months, a cruel, cold, uninviting place. A far cry from the Poland I had experienced in the hot summer months, with its seaside towns with sandy beaches, its cosmopolitan cities that party from dusk till dawn and a drinking culture not too dissimilar to England.

It was 11.50 a.m. and our train was making a slow approach into Katowice station. My sleeping partner woke up right on cue, claiming he had not been to sleep but was merely resting in a trance-like drunken stupor.

We disembarked from the train and made our way to the main hall of the station. The smell as we left the platform was rank. It reeked of urine and stale vomit. It was putrid and hastened our efforts to find a taxi. We made a sharp exit, following the way-out signs strategically placed along the passageway that linked the stairways to rail platforms.

The main entrance provided temporary shelter from the elements to an array of undesirables. Beggars, drug addicts and homeless people take up residence here quite frequently and as a result, Katowice station has the ignominy of being the most dangerous rail hub in Poland. For some reason, most main stations in Europe attract the lowlife of this world and it would be fair to assume that once under cover of darkness the problem would escalate to a grander scale.

I had made loose arrangements to meet a friend in Katowice. On my arrival I was to contact Piotr, a GKS Belchatow fan and writer for *To My Kibice* (This is Us, the Fans), a cult Polish football fanzine documenting life on the terraces in Poland. I had been in contact with Piotr for about six weeks prior to the game. Although I had never met him, he was in touch on a regular basis with information about the derby. He also gave me a brief understanding of the Ultra and hooligan mentalities that are ingrained into the Polish fan scene. I was really looking forward to hooking up with him.

Piotr had tried to explain the complex network of rivalries and friendships that have evolved amongst hooligan and Ultra groups in

Poland over the years. It's normal to see large groups of hooligans from different clubs unite together and fight against rival factions. The Wielkie derby is no exception and is in fact a prime example of this crazy Eastern bloc phenomenon.

At today's derby I could expect to see allies of Ruch from Widzew Lodz, Elana Torun, Apator Torun and incredibly, maybe even a right-wing firm from La Liga outfit Atletico Madrid could be making their way to this match. I was at the Madrid derby back in January and remember getting caught up in an outbreak of disorder outside the Calderon stadium prior to kick-off. A joint mob of around sixty Atletico and Ruch lads fought a ten-minute running battle with police escorting Real Madrid fans to the visitors' entrance. Inside the stadium, a large Ruch Chorzow flag was unfurled by the notorious right-wing Atletico Frente Ultras in the south *curva* thus indeed confirming an unlikely alliance. I also recall small Ruch flags hung over the advertising boards and a home-made banner advertising today's 'Wielkie derby'.

Ruch flags on show at the Estadio Vincente Calderon
confirming their alliance with Atletico's Frente

Gornik were no strangers to the herd mentality themselves and would be joined on the trip to the Slaski with allies of their own. Supporters of Wisloka Debica and GKS Katowice (a local alliance against Ruch) were expected to swell the ranks of the Zabrze hard core. Mix this lot with the thousands of police on duty and it made for a very interesting afternoon!

Windstorm Emma had shown no signs of abating. The wind and rain were unforgiving. Before dashing outside to the taxi rank I tried to ring Piotr to arrange a meeting point. However, with no signal on my phone, it wasn't to be. He did say in a previous e-mail that he was going to meet up with Gornik fans around midday at Zaleze, a small railway station on the outskirts of Katowice. But as the weather conditions were deteriorating by the minute, I was not prepared to take a chance and decided to head directly to the stadium in the hope of meeting him before the game at some point.

Dave spotted a free cab and attracted the driver's attention. 'Hello, mate, do you speak English?' said Dave. Our driver was about sixty years old and looked every bit his age. He had a tatty grey head, a moustache, which is compulsory amongst Polish cabbies, and Parker-esque (*Thunderbirds*) bushy eyebrows. He wore a flat cap and an old-style grey suit like the one you could imagine your great-grandad was laid to rest in. He had probably never been out of Katowice in his entire life so the chances of him speaking English were remote, and so I took over negotiations. '*Stadion Slaski prosze*?' And with the nod of a head, we were on our way.

The rain was pelting down and Katowice looked stereotypically bland, like a scene from an old black-and-white movie. Dave tried to interact with our driver by talking at him loudly so whilst he was getting on famously with his new-found Polish friend, I tried to take in the sights through a misted, rain-sodden taxi window that had never seen a car wash since its manufacture. Most of the buildings we passed looked worn, in need of maintenance, grey or made of red brick which had lost its colour due to a century of industrialised pollution. Talk of Katowice being upwardly mobile appeared premature if first impressions are anything to go by. In a city where time appeared to have stood still, the streets were crammed with bleak looking, hideously dated cuboid constructions and dilapidated Communist-style tenement blocks.

The Wielkie derby had attracted the lion's share of media attention. It was the ninetieth meeting between the two great rivals and Ruch Chorzow had not played Gornik Zabrze as the designated home team since 2004.

Ruch normally play their home games at the 15,000 (officially 11,000) capacity Stadion Ruchu. This stadium was built in 1935 as a replacement for the original stadium situated in another district of the city. Back then, the symbol of the stadium was an old Omega clock. The original timepiece dating back to 1939 is still in situ at the current stadium and although it was partly destroyed by rampaging Wisla Kracow fans, it does remain in working order.

After winning promotion back to the top tier in 2007, Ruch had problems obtaining a league licence because of mounting debt and no under-soil heating at Stadion Ruchu. At the end of delicate negotiations it was agreed that Ruch could play some games at their home ground but during the late autumn months to early spring, games would have to be played at the Slaski Stadion due to the extreme weather conditions in Poland.

Nobody wanted the most popular Silesian derby to be played at the 41,000 capacity Slaski Stadium but it was not a matter of choice. A relentless marketing campaign, firstly by Ruch fans then later by Gornik supporters, drummed up extraordinary demand to see the game. The match was officially declared as sold out weeks ago. This would be the highest attendance at a Polish league game for twenty-four years and what made it even more remarkable was the fact that the match was between 8th (Gornik) and 11th (Ruch) place in the league.

There was now an abundance of police activity on the roads around us so I guessed we couldn't be far away from our destination. A police helicopter hovered in the black skies above us and sirens seemed to be constant. I was beginning to think we had arrived in the middle of an incident. Our taxi driver was forced to take one detour after another, as many roads to the stadium had been closed for security reasons.

A convoy of armoured vehicles led by two huge military-style water cannons sped in the opposite direction with blue lights flashing and sirens blaring. They were swiftly followed by police cars and police motorbikes. Our driver tried to explain the situation to Dave. He even tried talking loudly, English style, but it was futile. We just couldn't get to grips with this language. We just smiled and nodded politely.

The stadium was now in sight so we asked our driver to stop. We paid him 60plz (approximately £15) for our thirty-minute journey and thanked him before heading to the nearest shelter.

My contact had given me instructions to collect our match tickets at the ticket office which could be located on the road to the stadium opposite the AKS Carrefour supermarket. As luck would have it, our nearest place to shelter was indeed the supermarket, just across the road from where our driver had dropped us off.

Once inside, we found the supermarket was part of a small complex of shops built within a mini shopping mall. I never thought I would find myself seeking refuge in a supermarket two and a half hours before the great Silesian derby but I cannot begin to explain how shockingly bad the weather was.

The shopping mall was extremely busy and I estimate over a thousand Ruch supporters were in there, each carrying or consuming some form of cheap alcoholic beverage. Upon further exploration of the mall we stumbled across a small pub. We decided to grab the only two seats left outside the bar and ordered a couple of pints of the local brew before braving the weather conditions and seeking out the ticket office.

I got talking to a couple of English-speaking Ruch fans sitting adjacent to me. They explained to us that the huge police presence was normal for a game between these two great rivals. The police convoy we had seen earlier was heading to Zaleze rail station in preparation for the 16,000 Gornik fans expected to arrive there. They explained that Gornik fans would arrive intermittently on several trains and then be transferred to buses where they would be escorted by police direct to the stadium.

The rain had eased off a little so we decided to brave the elements and try to locate the ticket office. We made our way down the road to the stadium opposite the shopping mall and somehow managed to stumble upon the ticket office, or lack of one. It literally was a table and chair covered with a large sponsored umbrella. I gave my name to the lady and after fumbling through a shoebox full of envelopes she came across one bearing my name containing two tickets for the game. With tickets in hand it was back to the mall where our seats in the bar were still warm.

It was approximately ninety minutes before kick-off and the mall was full to capacity. It was crammed with drunken Ruch fans sheltering from the rain. I could feel tension and apprehension amongst the local traders. The fans were noisy but not aggressive. Their behaviour was raucous but not abusive. They were drunk but not paralytic. It was derby day and singing loudly with an alcohol-induced ten-bob sway on is not a crime. I did however think trouble was looming when around fifty shaven-headed, muscle-bound hoodlums carved from granite marched into the mall through a rear entrance bellowing out loud, 'Hooligan, hooligan, hooligan!' They were a young skinhead firm all dressed in black hoodies, bursting with bravado and maxed up on testosterone. But with no Gornik around to inflict pain upon they disappeared into the early afternoon monsoon.

Skinheadism was at its peak in Poland in the late 1980s and early '90s. Chorzow in particular was a skinhead stronghold and the terraces were and still are to a lesser extent awash with skinhead firms promoting their right-wing and nationalist ideologies. Pro-German neo-nazi skinheads used to fight on the city streets with Polish patriot skinheads but rivalry was always forgotten on match days and the two groups would always unite at Ruch to fight with visiting supporters.

With only thirty minutes to kick-off we decided to drink up and join the noisy blue-and-white exodus for the short walk down the tree-lined road to the ground. The wind had dropped and we were now down to the occasional shower rather than the constant driving rain that was set to ruin the occasion. There was a huge police presence around the perimeter of the stadium, all heavily armed with an assortment of potentially lethal weapons. They carried three-inch-diameter clubs rather than the standard-issue baton carried by police in the UK. They were also kitted out in the finest protective clothing, together with riot shields and helmets with visors. I found it difficult to believe anybody could pick a fight with these brutes and win.

After talking our way through three heavily policed check points we finally arrived at our entrance and were just in time to see the latter end of the Gornik fans arrive. They were brought in on similar buses to the one Freddy Krueger drove in the classic horror film *A Nightmare on Elm Street.* Gornik supporters were hanging out of every window, all uniformly dressed in red–and-white scarves and red-and-white-striped beany hats that had been custom made for the game. It was a very colourful and chaotic entrance.

Dave made his way into the stadium whilst I had a quick look around to see if I could remember anything from my previous visit to this bleak and characterless construction back in 1997.

Stadion Slaski opened its doors on 22 July 1956. Poland played host to East Germany in a game they lost 0–2. It was initially designed to hold 87,000 spectators but actually attracted a record crowd of 120,000 for the Gornik Zabrze v Austria Vienna European Cup tie in 1963. It's the official home to the Polish national side and has a current all-seated capacity of 47,000.

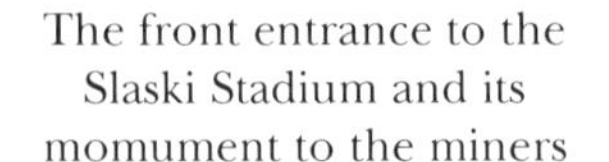

The front entrance to the Slaski Stadium and its momument to the miners

After my brief recollection of past memories I decided to make my way into the ground. With only ten minutes to kick-off, most of the supporters were inside by now which left me with a smooth uneventful access to my tribune. However, finding my seat was another story. I was passed from pillar to post by four or five different stewards before eventually spying Dave making small talk with one of the Polish journalists in the media sector. As nobody could actually find my seat for me I decided to sit on the soaking-wet spare seat at the end of the row next to Dave.

Cheerleaders from both clubs led the teams out to a thunderous reception. White streamers rained down on to the pitch and Ruch fans drowned out the announcement of the Gornik team with a relentless cacophony of boos and jeers. The blue-and-white army of Ruch fans to my right outnumbered the red-and-white legion of Gornik fans to my left by almost three to one. The official Zabrze ticket allocation was 12,000 but word on the street was they had over 16,000 supporters inside the stadium.

A carnival atmosphere greets the players as they emerge from the tunnel

Gormik supporters welcome their team

The Ruch sector before the start of the game

Gormik Ultras unfurl their huge club crest

Just before kick-off the Ultras set about displaying their choreography. Ruch fans unfurled four large flags, one of which was their famous blue-and-white club crest. At the other end of the stadium Gornik fans presented their *tifo*, also in the form of a huge flag bearing the club crest on a background of cleverly sequenced silver cards held up by surrounding Gornik spectators.

The meticulously organised Ultra groups pay for their own choreography. At Ruch, the Ultras fund the costing of their materials by collecting donations in and around the stadium and by selling unofficial Ultra merchandise at a small profit. They are a dedicated team of fanatics who devote a great deal of time to creating spectacular choreographed displays at Ruch games, ensuring a vigorous welcome for their team as they exit the relative calm of the players' tunnel.

As the game got under way Windstorm Emma came back into town for one last dance. I was thankful for being seated under the only covered part of the stadium at the rear of the players' entrance. The weather didn't dampen the spirits of the supporters though as they were in fine voice throughout. In the 28th minute Ruch supporters got what they came for, a goal against their bitter rivals.

The *Niebiescy* (Blues) erupted in celebration after Number 7, Cwielong, deservedly put his team in front and dashed towards his own supporters to celebrate a well-taken goal. Suddenly the dreadful weather conditions didn't matter any more, unless you're a neutral of course!

The Gornik supporters who were silent during the course of the goal celebrations suddenly burst into life with a terrace chant to the tune of the famous Beatles anthem 'Yellow Submarine', whilst jumping up and down together in tandem. However, not to be outdone, Ruch fans copied the chant twice as loud, jumping twice as high with backs to the field of play.

Eight minutes later and Brzeczec's equaliser sent the 16,000 Gornik collective into raptures, submerging them into a sea of madness as they embraced en masse. It was little more than Gornik deserved after scrapping their way back into a game that Ruch had completely dominated during the early exchanges.

Shortly before the interval the in-form home support embarked upon a flag-waving fest to the tune of 'Rivers of Babylon'. It was at this point that I noticed the large, intimidating black–and-white 'PSYCHO FANS' banner in the right-hand corner behind the Ruch goal. Both clubs have a similar-size fan base and both attract a voluble and active hooligan horde. Whilst Gornik's risk supporters (Torcida) are considered dangerous, there is absolutely no comparison with Ruch's Psycho Fans who are rated amongst the Polish fighting elite.

A Ruch flag-waving fest

The infamous 'Psycho Fans' banner

Psycho Fans is the infamous Ruch Chorzow fan movement who reside in sector eight of their home stadium and usually in or around sectors 38–40 at the Slaski stadium. This hard-core unit are solely responsible for orchestrating the incessant singing and chanting at all the blues games. When Psycho Fans sing, everyone in the stadium follows suit, culminating in a mosh pit of organised anarchy.

Founded in 1990, Psycho Fans has between 1,500 and 2,000 members and is the largest Ultra group in the stadium. Actively operating amongst them are up to 200 Psycho Fans hooligans and the reputation for extreme violence is their main asset. Prior to 1990, the lunatic fringe was known as *Ekipa Remontowa* (Renovation Squad) and this elite fighting core was at the forefront of football violence throughout the whole of the country. But despite the violent tendencies of the sizeable minority, Psycho Fans Ultras have a great relationship with the club and Ruch players go to their sector to thank them for their support after each match.

The ill-famed Renovation Squad played an integral part in the brutal underground Polish fight scene called *ustawka*, also known as barbecuing or grilling. Polish hooligan firms, numbering 20–100 and trained in mixed martial arts, would meet up at an agreed secret location, usually in a secluded forest, where they would fight without weapons until one firm was completely smashed. It's a sadistic fight club that goes way beyond the realms of spontaneous street fighting. It is, in essence, professional hooliganism, an unhinged game of last man standing ... and that takes cahoonas the size of ostrich eggs!

As a fan group, the most memorable day in Psycho Fans Ultras' history was last year (2007) when Ruch finally won promotion back into the top tier of Polish football after a four-year absence.

As a hooligan group, the most famous day in Psycho Fans' history was four years ago on 3 May 2004 in a second-division game against LKS Lodz in Chorzow.

During the half-time interval, police estimate an alliance of between 500 and 700 hooligans from Ruch Chorzow and Widzew Lodz (big rival of LKS) tore down fencing, invaded the pitch and using a range of makeshift weapons, fought a pitched battle with over 500 rival LKS Lodz hooligans for almost an hour.

Riot police really struggled to restore calm and at one point were subjected to a savage united attack by the whole of the rampaging mob. After being beaten and forced to make a hasty retreat from the stadium, they were left with no alternative but to use water cannons and rubber bullets to gain control of one of the worst sporting riots in Polish history.

All together, media reports confirmed sixty-one police officers were injured (five hospitalised) and in excess of 160 supporters arrested, fifty-three of them for attacking police officers. Needless to say, the relationship between the police and Psycho Fans remains very poor because of that incident and at most games Psycho Fans provoke the police by singing their song, '*Zawsze i wszedzie policja jebana bedzie*' (Always and everywhere f*** the police).

Due to the fragile and ever-deteriorating relationship between law enforcement and Polish supporters in general, the majority of stadia tend to be policed by private security companies. It is widely recognised that a high-profile police presence within the confines of the stadium increases tensions and although officers are deployed to keep order, their reputation for being overly aggressive has in the past often been the catalyst for large-scale disturbances.

Half-time couldn't come quick enough. The weather was again deteriorating and I am certain the players were as overjoyed as we were to hear the referee's whistle signal the end of a very entertaining first half of low-quality, high-octane football. For all the hype and hysteria surrounding this bitter grudge match, we mustn't forget what the dedicated supporters brought to the stadium. On a treacherous afternoon, in a game notoriously characterised by extreme fan violence, both sets of supporters had partied like their lives depended on it and had been a real credit to their clubs.

I took advantage of the break to try and locate a drier vantage point deeper into our tribune. Although we were under cover, the blustery wind drove the rain into our direction. But a quick glance at the vast majority of spectators without cover made me feel a whole lot better.

They were soaked from head to toe. They couldn't have been any wetter had they bathed in the rain. It wasn't just wet rain either. It was bitterly cold rain, the sort that chills your bones!

As the players returned to the field Ruch fans displayed three large hand-painted murals to my right. The central one had a black background bearing the club crest, flanked either side by black-and-white murals of two young men, Rajmund and Remik. At first I thought they were two ex-players but was later told, by 'old-school' and lifelong Psycho Fan Kroncic, the very sad story behind the tribute.

Rajmund and Remik were two young Ruch supporters brutally murdered by Gornik thugs in separate incidents. On 17 May 1997, 19-year-old Ruch supporter Remigiusz Thiem, known locally as Remik, was kicked unconscious by rival Gornik hooligans and brutally thrown to his death off a railway bridge. Once word of this horrific act had spread amongst Ruch fans there was talk of a *smierc za smierc* (death for a death) mentality and police feared the worst. Fortunately the inevitable visceral reaction never materialised.

Relations steadily worsened between the two sworn enemies but sank to an all-time low when five years later another Ruch supporter was killed after clashes with Gornik thugs. On 10 August 2002, 16-year-old Rajmund Drynda, from the Halemba district in the southern part of Ruda Slaska, was seriously injured after hooligans from Gornik Zabrze attacked a small number of unarmed Zaglebie Lubin supporters bearing no colours and not looking for trouble (Ruch supporters had a friendship with Lubin fans). Rajmund was hit in the leg with one of three distress flares fired at the group just after they got off a bus taking them to the Lubin v Gornik match. He was so badly burned in the attack that surgeons reportedly had no alternative but to amputate the young boy's leg. Rajmund died in hospital from his injuries just over a week later.

Rajmund and
Remik R.I.P.

On the derby after Rajmund's death in the autumn of 2002, Ruch fans collected hundreds of Gornik scarves and burned them on the terrace fencing before the game, with one transparent Ruch banner proclaiming '*WY PALICIE MY ZABIJAMY*' (You buy them, we burn them). In the next derby at Gornik six months later, supporters retaliated by displaying a transparent banner of their own pronouncing '*WY PALICIE MY ZABIJAMY*' (You burn them, we are killing).

In the days after the derby, sick graffiti appeared all around the Ruda Slaska district: Gornik 2 Ruch 0 in reference to the two young murdered supporters. This region is the biggest war zone between Ruch and Gornik fans and is quite often turned into a battleground by rival hooligans living there. Ruch supporters have boycotted all games at Gornik since the spring of 2003 and have no intention of returning. Psycho Fans say, '*Nie dla derbow z mordercami*' (No derbies with the murderers!)'.

To some people 'football is life'. How ironic then, that two young Ruch supporters with their whole lives ahead of them lost them to football. Rajmund and Remik R.I.P.

The use of weapons in gang fights between rival hooligans has been a huge problem in Poland and the primary cause of most football-related fatalities. In December 2004, Lech Poznan hools invited mob leaders from hooligan firms across the country to discuss the frequent use of weapons during fights between rival gang members. In a pub adjacent to the stadium of Lech, representatives of some seventy football firms gathered together and agreed to fight with only fists and feet! Soon after the groundbreaking meeting, the 'Poznan Pact' was embraced by almost every Polish firm. There were, however, exceptions. Ultra-violent Krakow rivals Wisla and Cracovia didn't accept the arrangement. Also hooligans from Ruch Chorzow and Gornik Zabrze weren't wholly convinced, but in the end, they agreed. Unfortunately, the Poznan Pact came too late for Rajmund and Remik.

The second half began in the same fashion as the first half. Ruch were once again the dominant force and their pressure forced an early corner. Only two minutes had elapsed when Grzegorz Baran headed into the Gornik goal, much to the dismay of the Gornik fans at the rear of it. Cue tribune-trembling celebrations of the masses!

With the second half barely fifteen minutes old and Gornik struggling to stay in the game, the red-and-white hordes behind the goal to my left started to simultaneously light hundreds of luminous red flares. It started in the bottom corner behind a Torcida (Zabrze Ultra group) banner and quickly spread throughout the stand. It was a jaw-dropping, pre-planned pyrotechnic show of the highest magnitude. It really was a spectacular sight and both Dave and I could feel the heat generated by these flares up in our stand on the halfway line.

Gormik supporters turn the visitors section into a blazing inferno

Pyro shows used to be commonplace at all league games in Poland but the authorities banned them because rival fans used them as weapons. It therefore begs the question, how did two to three thousand Gornik fans manage to smuggle flares into the stadium?

Ruch supporters haven't used pyro at their games since 2007 because their club got fined and fans had to serve a four-match away ban. 'It just isn't worth it,' according to Kroncic. 'Ruch are victimised for pyro use whilst others get away with it.' He firmly believes it is because of the club's Silesian identity!

Shortly after the pyro show Ruch made it 3–1. A great move from midfield left Nowak clear in front of goal and a sublime finish found the roof of the net. Cue another avalanche of delight in the blue-and-white sectors of the Slaski.

With local pride at stake and 16,000 devastated visitors to appease, Gornik threw everyone forward in search of little more than divine intervention. And in an adrenalin-fuelled close to the match, with just seven minutes to go, an unlikely equaliser became a distinct possibility when Zahorski's well-placed header reduced the deficit to a solitary goal. But despite the fresh impetus from a rejuvenated Gornik team, an extremely vocal visitors' sector and a last-minute red card for Blues midfielder Marko Bajic, it wasn't enough to stop a determined and desperate ten-man Ruch holding out for a well-deserved derby victory against their eternal rivals. It was a result that restored Ruch to their rightful position as the top team in Silesia and secured the weekend's bragging rights for their cold and soaking-wet die-hard supporters.

Both sets of fans contributed greatly to a keenly fought contest in appalling weather conditions. The atmosphere they create at these games is extraordinary and it becomes quite apparent that players feed on the adulation of their supporters. The sell-out crowd was constantly singing, chanting and waving flags. As much as she tried, even 'Windstorm Emma' couldn't dampen the spirits of these loyal servants. Derby day is the most important and eagerly awaited date in any football calendar. After today's offerings it is easy to understand why.

To these two sets of supporters, football is indeed life!

The Green Mile … and a half

O Classico

Game: Benfica 2 – 0 Sporting Lisborn
Venue: Estadio de Luz
Date: 27 September 2008
Attendance: 60,002

'*Filho da puta – filho da puta – filho da puta*' (son of a bitch), screamed the 2,000-strong Sporting *cortejo* as they were escorted through the Benfica-infested neighbourhood on their way to the cathedral of football, Benfica's 'Stadium of Light', one of the world's most iconic football stadia. *Benfiquistas* living in the high-rise tenement blocks booed and whistled at their adversaries below whilst neighbouring *Sportinguistas* retaliated by cheering, applauding and spinning green scarves above their heads. Like any two-team city, the rivalry is intense and passions run high whenever these sides meet. There are no friendly neighbours on match day, just disciples of the enemy.

The Derby da Capital celebrated its centenary last year but the rivalry that was created at the beginning of the twentieth century has shown little sign of abating. The two teams involved may no longer be the powers they once were, but with 80 per cent of the Portuguese population supporting *Os Leoes* (The Lions) of Sporting or *As Aguias* (The Eagles) of Benfica, it is Portugal's most eagerly anticipated football fixture.

With only three league titles between them in the last fifteen years and no European success since Benfica lifted the European Cup in 1962, topping the bragging-rights table is the only consolation left for the long-suffering supporters of both teams. Only a *Benfiquista* or a *Sportinguista* can fully understand the importance of this game.

While Benfica claim to be the people's team, aristocratic Sporting have a history of affluence and elitism. Largely funded and guided by a wealthy local landowner the Viscount of Alvalade, Sporting Clube de Portugal was formed in 1906. They adopted the raging lion of another club patron, Count Don Fernando de Castelo Branco, as their crest and symbol of the club and aimed to create Europe's principal multi-use sports club.

December 1 1907 saw the first meeting between the two Lisbon giants. It was also the game in which Sporting players changed from their original all-white strip into a striped green-and-white jersey with white socks. It was a new kit that was to become synonymous with the formation of Sporting and was reproduced 100 years later to celebrate the club's centenary in 2007. Played out in treacherous weather conditions, a Sporting team containing eight former Benfica players ran out 2–1 victors, heralding the start of an eternal rivalry that has lasted over 100 years.

The 1938 reformation of the Portuguese football championship saw a new league format introduced and so began the *Campeonato Nacional da Primeira Divisao.* Although Porto won the first two championships, it wasn't long before the Sporting juggernaut took to the road. The years between 1946 and 1954 proved to be the most successful period in the club's history, with seven league titles in eight seasons.

Correia, Vasques, Travassos, Albano and the prolific Fernando Peyroteo made up the legendary Sporting forward line nicknamed *Os Cinco Violinos* (The Five Violins) and were the five key players instrumental in Sporting's success. They were a formidable attack-minded unit blessed with a telepathic-like chemistry. During the 1946–47 championship-winning season, this deadly collective helped Sporting score an amazing 123 goals in 26 matches, an unprecedented average of almost five goals per game.

The early 1950s saw the introduction of the European Champions Cup. This prestigious cup competition was originally commissioned by French-based *L'Equipe* and did not require participants to be champions of their own domestic league. Entrants were invited into the tournament based on their prestige and fan appeal.

Despite Benfica finishing the 1954–55 season as Portuguese champions, it was Sporting who had the distinction of playing in the first ever Champions Cup game and despite a gutsy first-leg 3–3 draw with Partizan Belgrade in Lisbon, the Lions succumbed to a disappointing 8–5 aggregate defeat in Yugoslavia that saw them dispatched from the competition at the first hurdle. Being overlooked for entry into the inaugural Champions Cup at the expense of their wealthy neighbours was a contentious decision that further intensified Portugal's greatest sporting rivalry and still irks Benfiquistas over fifty years later.

In 1956 Sporting opened their new stadium. It was named Estadio Alvalade in honour of Jose Alvalade, the grandson of Viscount Alvalade who was instrumental in the club's formation.

A decade later, Sporting defeated MTK Budapest of Hungary 4–3 in a two-legged final to become Portugal's only ever winner of the now defunct UEFA Cup Winners' Cup, their one and only European success to date.

It was mid afternoon when Dave and I arrived at the Alvalade and the Sporting Ultras were already out in force. We headed straight for the Juve Leo Ultra bar, home of Sporting's largest and Portugal's oldest Ultra group. Their HQ is situated under the steps directly outside the stadium and is the preferred meeting place for the hard-core Sporting Ultras before games. It's a small bar, not much bigger than a large double garage, but you can get a cheap beer and soak up the Ultra mentality of the Sporting supporters.

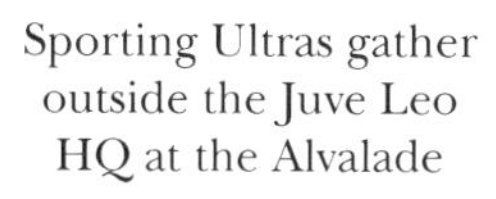

Sporting Ultras gather outside the Juve Leo HQ at the Alvalade

It was here we met 32-year-old Sporting militant and proud Juve Leo member Jose. He is a lifelong Sporting fan who was introduced to *os melhor jogo* (the beautiful game) by his father as an innocent eight-year-old back in 1986. He was addicted almost immediately. Six-foot-tall mesomorph Jose was keen to show off his Sporting tattoos. He whipped of his Sporting shirt to proudly reveal his Juve Leo tattoo perfectly positioned on his right shoulder blade. 'Juve Leo is my life,' he proclaimed. 'Tonight's derby will show you the strength of passion we have for the game and you will see just how much victory means to the supporters when the game is done.

'Come, let's get a beer,' insisted Jose, 'and I will tell you about Juve Leo.' We followed Jose's path as he shouldered his way to the bar, shaking hands and high-fiving his pals along the way. He introduced us to his friends as two crazy English guys who had come to see Sporting kick the ass of the *Lampioes*, the Sporting nickname given to Benfica supporters in reference to their Stadium of Light home. Jose got the beers in and we sat on the steps above the bar.

'This is a unique occasion you are never likely to forget, so let's start at the beginning,' said Jose. 'Sporting has 300 official fan houses [supporters' clubs] and 100,000 club members worldwide. We have only four recognised fan groups at the club, Juve Leo, Directivo Ultras XXI (DUXXI), Torcida Verde and Brigada.' And with that he pointed to the different banners draped around the stadium forecourt belonging to each of the groups.

'My group, Juventude Leonina [Juve Leo for short], are the biggest and most respected. We were formed in 1976 by the sons of Joao Rocha, a former Sporting president. Our name, meaning 'Lion Youth', was given to us because our symbol is a lion and the group was created by young supporters. We also have the face of a young boy on our banners. He represents all the Sporting youth. Football is our life and we bring the stadium alive with our passion for the team. You must come to the Alvalade for the home game with Benfica,' he pleaded. 'You will see a partisan devotion like no other. It is a great atmosphere, like nowhere else in Portugal.'

Juve Leo also has a dark side. Group 1143 is a small nationalistic skinhead group named after the year Portugal was founded and is said to be a splinter group within Juventude Leonina. Their leader, Mario 'M', also the leader of the Hammerskin Skinhead Movement, has been in preventative custody for some time now whilst awaiting trial for a number of offences including racial discrimination, abductions, illegal ownership of weapons and the spreading of neo-Nazi propaganda.

'Mario is a very dangerous person,' said Jose. 'Their group is not something I, nor many others, agree with but we just don't get involved with them or their beliefs. Most clubs in Portugal have racist groups but fortunately they are very much in a minority.'

Two years after the formation of Juve Leo, Sporting gained another supporters' group called Torcida Verde. They are a small group but have a great reputation for producing huge banners and creating great *tifosi*.

In 2002, an internal problem between the leading members of Juve Leo resulted in the exit of hundreds of Ultras. They wasted no time in setting up a rival group, calling themselves Directivo Ultras XXI. The acrimonious break-up resulted in sporadic outbreaks of violence on the terraces as opposing factions fought out a bloody turf war. Nowadays, differences have been resolved, scores have been settled and Sporting are united again, all pulling together for the same cause. Directivo has grown into one of the biggest ultra groups in Portugal and take their place on the north stand of the Alvalade.

Brigada is the last and smallest of the recognised groups at Sporting. They have only a few members at present and were created by some disgruntled guys who left Torcida Verde.

Time was getting on and police numbers became more visible. Around 1,500 or so supporters gathered on the stadium concourse and were making their presence felt by singing loudly and lighting up luminous red flares. Although the rivalry is intense and the hatred unbearable at times, fan violence in Portugal is relatively rare in comparison with other European countries. The O Classico has provoked disorder in the past, but they were mainly isolated incidents and dealt with meticulously by the infamous Portuguese riot police.

A terrible accident at the 1996 Portuguese Cup final between the two Lisbon superpowers led to the death of Sporting fan Rui Mendes. The 36-year-old father of two was tragically killed after being hit in the chest by a flaming distress flare launched from the Benfica sector. The game continued in a tense atmosphere and although Benfica went on to lift the trophy, defeating Sporting 3–1, celebrations where somewhat muted once news of Rui's death reached the players. The whole tragic episode sent the Portuguese footballing world into mourning, briefly uniting the red and green halves of the city.

The green army were in fine voice and the carnival atmosphere that surrounds these famous games got into full swing as supporters let off firecrackers and lit flares. The Ultra bar was rocking and singing fans began to pour out to join in the mass exodus for Benfica. Jose said his goodbyes and joined the rest of the Juve Leo boys as they organised themselves with military precision for the two kilometre walk to Estadio de Luz.

Fully kitted armed police moved in to surround the *cortejo* and police riot vans, driving very slowly with lights flashing, led from the front and followed from the rear.

Sporting received around 2,500 tickets for today's game, almost a quarter of the allocation they got pre-Euro 2004. In the 1990s it was not uncommon to see a mass invasion of around 10,000 visitors but new laws were established after the European Championships, enforcing a meagre allocation of only 2,500–3,000 tickets for any visiting team. Tickets for the derby were distributed amongst the official supporters' groups with the Juve Leo boys gaining the lion's share of around 1,500. The same rule also applies for Benfica fans when they play at the Alvalade.

The *cortejo* was escorted by the *Policia* from the confines of the Alvalade, led by Torcida Verde and their banners, followed closely by Directivo Ultras and last but not least, the colourful and noisy Juve Leo group.

Torcida 1984 leading the *cortejo* from the confines of the Alvalade

A one-hour, mile-and-a-half parade lay ahead and the sea of green cranked up the noise levels. The *cortejo* had a real sense of purpose about this journey. They were singing loudly, chanting, igniting flares and showing off their signature flags and banners. Traffic came to a temporary standstill as they put on a real show for the gawping passers-by and the residents who lived en route. The nearer we got to the Luz, the louder and more animated the Leos got.

The Juve Leo Boys en route to the 'cathedral'

Plain clothes *Policia* wearing stab-proof vests walked ahead of the armoured police vehicles in small snatch squads. They would periodically sprint down many of the adjoining streets with batons drawn, chasing away any would-be Benfica hooligans looking to ambush the carnival-like *cortejo*. Their would-be attackers never even got close to the visitors. They were dealt with swiftly and efficiently by the experienced and often brutal Portuguese football police. Manchester United fans can pay testament to that after being set upon and shot with rubber bullets in a completely unprovoked attack by Portuguese riot police after a European Cup quarter final in Porto, back in March 1997.

Newly appointed Benfica manager Quique Sanchez Flores leads a stuttering Benfica team into his first ever Lisbon derby tonight. Expectations from the home crowd will be high after a poor start to the Spaniard's reign. Once a proud bastion of invincibility, the Stadium of Light's fear factor has been slowly eroded, leaving the team vulnerable and profoundly lacking in confidence. Benfica have drawn two of their opening three league games and lost 3–2 at Napoli in their first-round first-leg UEFA Cup tie. In contrast, Sporting have a 100 per cent win rate from their opening three games and haven't lost at Benfica in their last three visits. The atmosphere in these games is unique but today I sense there is going to be even more anxiety attached to it for *Benfiquistas*.

Football in Portugal is big news. There are three daily newspapers devoted to football that, together with non-stop television and radio media coverage, provide regular updates for the football-crazed masses here. The press attend Benfica's training complex every day and the club provides a press conference after each session. The hacks never let the facts get in the way of a good story.

In the lead-up to the derby, historical results, statistics, facts and everything that concerns Sporting–Benfica dominates the Portuguese media. Youngsters in schools and colleges throughout the whole of Lisbon morph into soothsayers and spend much of their time forecasting results and predicting line-ups. The supporters in work talk about past derbies; Sporting fans hark back to the unprecedented 7–1 demolition of Benfica in 1986 and *Benfiquistas* evoke memories of the derby they won 6–3 at the Alvalade in 1994. It's a case of total football madness on a national scale.

Post-derby media coverage is almost the same. The following week is glorious for the winners, shame for the losers and victorious supporters wallowing in the result until at least the next meeting between the two teams.

The pressure at both clubs is immense and the thirst for success grows with every barren season. Flores is the eleventh manager to take the Benfica hot seat in ten years as the club seek to bring back the glory days. After a disappointing start to the season, a defeat in today's derby will do little to inspire confidence and could spell the beginning of the end only four games into a new league campaign. *Benfiquistas* are notoriously fickle and do not tolerate failure.

I could see the stadium on the horizon so I jogged ahead of the cortejo and awaited their arrival at a busy intersection close to the ground. Riot vans emptied and the tetchy occupants donned their crash helmets and riot shields in preparation for the imminent arrival of the noisy neighbours. Benfica fans started to congregate in the same area but were ushered away. Those who didn't take to the softly softly approach were promptly set upon by impatient officers eager to dish out several bone-crunching blows to the lower legs. Ouch! Needless to say, it worked a treat.

The impressive 65,000 capacity Estadio de Luz, home of Benfica

Os Verde e Brancos (The Green and Whites) were now deep into enemy territory and once again in fine voice, much to the annoyance of their hosts. 'SLB-SLB-SLB,' chanted the 200-strong Benfica welcoming committee. But their chants fell on deaf ears as they were vastly outnumbered and outsung by their more lively counterparts. Benfica Ultras were becoming increasingly agitated. They were loudly whistling and jeering to try and drown out a song they were being taunted with by the arriving Sporting contingent. One of the Ultras' photographers at the intersection roughly translated for me:

> Feel the smell that scares away the dogs, it's a smell of *Lampioes* and their fu**i*g mothers ... it's the smell of sh*t that comes from there (Estadio da Luz) ... its so intense that you can't take it out with acid ... *Lampiao* pig, *Lampiao* faggot, you are the shame of Portugal ... you're miserable and retarded, and you need to give your ass to Eusebio ... Benfica is shit, Benfica is shit, Benfica is shit ...

Of course, it sounds better in the native tongue, footie songs always do.

The visitors were escorted left at the intersection and under the bridge to the away sector. Scuffles broke out as flares were lit up and thrown at the police from within the Juve Leo group. Police made several arrests which further antagonised the visitors leading to a number of missiles being thrown at police officers who were doing their utmost to keep a minor situation from spiralling out of control. More officers were drafted in and the Sporting Ultras were eventually shepherded into the visitors' section in single file.

Riot police greet the arriving Sporting *cortejo*

Sporting fans are held by police at the intersection as the stadium prepares for their arrival

I decided to exit the area and head for the ticket office to pick up my accreditation for the game, kindly arranged by my good friend in the media Irwin Fletcher. I called Dave and arranged to meet him at the entrance to the accreditation centre before making my way pitch-side for an optimum view of Portugal's biggest derby.

Designed by architect Damon Lavelle, the 65,000 capacity Estadio da Luz was built in 2003 and hosted the European Championship final in 2004. It was given a five-star rating by UEFA and is without doubt one of the world's finest stadia. However, the building of this cutting-edge multi-sports complex was dogged by controversy. Allegations of corruption, alleged phantom payments and a debt of £60 million almost led to the demise of the sacred Lisbon giants who are firmly established as a national institution.

But this is Benfica we are talking about, Portugal's favourite son, and somehow, with enough jiggery pokery to confuse a Philadelphia lawyer, they managed to pull through. They even managed to persuade a government hounding them for an unpaid tax bill to provide the club with a £16 million grant to fund the building of the new stadium.

Only two years prior to the completion of the new stadium a Portuguese judge ordered the club's assets to be frozen while investigations continued into alleged embezzlement involving former club president Joao Vale e Azevedo. During his tenure at Benfica, the club ran up massive debts and at times was unable to pay outstanding tax bills or players' wages. He was alleged to have embezzled at least £680,000 from the club and laundered the money through offshore bank accounts.

Prosecutors confirmed they were investigating the transfer of Russian goalkeeper Sergei Ovchinnikov from Benfica to FC Alverca. It was reported that part of the money was used as payment for the 45-year-old lawyer's luxury yacht, aptly named *Lucky Me!*. Azevedo persistently maintained his innocence but the courts convicted him in April 2002 and imprisoned him for four and a half years. It was an almighty setback for the man once lauded as Benfica's saviour.

Six years later and the controversy surrounding Azevedo's iffy dealings still rages. Freed by the Supreme Court after serving only two years of his sentence, the former club president now resides in the UK. An international arrest warrant was issued in June 2008 requesting Azevedo's extradition back to Portugal to face fraud and document forgery charges relating to mismanagement of the team's finances. He is currently appealing extradition proceedings and remains under house arrest in the UK.

Sporting fans have always cried foul play, often accusing their sworn enemy of being in cahoots with leading political figures and governing bodies. The many allegations of corruption and bribery levelled at Benfica do nothing to dispel their neighbour's conspiracy theories.

The deep reservoir of resentment doesn't just lie with the supporters. Officials from both clubs often show their disdain for one another by publicly trading insults through the media. During Bobby Robson's ill-fated reign at Sporting in the early 1990s, club president Jose de Sousa Cintra forbade him from scouting at Benfica. *Times* journalist Rick Broadbent quoted Sousa Cintra's rant at Robson: 'You don't go there,' raged the president. 'We hate them.' That was before he barged uninvited into the Sporting dressing room at half-time in the derby game and offered to double his players' win bonus.

Benfica's signing of former Sporting starlet Paulo Futre was the catalyst for another very public spat between the two warring boards. Apopleptic with rage, Sousa Cintra tried to sign three Benfica players, Paulo Sousa, Antonio Pacheco and Joao Pinto in a cynical ploy designed to create unrest. He was successful with the Sousa and Pacheco signings but Benfica won Pinto over by offering a superior financial package. Public insults were traded and a huge row between the two boards ensued but it was Benfica who had the last laugh as Pinto scored a hat-trick in the final derby of that season.

Pinto did, however, sign for Sporting some seven years later and went on to achieve the almost impossible. He achieved iconic status on both sides of the divide. During the 1990s he was the primary Sporting hate figure and fan favourite at Benfica, even more so after snubbing Sporting's big-money offer in the much publicised 'hot summer' of 1993.

At the end of Euro 2000, Benfica president Azevedo released Pinto from his contract making him a free agent. After turning down several offers from abroad and a late bid from Porto, he chose to join Sporting on a free transfer. This is the equivalent to Steven Gerrard joining Manchester United after an illustrious career at Liverpool. Sporting fans were delighted and a huge reception awaited him on his debut at the Alvalade.

His first derby in Sporting colours at Estadio da Luz resulted in Benfica's unforgiving fans booing and jeering their former idol relentlessly. However, the following season, Pinto rolled back the years and in a glorious run, missing only one game, he helped Sporting to their eighteenth and last Primeira Liga title. Four times Portuguese Golden Boot Winner Mario Jardel described Pinto as the 'father of the team'. After finishing his career, Joao Pinto won the respect of both Sporting and Benfica fans, because, despite crossing the divide, he always gave 100 per cent for both clubs. Pinto has cemented his place in history as a true legend of Portuguese football.

The unforgiving animosity between the two clubs can be traced back to their formative years in the early 1900s, when the traditionally bourgeois officials and patrons of Sporting took every opportunity to cock a snook at the working-class following of Benfica. Like so many derbies, the O Classico has endured its fair share of controversy over the years. In a meeting between the two sides in July 1911, it is believed that Sporting declined to welcome Benfica to their football ground, proclaiming the underclasses from Benfica were not worthy of playing at their sacred stadium. Although class distinctions no longer apply, the many distasteful events of the past live long in the memory of supporters.

Despite Sporting being the more dominant club during the early exchanges, it was Benfica who eventually flourished and went on to become the superior team and the most successful football club in Portuguese history. The 1960s saw the start of a period of dominance that would span the next three decades. It was a trophy-rich era that saw Benfica rewrite the history books and cement the club's standing as one of the greatest sporting institutes in the higher echelons of world football. One player in particular, Eusebio de Silva Ferreira or quite simply Eusebio, was instrumental in Benfica's rise to prominence. Signed in acrimonious circumstances in 1960 by Benfica's Hungarian team coach, Bela Guttman, Eusebio would go on to be one of the world's greatest and most famous players.

Eusebio started his career in Mozambique with local team Sporting Club Lourenco Marques. Ironically, the team was formed by Sporting CP fans and used as their own feeder club. Given the 'heads up' by an old friend from Sao Paulo, Guttman convinced his president to part with $20,000 to take a calculated punt on the unknown 18-year-old striker. His arrival in Lisbon sparked an acrimonious fight for his registration as Sporting were adamant Eusebio belonged to them. Benfica however, had other ideas and in a cloak-and-dagger operation straight out of the movies, they promptly removed him from the media spotlight and allegedly hid him away in a small Algarve village.

Seven months later with the legal process exhausted, Eusebio was officially unveiled as a Benfica player, much to the annoyance of their neighbours. Sporting conspiracy theorists still to this very day insist Eusebio belonged to them and was kidnapped by the enemy!

At the age of 20, the 'Black Panther' scored twice in the 1962 European Cup final to inflict a 5–3 defeat upon Di Stefano's great Real Madrid side. It was Benfica's second European Cup triumph in succession and a result that made the footballing world sit up and take notice.

In his fifteen years at the club, Benfica won eleven league titles and five Portuguese Cups, and contested five European Cup finals, winning two and losing three of them – AC Milan (1963), Internazionale (1965) and Manchester United (1968). On a personal note, he won the European Player of the Year award in 1965, was top scorer in the 1966 World Cup finals in England and won two European Golden Boot awards for being Europe's top goal scorer. With an unprecedented 727 goals in 715 matches, he is indeed a living legend and the club paid tribute to his exploits by erecting a bronze statue of him outside the stadium.

Eusebio de Silva Ferreira

Before the Eusebio era both Lisbon teams were adjudged to have had equal support. But the publicity generated by arguably the world' greatest striker contributed greatly towards Benfica officially becoming the world's best-supported team. It is said that you will find a *Caso do Benfica* (Benfica Supporters' Club) in almost every municipality in Portugal.

In November 2006, the Guinness Book of World Records confirmed Benfica as the biggest football club in the world with a staggering 160,398 paid-up members. That figure is now said to have exceeded the 200,000 mark worldwide, a phenomenal achievement for a club that is no longer considered to be among Europe's elite or even the best team in Portugal.

With just thirty minutes to kick-off, the stadium was beginning to rock. The 2,500 excited visitors crammed into the corner of the Bancada Coca Cola Stand were fully geared up for the impending war. Banners on show, flags waving, scarves swirling and faces painted, they traded insults with the home fans to their left. Police wearing protective gear formed a cordon down both sides of the visitors' section, segregating them from the testosterone-fuelled Benfica Ultras frothing at the mouth around them. Football is all about two sets of supporters being passionate about their team but sometimes high-octane games between cross-city rivals end up hitting the headlines for all the wrong reasons.

High expectations – The Sporting sector cranks up the noise level before kick-off

Where Eagles Dare –
Juve Leo Killers

A badge for life – Juve Leo boys

A huge Benfica roar was reserved for the club's famous mascot, Vitoria (Victory) the eagle. Dressed with red-and-white ribbons hanging from his talons, the eagle made his flight around the stadium as he does every home game. His handler, wearing a Benfica kit, runs around the pitch following the bird's flight path around the da Luz before sinking to his knees to welcome back his feathered friend.

Benfica players emerged from the tunnel to a standing ovation and thunderous applause from a near-capacity crowd of 60,000 delirious *Benfiquistas.* The famous opera-like Benfica anthem, Ser Benfiquista, was played loudly through the public address system and despite a valiant effort, could not be drowned out by the whistling and cat calls from the Sporting section.

> *Ser Benfiquista*
> *Sou do Benfica* (I am from Benfica)
> *E isso me envaidece* (and that flatters me)
> *Tenho a genica* (I have the agility)
> *Que a qualquer engrandece* (that to anyone I can be big)
> *Sou de um clube lutador* (I am from harsh club)
> *Que na luta com fervour* (that in the struggle with ardour)
> *Nunca encontra rival* (never is rivalled)
> *Neste nosso Portugal* (in our Portugal)
> (*refrão*/chorus)

Ser Benfiquista (To be Benfiquista)
é ter na alma a chama imensa (is to have on your soul the internal flame)
que nos conquista (that conquers us)
e leva à alma a luz intensa (that brings to the soul an intense light)
do sol que lá no céu (from the sun way in the sky)
risonho vem beijar (smiley comes to kiss)
com orgulho muito seu (with his own particular pride)
as camisolas berrantes (the garish shirts)
que nos campos a vibrar (that on the fields vibrate)
são papoilas saltitantes (are jumping poppies)

In the book *Monastros Sagrados* (Sacred Monsters), authors Vasco Pedro and Ricardo Galvao claim the first Benfica anthem was written in 1929 and was called 'Avante Benfica' but was abandoned due to the nature of the wording that could have been deemed inappropriate.

The current anthem was written especially for Benfica by Paulino Gomes Junior and is said to be the only club anthem sung by a tenor. Famous Portuguese tenor Luis Picarra had the honour of debuting 'Ser Benfiquista' on 16 April 1953. He sang to an audience of 6,000 *Benfiquistas* at the Pavilhao dos Desportos at an organised fundraising event to raise money for a new stadium. Classical musician Antonio Vitorino de Almeida recently wrote a symphony to commemorate the club's centenary.

Both sets of supporters had huge banners and giant flags and used their own chants to compete for oral dominance. The Benfica faithful were even more boisterous than usual and the No Name Boys in the left corner of Bancada Sagres ignited a host of luminous flares and let off smoke bombs, contributing to an atmosphere worthy of a cup final.

Fever pitch in the home sector

'Ser Benfiquista' – The crowd go opera

The teams are announced and kick-off is almost upon us

The No Name Boys are Benfica's and Portugal's most feared and notorious fan group. Known for their English name and using a badge comprising of two reversed Ns, they were formed in 1992 after an internal falling-out between the leaders of Benfica's only recognised fan group, Diabos Vermelhos (Red Devils). Disagreements rapidly escalated into violence, followed shortly afterwards by all-out war, as the rival groups fought for control of the terraces. It was reported that the Diabos club house was burned out in an arson attack and one of its members stabbed by a member of the No Name Boys group.

It was a flare shot from the No Name Boys section that tragically killed the Sporting fan in the 1996 cup final and subsequently led to the club stopping their funding and casting them out. After being disowned by the club, the No Name Boys became public enemy number one and the most-hated fan group in Portugal. The leaders of the group made the decision to shun publicity and cut themselves off from the outside world. They shut down internet sites, ceased publishing NNB material and adopted a siege mentality.

Their motto to this day is '*Nos nao existimos*', meaning 'We don't exist'. They don't co-operate with match-day police or club officials and are the only supporters who travel to away games independently. They have an intense rivalry with Juve Leo and few derby matches pass without incident between the two.

The relationship between the No Name Boys and Diabos has since been repaired and both have an equal footing at the da Luz. NNB occupy the corner of Bancada Sagres and the DV headquarters are at the opposite end of the stadium in the corner of the Bancada Coca Cola. Each has a different Ultra mentality, with Diabos famous for their great choreography and No Name Boys renowned for their vocal support. The No Name Boys, however, are still not recognised as an official fan group by the club and continue their clandestine existence.

A huge Benfica roar marked the start of the game but it was Sporting who came close to scoring inside the first minute when Djalo shot wide after getting on the end of Veloso's excellent pass. Benfica hit back almost immediately when Cardozo's long-range effort almost caught out Sporting keeper Rui Patricio.

The 2,500 Sporting Ultras were outsinging their neighbours and the players responded by dictating the early pace of the game. Some clever passing play had the hosts chasing shadows at times but Sporting only had the one shot at goal to show for their early domination.

'Benfica ... Benfica ... Benfica,' the chant grew louder and louder as home fans rose to their feet in an attempt to lift the players. Now it was Benfica's turn to get on top, playing a tidy passing game. Former Arsenal player Jose Antonio Reyes was chief tormentor and was unlucky not to slip Gomes through on goal just before half-time.

Benfica turned the screw after the interval, completely dominating proceedings. In an attempt to break the deadlock, Flores made his first substitution of the game, replacing the tired-looking Gomes with the experienced Argentinian attacking midfielder Pablo Aimar. It proved to be a masterstroke. Less than ten minutes later, it was the tricky Aimar who provided the pass for the impressive Reyes to curl home a shot giving Benfica a well-deserved 67th-minute lead.

The home crowd went nuts. The Diabos Ultras ignited luminous flares and set off smoke bombs as they danced around hugging and kissing each other, before turning on the Sporting fans to their right, hurling abuse and making lewd hand gestures. Sporting fans were clearly antagonised and surged forward to remonstrate but it was nothing more than handbags.

Gooooaaaaaaaallllllll –
1–0 Benfica

The whole stadium erupted into song, 'SLB-SLB-SLB,' and it wasn't about to get any better for disconsolate-looking Sporting fans. The smoke hadn't died down from the first goal celebration when less than five minutes later, Martin's cleverly floated free kick was headed into the back of the net by Benfica's Brazilian defender Sidnei.

The ecstatic Benfica fans, delirious with joy and still exhausted from their first goal celebration, still managed to conjure up enough energy to hug and kiss everyone around them before unleashing a roar of delight upon the players below. A Benfica team wallowing in a sea of averageness less than 24 hours earlier, now looked odds-on favourites to destroy their neighbours' 100 per cent win record. Two minutes later, man-of-the-match Reyes, who received a well-deserved standing ovation, was replaced by the young, highly regarded winger Angel di Maria. Sporting players looked totally demoralised and I had seen nothing in their second-half performance to suggest they could come back from a 2–0 deficit with only 15 minutes left on the clock.

Gooooaaaaaaaallllllll –
2–0 Benfica

With the game deep into injury time, the referee looked at his watch. Put his whistle in his mouth. Glanced at his linesman and with the authority of a sergeant-major etched on his face, blew for full time, signalling the start of mass hysteria in the stands. Flores punched the air in delight, Benfica players celebrated like lottery winners and 60,000 *Benfiquistas* hugged each other in equal states of joy. In contrast, the Sporting players, heads bowed, walked slowly over to the vocal green-and-white army and showed their appreciation for terrific support. After a brief but sincere handclap, the team trudged wearily off for a behind-closed-doors dressing down from manager Paulo Bento.

Between them the Sporting–Benfica duopoly has claimed forty-nine league titles and forty-three Portuguese Cups. But their unprecedented domestic domination has in recent years been unceremoniously gatecrashed by northern upstarts FC Porto. The year 1985 saw the start of a new dawn in Portuguese football as the big two became the big three. Benfica's record of thirty-one league titles is now the target for a Porto team that has been crowned league champions sixteen times in the last twenty-three years. Add eight Portuguese Cups, two European Cups and a UEFA Cup in the same period and it confirms the monumental task that lies ahead if Lisbon is to avoid a power-shift to the north.

Os Encarnados (The reds) will be dancing on the streets of Bierra Alto long into the early hours whilst *Os Leoes* will surely be conducting a post mortem over supper. Sunday's sports pages will be dedicated to *Benfiquistas* worldwide, whilst over at the Alvalade, Paulo Bento will find out that 'hell hath no fury like a football supporter whose team has just lost the local derby'!

Desperately Seeking Dinamo

The Marele Derby

Game: Dinamo Bucharest 1– 1 Steaua Bucharest
Date:1 November 2008
Attendance: 15,200

At first sight Bucharest is a chaotic mix of traffic-congested streets, sullied concrete apartment blocks and eye-catching Communist buildings that dominate the city's skyline. The capital only came into its own shortly after Romanian independence and was almost completely redesigned by French-trained architects who were responsible for the Paris-themed makeover.

The centre of Bucharest is a short cab ride from the airport and the first historical monument you see is The Arcul de Triumf. Situated in the middle of a busy intersection adjacent to Herastrau Park, this section of carriageway is known locally as the 'Bucharest Champs-Elysées'. The arch is a granite imitation of the Arc de Triomphe in Paris and was built in 1935 to replace an earlier poorly constructed arch made from wood. The original arch was built in 1922 to commemorate Romania's war dead and the new arch is now the centrepiece for army parades on national holidays.

Romania, Bucharest in particular, has become synonymous with stray dogs, many of whom appear mangy and malnourished and exist only through the pity of strangers who feed them leftovers. When the brutally efficient Ceausescu was in power, thousands of Bucharest residents were cruelly evicted from their homes and much of the city was demolished to make way for the construction of dingy apartment blocks in which former homeowners were forced to set up a new place of abode.

In addition to losing their homes, a compulsory ban was also imposed forbidding residents to keep their cats and dogs. Anybody who declined the opportunity to have their pets put to sleep let them run free. Consequently, there are some half-million stray dogs roaming the streets of Bucharest today.

We had a rendezvous with my Romanian contact Lex at 15.30 hrs. Lex was a youthful twenty-something hard-core Steaua Bucharest Ultra and I was meant to hook up with him earlier but he had to meet another guest for today's derby, from Nuremberg in Germany. Although only young, he was part of the old-school Stil Ostil Ultras, one of the first Ultra groups to grace the terraces at Steaua. Unfortunately, the older members of Stil Ostil were forced into dissolving the group after suffering long periods of intense, politically motivated police repression. Nevertheless, they still remain loyal to their colours and most of them take their place on the south curva on match days but have no banner on display at the stadium to mark their presence.

Lex and his young German friend arrived on time and after brief introductions we took a taxi to meet the mob. It was a brief ten-Leu journey down one of the many tree-lined boulevards deep into the heart of Steaua territory. I could see the Ghencea in the distance just after the large imposing cemetery on the right. Brian pointed out at least a dozen funeral parlours conveniently located adjacent to the perimeter wall surrounding the graveyard. Incongruously garish signs depicting coffins and promises of low prices hung shamelessly outside each *servici funerare* (funeral directors). Coffins of all shapes and sizes were on display, lining the footpath outside each shop. It was just lacking the proverbial Romanian barrow boy doing his Del Boy sales pitch!

Our taxi driver pulled over just across from Steaua's stadium. I paid the driver and Lex took us to the rear of one of the many small buildings lining the highway. I could see a tidy crowd encamped ahead of me talking and drinking but no sign of a bar. It turned out to be a gathering of around 50–60 Steaua risk supporters, a mixture of old-school and youth, who were boozing and discussing their plan of attack on their hated rivals, Dinamo. After familiarising ourselves with the main faces, we were warmly accepted into the group and handed a beer each with a licence to help ourselves to their plentiful supply as and when required.

I was introduced to Robert, a casually dressed stocky lad in his mid twenties, with rapidly greying hair that made him look older than he actually was. Robert's English was impeccable and as we became engrossed in conversation, he told me that he had spent a few years in England in his youth. Unfortunately for him it was at Her Majesty's Pleasure, detained in the palatial surroundings of the majestic HMP Walton in Liverpool. This would of course explain Robert's comical hybrid Scouse–Romanian twang.

He was a friendly bloke who enjoyed his time in the UK and dreamed of going back there one day, but wasn't sure if immigration would allow him back into the country. We had a good chat about the company he kept and the city-centre bars he used to frequent before he was incarcerated.

Robert introduced me to Sveeni, one of the older lads in the group. He was a tall brute of a man, easily weighing 250 pounds and built like the Terminator. Scary-looking and in his late thirties he looked a real handful but I found him to be an extremely nice bloke which totally personifies the reason why you should never judge a book by its cover. We had only been talking for five minutes and I had the offer of a room at his home and a night out on the town. But as we were only in Bucharest for the evening and we already had a hotel, it was an offer that I had to politely decline.

Sveeni confided in me what he did for a living. I couldn't believe it; he was one of the 'other people' (police officer)! I naturally thought it was a wind-up, but Robert insisted it was true, the gamekeeper had indeed turned poacher. Despite his allegiance to the state, he didn't hide his disdain for his employers. 'ACAB,' laughed Sveeni. To him it was just a job that paid the bills.

I asked Robert and his mates if they followed the English Premier League, but they didn't. Most, like Lex, had no interest in modern football. In fact, they hated it! They firmly believe that money is killing the game and everything it stands for.

'Every year it is the same,' said one of the lads. 'The big clubs send their people to the smaller clubs and relieve them of their best talent for a pittance. How are we supposed to compete with the best teams in Europe when they steal our talent?' he asked angrily. I had to agree with him. Small clubs like Steaua have inadvertently become feeding academies for the elite clubs and like most of the other minnows who qualify for the money-spinning Champions League competition, are only involved to make up the numbers. I could genuinely understand the frustration. Much wealthier clubs had relieved Romanian teams of many talented players in recent times. Steaua lost two of Romania's most gifted footballers, Gheorghe Hagi, arguably Romania's most celebrated player, and the fantastically skilful striker Adrian Ilie, nicknamed The Cobra because of his lightning speed.

Dinamo had also fallen prey to the lure of Western cash, having lost Cosmin Contra and the prolific but controversial Adrian Mutu. Unfortunately, money talks! One minute your local hero has just bagged the winner against your hated derby rivals, the next minute the offer of a bigger pay cheque, European football and increased self-fulfillment, and it's *adios amigo!*

It was approximately 4.30 p.m. when the lads decided to make a move. A few of the Steaua mob had been trying to contact the Dinamo boys by phone but had no joy. This motley little crew was in no mood for waiting and patience was wearing thin, so it was time to seek out Dinamo on their own manor in the north-east of the city.

Today's turnout was top-heavy with the core of a casual youth firm from the south *curva*. It was a mixture of Ultras and hooligans who on derby day are one in the same. The Romanian Ultra movement has a relatively short history and only really came into existence after the death of Ceausescu at the end of the Communist era.

The perception amongst most people is that Ultra is just a euphemism for hooligan, when in fact according to Lex and the boys, this is quite simply not the case. Being an Ultra in Romania is a way of life. It's a fight against repression. It's a healthy escape from normal life. It's an opportunity to vent extreme passion and emotion. The main focus of the Ultras is to transform the stadium into a colosseum of invincibility. They paint banners, make flags, use pyrotechnics and provide a quality show before, during and after the match. They sing with passion at every game and the use of pyro enables them to create a vast, colourful Spector-esque wall of sound that is unique to the Ultra mentality.

Although stadia have been the focal point of many serious clashes, hooligans tend to be more active in the streets, seeking both spontaneous and organised violent disorder with rival thugs. The propensity for football violence is bordering on endemic throughout the whole of Eastern Europe and in the absence of decisive action from Romanian football's ruling body, fan violence is escalating towards a national emergency.

The Titan Boys were the first main hooligan firm to attach themselves to Steaua back in 1996. Skins Berceni, a small but dangerous skinhead mob, followed shortly afterwards. They were formed by members of the now defunct Stil Ostil group. Nowadays, the recently established E.R.A., an acronym for Elita Ros Albastra (Red and Blue Elite) are the principal hooligan group. Some of the older lads from the original Titan Boys unit are now an active element within this dangerous little firm and they reside on the north *curva*.

This local derby, one of three in Bucharest, is steeped in acrimony and is without question the most volatile game in the Romanian calendar. Both sets of supporters have a penchant for violence and this hot-tempered meeting between Romania's two most successful clubs rarely passes without incident. Being a Steaua supporter means despising Dinamo and vice versa.

Since the fall of the Iron Curtain in 1989, Romanian football has been consumed by fan violence and the capital, Bucharest, has become a city overwhelmed by hooligan incidents. One of the most serious outbreaks of disorder occurred at Steaua's Ghencea stadium in May 1997. A huge police presence was mobilised for the game in anticipation of the crowd trouble that is a constant feature of this fixture. Shortly before the start of the match, Dinamo thugs set fire to the south stand destroying hundreds of seats, delaying the game and forcing the evacuation of 2,000 supporters. Around thirty fans were arrested but, luckily, no serious injuries were reported.

More recently, in November 2007, supporters from both teams fired flares at each other and threw smoke bombs on to the pitch as disorder threatened to force the abandonment of the derby at the Ghencea. Both teams had to suspend their warm-up prior to the start of the game as police used tear gas to prevent fans from ripping seats out and throwing them on to the pitch.

The game was also halted on several occasions and players retreated to the safety of the dressing rooms to avoid inhalation of dense acrid smoke that had poisoned the evening air. Police eventually restored order within the confines of the stadium only for it to continue after the match in the surrounding area. As rival fans rioted, television footage showed fans smashing windows and destroying nearby property.

Bucharest's first Ultra group was the right-wing Armata Ultra (AU – Ultra Army) of Steaua Bucharest. Formed in 1995, AU was the vanguard of Ultra culture in Romania and set up home on the north *curva* of the Ghencea for over six years. Membership swelled to an unprecedented 4,000 Ultras and their away support was unrivalled anywhere in the country.

Sadly, a huge internal dispute led to the group's demise and AU was officially dissolved in 2001. Although no longer active, AU had such a profound effect on those who shared their terrace ambience that its influence lives on inside the hearts of many of its former members.

The Ultra movement is dependent on youth. As good 'Old Father Time' catches up and takes its toll on us, it becomes natural to prioritise what is important in life. Casual relationships morph into marriage. Children are born and one's life undergoes seismic changes. Financial constraints become more prevalent and ultimately priorities change. Leaderships and responsibilities have to be passed down to the next generation to uphold the historical traditions and values of the club and its supporters. At Steaua, the Ultra movement is still strong and despite a seething contempt for the owner of their club, where for many football is life, they continue to support the team with a passion than runs deeper than a concern for a turn in profit.

The start of Ultra culture at Dinamo, as with Steaua, can also be traced back to 1995 when small Ultra groups like Dracula and Rams Pantelimon appeared on the north *curva*. A year later in 1996, Nuova Guardia, Dinamo's most powerful Ultra group, was created and they also took up residence on the north *curva*.

Officially known as the Peluza Catalin Hildan, the north *curva* is named after the famous young Dinamo player and captain Catalin Hildan. Hildan suffered a fatal heart attack mid way through Dinamo's friendly game with Oltenita and tragically passed away at the tender age of 24. He was worshipped by Dinamo supporters and will always be remembered for being instrumental in securing the Romanian league title for the club in 2000, marking the end of a nine-year barren spell.

Nowadays, there are lots of Ultra groups attached to both clubs. Some have more power than others, some have more members than others, but all have one thing in common: their hatred for each other's club. It's a hatred that quite often degenerates into pure unadulterated violence.

> Steaua Ultras in Peluza Nord (north *curva*) – Desant, TK, Nucleo, Tineretului Korp, Insurgentii, Armata forty-seven and Roosters.
>
> Steaua Ultras in Peluza Sud (south *curva*) – Ultras, Glas, Vacarm, Stil Ostil, Banda Ultra, Era, Outlaws, Hunters and South Boys. Ex-Titan Boys, ex-Skins Berceni and ex-Gruppo Apparte present in South but with no banner.
>
> Dinamo Ultras in Peluza Nord – Nuova Guardia, Front 48, Dogs of War, Mad Men, Tifosi Ultra, Supras, Panzer, Supreme and Energizatii.
>
> Dinamo Ultras in Peluza Sud – Brigate and Boys.

Despite portraying a united front, it's not uncommon to see a power struggle between rival Ultra groups within the same club. In August 2005, Steaua Ultras residing in the north stand attacked fellow Steaua Ultras in the south stand and a violent stand-off ensued. The north stand came out on top due to the larger numbers but the fall-out from that incident created a chasm between the north and south stands. The leader of the Ultras in the north declared that the south stand did not exist and refused to recognise them as Steaua supporters.

Conflicts between Ultras often occur because of the way fans choose to support their team. Collectively, Ultras share the same passion for supporting their team, but independently, many Ultra groups have their own beliefs and prefer to stamp their own unique identity within the collective. They are self-funded, organise their own travel to away matches and feel they have a right to criticise the club or its players should the need arise. It's a maverick attitude responsible for creating tension with other Ultra groups and quite often spills over into violence.

There are three major teams in Bucharest – Steaua, Dinamo and Rapid. Football culture has a lengthy tradition in this madhouse of a city but the main derby in Bucharest, or Romania for that matter, is the Marele derby contested between the two best-supported teams in the country. Steaua and Dinamo, both founded by Communists, have won 41 titles between them, Steaua on 23 and Dinamo on 18.

Steaua, formed in 1947, were known as the army team and always had the support of the despised but all-powerful Ceausescu family until the Romanian revolution led to their execution in 1989. They are without doubt the most popular team in the whole of Romania with up to 40 per cent of the country claiming to support them. They play their home games at the Stadion Ghencea situated in Ghencea, in the south-west on the outskirts of Bucharest. The stadium is now the only link to the army as the ground is owned by the Ministry of Defence.

Not content with domestic success, Ceausescu bankrolled the club on to the world stage and Steaua went on to contest two European Cup finals in the 1980s. They won the 1986 final on penalties after drawing the match 0–0 against Barcelona in Seville, making them the first Eastern European team to lift the trophy.

Steaua goalkeeper Helmuth Duckadam was the star of the show, performing heroics by saving all four Barcelona penalties. Only 200 travelling supporters witnessed this momentous occasion and although each one was vetted by the Securitate, forty of them still defected to the West.

Back home, Bucharest went into meltdown. The team enjoyed a heroes' reception as jubilant supporters walked to the airport in droves to greet the team's arrival. Thousands of well-wishers cheered the team from the city streets in extraordinary scenes never seen before anywhere in the Eastern bloc. Steaua also went on to play in the 1989 European Cup final but were well beaten 4–0 in the Nou Camp by a classy AC Milan side in a very one-sided game.

Dinamo were formed a year later in 1948 and represented the Ministry of the Interior (Securitate), better known as the 'Secret Police'. Although Steaua claim to be the dominant force and Dinamo may not carry the European prestige of their neighbours, *Cainii Rosii* – the Red Dogs – should not be underestimated. They have amassed a significant trophy haul themselves – 18 league titles, 12 Romanian Cups and one Romanian Super Cup make up a proud 60-year history. Dinamo play their home games at the 18,000 capacity Dinamo Stadion, commonly referred to by Steaua fans as *Groapa* (The Hole).

During the Steaua-dominated mid to late 1980s, a period that incidentally coincided with the damnable Ceausescu family's allegiance to the club, the *Dinamovisti* pointed an angry accusing finger at the Ceausescu regime. Dinamo conspiracy theorists insist that teams simply 'gave up' and failed to compete against Steaua because of the threat of violence and incarceration from the brutal Ceausescu dictatorship.

Between June 1986 and September 1989, Steaua went 104 games unbeaten over the course of three entire seasons – 88 wins and 16 draws – quite possibly a world record for the longest unbeaten sequence in top-flight football. They also won five championships in a row between 1985 and '89.

The Romanian revolution of 1989 saw the overthrow of the Ceausescu family and marked the end of an era of domination by Steaua. The dictatorship left behind a legacy of success many believe was built on corruption and for that reason alone, Steaua's incredible trophy haul will always be tainted.

After much debate between leaders and some frantic mobile-phone activity we were on the move. Destination, Dinamo! It was a warm autumn afternoon and we walked through a number of parks before cramming on to a single-decker bus. All sixty of us! Like sardines in a can and with the temperature rising by the second, Brian and I set off on a journey into the unknown with our new-found friends.

A couple of stops later, we disembarked and made a dash for the nearby tram stop. Lex explained to me that we were heading for a rendezvous with another group of Steaua lads from the north *curva* before heading off to Dinamo in one big firm. Several stops later and still undetected by the law we departed the tram, crossed the busy intersection and walked to the entrance of one of the many city-centre parks where two large white box vans appeared to be waiting for us.

The drivers entered into dialogue with the leaders of the group but tempers quickly became frayed. Voices were raised and fingers were pointed in what appeared to be a very animated exchange. According to Lex, it was a case of 'too many chiefs and not enough indians'! Some of the mob wanted to walk, some wanted to catch the metro and some wanted to go in the vans, so we chatted amongst ourselves until the powers-that-be came to a decision.

After some seriously disorganised deliberation, it was agreed that we would all travel by metro to meet the other boys from the north *curva.*

The station guard didn't stand a chance as a marauding mob of around sixty ticketless lads charged through the entrance and down on to the platform. We travelled a couple of stops to a place called Titan and as we emerged menacingly from the bowels of the metro station into the early-evening darkness, we were greeted by another forty Steaua lads.

We were now about 100 strong and I could sense violence in the air. Some of the younger lads started to break up park benches and pick up just about anything that could be used as a makeshift weapon. Mobile-phone activity reached saturation point as rival supporters frantically organised the perennial prematch territorial hoolie-fest ahead of our arrival at the stadium.

We left the park and made our way through a maze of high-rise apartment buildings. There was a noticeable quickening of the pace as the mob approached the estate's exit and the mood had changed from one of excitement to one of apprehension and aggression. Lex took a call from one of his pals at the front of the mob who confirmed that Dinamo had arrived at the agreed location and we were literally minutes away from serious confrontation.

Cue the primeval roar and the welcoming horde we had befriended only a few hours earlier, had become instantly radicalised and surged forward into the busy carriageway. A series of loud explosions broke the early-evening tranquility and a steady stream of luminous red flares were being tossed back and forth by the two warring factions hell-bent on inflicting bodily harm on one another. Wearing baseball caps, hoodies and scarves wrapped around their faces to protect their identities, this faceless terrace persuasion upped their momentum and set about humiliating Dinamo on their own turf.

The Dinamo firm, around thirty-handed, completely melted and ran for their lives without so much as a second glance. The Steaua boys, by now a baying mob, progressed deep into Dinamo territory at will and like a destructive wind, wontonly vandalised everything in front of them.

They even split up into smaller groups and searched down every side street in their relentless pursuit of confrontation but there were simply no takers. With hooligan-infested streets and lawless anarchy, it was a scene reminiscent of the early 1980s match-day hooliganism in the UK, when football violence was at its apex.

As I reached the first major junction on the busy main road, the first of many police cars arrived on the scene. Panic stricken, the police officers were more intent on providing sanctuary for the innocent passers-by caught up in the pandemonium rather than dealing with the lads running amok. I saw one petrified lady and her two hysterical children seek refuge in that police car, where they were forced to stay until the cavalry arrived to restore order.

Blue flashing lights appeared on the horizon and the wail of blaring police sirens cut through night air. I began to get a little edgy. I was on my own and having to navigate my way through small mobs of lads coming from all directions and then contend with the area being flooded with police officers looking for somebody to blame. I breathed a sigh of relief when I saw Brian standing in the central reservation beckoning me forward. Seconds later, I spotted Lex on the opposite side of the road just as he was about to call me.

We crossed over the debris-strewn road and discussed the night's events together. Lex was buzzing! Consumed with adrenalin, he couldn't keep still as he boasted about the early-evening antics that had completely paralysed the local neighbourhood.

The Steaua mob, around 100 in total, had shrunk considerably by the time a full complement of police reinforcements arrived. Eager to avoid detention, many of the lads blended in with the crowd or fled down one of the multitude of side streets in the area. Meanwhile, the forty of us left loitering at the top of the boulevard were completely surrounded by police cars and beat bobbies. Dismayed by the prospect of imminent arrest I told Lex that I was going to slip out of the police cordon and view proceedings from the opposite side of the carriageway. 'Don't worry,' he assured me, 'it isn't a problem. The police can do nothing. They will secure the area and then escort us directly to the stadium.'

After a brief exchange between senior officers the decision was made, as Lex predicted, to escort us to the stadium. So flanked either side by officers on foot and led down the boulevard by a convoy of police vehicles we were frog-marched slowly in the direction of the ground. Unremorseful about their prematch riotous behaviour, the Steaua boys further antagonised their unwanted guardians by goading passing Dinamo supporters. '*Dinamo Bucuresti unde mortii ma-tii esti, Dinamo Bucuresti unde mortii ma-tii esti?*' (Dinamo Bucuresti where the f**k are you?) chanted the lads at the front. It was a chant that reverberated throughout the whole of the mob and got louder with every stride. If Dinamo hools were looking for a rematch, this lot wouldn't need asking twice. With or without a police escort!

Restless and bored, some of the younger kids started to play up. One lad in front of me somehow managed to snatch a police officer's baton from his utility belt. It was passed back and forth whilst the red-faced copper tried frantically to retrieve it. The situation was rapidly descending into a farce and was only resolved after intervention from his colleagues.

Mobile-phone activity became quite apparent and the evening began to adopt a Groundhog Day-esque feel about it. Some of the Steaua lads made a concerted effort to tool up by collecting missiles and rummaging through litter bins for discarded bottles. One eagle-eyed officer at the side of me was on the ball and alerted his colleagues who demanded an end to the nonsense with immediate effect. Pleas for calm fell on deaf ears and with a total disregard for the law, the pace gathered momentum and the collection of makeshift weapons and missiles continued without restraint.

Lex had got word that Dinamo were in the vicinity and planning an ambush. He pointed out that most of the older and stronger Steaua boys had made their way to the front of the mob in preparation for any snide attack. 'It is better that the older boys are at the front,' said Lex. 'It gives the youth the confidence to fight'.

We had been walking for a good half-hour and there was still no sign of the stadium. I got talking to one of the Steaua lads walking alongside me. He was quite blatantly holding a telescopic cosh in his hand with no concern that he may be arrested by the local plod. 'Where did you get that from?' I asked. 'I took it from one of the Dinamo boys earlier,' he bragged. 'It's no problem. Sometimes you win and sometimes you lose. This time I win,' he said, smirking. I had to admire his bravado; he was cocky and very self-assured!

Bang, bang, bang! First a burst of loud explosions, followed swiftly by the rat-a-tat-tat of fire crackers and then a roar of primal aggression. We had just been ambushed by the Dinamo boys eager to lock horns and gain revenge for their earlier humiliation. More explosions followed and swathes of red signal flares lit up the night sky as they rained down upon us.

Dinamo had turned up around forty-handed but this time they came tooled up for the occasion. Taser guns were discharged by the head-cases at the front of the Dinamo firm and the Steaua boys were forced into a reluctant but hasty retreat. It became quite apparent that in the interest of self-preservation, Brian and I may just have to get involved if we were to come out of this melee unscathed. Despite the obvious threat of grevious bodily harm, brought about by our unenviable but self-inflicted predicament, we had no immediate regrets. Because as Neil McCauley (Rober De Niro) quite rightly points out to Lt. Vincent Hanna (Al Pacino), during one of the most iconic movie scenes of the twentieth century – We didn't have to be here, we both knew the risks. It rains … you get wet! (*Heat* – 1995)

I marched forward into the fray and as I came to within five metres of conflict, disaster struck. Somebody in the high-rise apartments above hurled what I hoped was a bucket of water through the window and scored a direct hit upon several of us. As you can imagine, my first thoughts were that I had been covered by the contents of some Romanian gypsy's bedpan! Thankfully, upon closer examination it proved to be clean water. Result!

Meanwhile back at the riot, Steaua had halted their retreat and poured forward with purpose and sheer determination. Dinamo were slowly but surely being pegged back on to the back foot but this time, unlike in the previous encounter, they were putting up a hell of a fight. It was a surreal moment. Two sets of supporters fighting out an imaginary territorial battle without fear of consequence. And despite the risk of serious injury or worse, it was an unnatural act they all seemed to revel in.

After five minutes of insanity the lame and uninspiring keystone cops had finally plucked up the courage to have a go themselves and were cracking heads like it was going out of fashion. It was now a three-way fight and just as it looked to be spiralling completely out of control the Jandarmeria arrived on the scene in the nick of time.

Also known as the 'militia', these paramilitaries have a reputation for being the hardest, most brutal cops in the whole of the Eastern bloc and the supporters from both clubs have a long history of violence against them. Fan movements harbour a deep-seated hatred towards the police in Romania; they are considered the proverbial arch enemy of all Ultra groups and the acronym ACAB (All cops are bas**rds) can be seen sprayed randomly all over the city.

There is a severe mistrust of the police force amongst football supporters in Romania. Disproportionate police operations at matches often result in exaggerated actions against spectators, especially the Ultras. Baton-wielding militia dish out severe beatings to all and sundry on a regular basis and stand accused of failing to make the distinction between the violent minority and real fans.

In 2002, Steaua Bucharest played away at Petrolul Ploiesti and a travelling Steaua supporter was shot in the neck by a rubber bullet after security forces fired indiscriminately into fans after disorder broke out. Trouble flared again at the same fixture in 2004 and a Steaua fan had to be resuscitated where he lay after being viciously beaten by a group of over-zealous police officers. That same month at the normally acrimonious Dinamo v Steaua derby, rival Ultras put aside their differences and showed the solidarity of the Ultra movement by taking part in a preorganised protest called 'Ultras' Resistance'. The visitors' (Steaua) sector unfurled a large mural portraying four of Romania's most popular Ultra groups, whilst the home supporters (Dinamo) risked the wrath of the law by continuously chanting anti-police songs for the duration of the match.

The alleged attacks continued and the LPF (Liga Profesionista de Fotbal), headed by the vehemently anti-Ultra Dumitru Dragomir, were instrumental in bringing in new laws to repress the Ultra movement. Persistent police repression, including savage beatings, unwarranted detention, stadium bans and unjust prison sentences, have taken their toll on the followers of Romania's most popular spectator sport.

In September 2007, up to 1,500 Ultras representing teams from all over Romania stood together and marched through the streets of Bucharest in protest at the new laws. Steaua, Dinamo, Rapid, Craiova, Vaslui, Brasov, FC National, Petrolul Ploiesti, FC Arges, Bacau, Arad and Timisoara all had Ultra groups at the march. It's also worth mentioning that Ultras from Arad and Timisoara had travelled in excess of 600km to take part in the protest. Although the protest almost certainly fell upon deaf ears, this unlikely alliance against the common enemy showed the authorities that the Ultras do have a voice and will not be bullied into submission by their repressive regime.

A politically motivated media campaign portrays Romania's Ultras as football terrorists. Organised football supporters' groups are viewed as public enemy number one and treated like scum. There appears to be no distinction between supporters and hooligans. All are treated with disdain, assaulted regularly and subject to unjustified repression. In the derby at the Ghencea in 2007, supporters claim that over 700 Ultras from Dinamo were detained in the visitors' section for four hours after the final whistle, before being taken to the police station and held in custody for a further four hours. All were released without charge in the early hours of the morning with no justification for their detention.

In the face of adversity, the Ultras continue to fight the good fight in their attempt to change public perception of them. United in a common cause, spirits will not be broken and the protests will continue. Whilst there is undoubtedly a hooligan influence within the Ultras and occasionally you do see the ugly face of the beautiful game, I firmly believe that for the vast majority of Ultras, football is a way of life and they genuinely have the best interests of the club at heart. For the Ultras of Steaua Bucharest, football isn't more important than life, 'football is life'; it's what they live for!

Back at the war zone, the Jandarmeria's presence had an instantaneous effect. They arrived in haste, twenty-four at a time, in specially customised armoured police trucks. The storm troopers steamed straight in to the warring factions, cracking heads first and asking questions later. The Dinamo lot, bloodied and bruised, scarpered faster than wildfire and the rest of us were firmly rounded up, prodded, poked, clubbed and 'ordered' to remain static until the area was secured. Surrounded by a vicious-looking military task force, resistance was futile. The ice-cold Jandarmeria looked like they were kitted out for military conflict. They were protected from head to toe with protective padding, stab-proof (maybe bullet-proof) vests, balaclavas, visors and tin hats. They were more than prepared for anything any football hooligan could throw at them.

The capital's media turned up at the scene in legions. Camera crews jostled for prime position and the tabloid photographers thought Christmas had come early. The media frenzy had begun and the Steaua contingent being detained by security forces was the focus of intense scrutiny from story-seeking hacks looking for a sensational headline. It was complete madness. Tonight's image of violence and thuggery did little to support claims of police repression and the anti-Ultra Bucharest media would no doubt revel in the prearranged fan violence and broadcast damaging news reports throughout the whole of the country, once again further tarnishing the reputation of the Marele Derby and the Ultras who uphold the traditions of their extreme fandom.

Steaua Bucharest was bought in 2003 by Machiavellian entrepreneur Gigi Becali, one of Romania's richest men with an estimated 1 billion-euro fortune. He started his working life as a shepherd, sold his sheep and with the money it is alleged that he bribed the Romanian National Army in order to buy prime real estate surrounding Bucharest. Now a very successful businessman, it is widely believed that he holds aspirations to become the president of Romania.

The *Militarii* are in disarray on the domestic front and haven't won in seven matches. They were also recently eliminated from their National Cup by a team from the second division. To make matters worse, Steaua legend Marius Lacatus resigned his position as manager after a 3–5 home defeat to Lyon in the Champions League the previous week. Lacatus was a fans' favourite and scored 98 goals in 357 appearances for Steaua. He signed for Steaua in 1983 and spent his whole career there with the exception of a short, unsuccessful spell in Italy with Fiorentina (1990–1991) and in Spain with Real Oviedo (1991–1993).

Becali bore the brunt of the fans' anger at Steaua's last home game. The contempt he showed towards his own supporters was unprecedented. Steaua Ultras protested and sang songs demanding the owner leave the club. They hate him and their protests were likely to escalate in the coming weeks. Fans claim that Becali takes little interest in Steaua and hasn't got the club in his heart like them.

According to Lex, nobody had heard of Becali before he bought the club and he just used Steaua as a medium to generate publicity for himself through the media. Despite his extreme wealth, he continues to buy cheap, mediocre players but expects Steaua to make progress in Europe's premier competition. Gigi and his cronies seem to have lost sight of what Steaua stands for and it appears that fans are at the back of a very long queue when it comes to priorities. His failure to understand the fans and what their club means to them is likely to bring about his downfall sooner rather than later. Steaua is not a brand or a franchise. It's a religion; a way of life!

Lex accused Becali of having a vendetta against the Ultras who challenged his leadership. Word on the street was that he planned to go into every high school in Bucharest to recruit youngsters in the hope of forming new pro-Becali fan groups who would change the image of the club. Out would go the skinheads, tattoos, flags, banners and pyrotechnics. In would come the clean-living middle classes with no soul, marking the beginning of the end of the Ultra movement at this famous club.

Because of the animosity shown towards him, the politically driven Becali issued a statement to the Bucharest media threatening to deny Steaua fans the opportunity of seeing today's match by withholding tickets for the game. This only succeeded in further infuriating Steaua supporters who issued a statement of their own, stating their intention to travel to the derby, with or without Becali's tickets. And true to their word, supporters carried out their threat and travelled en masse without tickets. The group I was with were also ticketless but the police officer in charge of escorting us to the stadium confirmed tickets would be delivered direct to the escort by courier. Becali's bluff had obviously been called, probably on the orders of the police, who feared that withholding tickets would have resulted in further outbreaks of violence on a grander scale.

The courier arrived around an hour before kick-off and after fighting his way through the sizeable gawping crowd, tickets were handed out gratis to all the Steaua fans being held by the Jandarmeria. Once we had our tickets in hand we opted to make a move. Time was of the essence and we didn't want to miss the kick-off so we thanked Lex and the boys for looking after us and slipped out of the escort in the guise of tourists unwittingly caught up in the night's disturbances. Brian and I walked calmly out of the escort and we made our way to the rear of the security cordon. Nobody gave us a second glance, so we crossed over the road, walked around the back of the armoured police vans and headed in the direction of the stadium floodlights that lit up the night sky at the top of the carriageway.

With kick-off time almost upon us, crowd congestion was at saturation point and the noticeable police presence was doing very little in the form of crowd management. There were no conspicuous signs for non-Romanian-speaking supporters and it was almost impossible to move in any direction of your own free will, so we stopped to gather our thoughts.

As we were trying to determine the best point of entry, we stumbled upon what appeared to be the stadium offices. We opened the glass-fronted door and approached security in there. I explained to the 80-year-old relic masquerading as head of security that we were from the UK and looking for the correct entrance into the stadium. He couldn't speak a word of English and for some reason got the impression that we were officials of some description, because he marched us straight to the front of the queue and through a side gate without asking to see our tickets. Fortuitously, it was a job well done and we were in the stadium a good forty minutes before kick-off.

The stadium was built in 1951 and looked old and dilapidated. It was a fairly basic concrete bowl design with a 15,300 all-seated capacity. The running track surrounding the pitch has seen better days and the east stand is the only part of the ground that had any form of cover. The roof looked like a substandard late addition and the steel works that support it clearly obstructed the view of anyone sitting in their vicinity. The oversized, outdated pylon floodlight system completed this unremarkable piece of ugly-tecture.

To the left of me was the Peluza Catalin Hildan (north stand), home to the revered Nouva Guardia, Dogs of War, Mad Men and Supra Ultra groups. Their banners were draped proudly over the security fencing along with many other colourful flags and painted sheets belonging to the vast array of Dinamo supporters groups. This section has a reputation for housing Dinamo's most hostile Ultras and risk supporters and can be quite intimidating for visiting teams and their followers.

Dogs of War

Supra Ultras

Mad Men

To the right of me was Peluza Sud (south stand). Visiting supporters are housed in the corner of the same stand but security fencing, an empty section of terracing (no-man's-land) and around 100 fully equipped militia segregate rival factions.

No mans land – I predict a riot!

It was nigh on 8 p.m. and kick-off time was almost upon us. We still hadn't managed to locate our seats so had to watch the opening exchanges from an obstructed view high up in the west stand. The Ultras in the packed north stand displayed a long banner proclaiming, '*DINTOTDEAUNA TRAIM UNICUL DERBY LA INTENSITATE MAXIMA*' (We always live the only derby at the maximum intensity).

As the players entered the pitch the whole stadium erupted into a deafening roar and despite its meagre capacity, fans from both teams helped turn the stadium into a seething mosh pit of noise. Red distress flares lit up the north stand and a barrage of ear-splitting firecrackers were hurled on to the running track.

Over in the visitors' section, Steaua commenced their *tifo* by letting off several coloured smoke bombs and then unfurling a huge banner that covered the whole away end with the inscription '*MUIE DINAMO*' (F**k you Dinamo). In retaliation to the derogatory banner, the Dinamo fans in the north flung a salvo of distress flares in the direction of their cross-city adversaries and drew them into an angry confrontation. Fences were shaken, coins were thrown and insults were exchanged but the empty terraces segregating the two sets of rival supporters did its job almost to perfection.

Muie Dinamo – a message for the home team

With the stadium almost full to capacity it was nigh on impossible to get to our seats so it was time to improvise. In a private conversation that I had with one of the club officials I managed to get Brian a different seat in the west stand and blagged myself a fluorescent bib giving me access to the pitch.

Just as I was being escorted to the access gate at the bottom of the west stand, a huge roar went up to my right. Steaua had scored and their supporters were going crazy. I urged my chaperone to show some urgency and get me to pitch-side so that I could witness their celebrations at close quarters.

I did a Usain Bolt and sprinted around the running track towards the south stand just in time to see the Dinamo fans react badly to conceding an early goal. A sustained five-minute period of missile throwing commenced and only police intervention put a stop to it. Meanwhile, Steaua fans continued their celebrations by repeatedly chanting the timeless classic, '*Dinamo Bucuresti unde mortii ma-tii esti?*' (Dinamo Bucharest, where the F**k are you?) much to the annoyance of the home crowd.

It was a dream start for the new manager, ex-Steaua player and Romania's most capped player Dorinel Munteanu. This was Munteanu's first Bucharest derby and a victory at Dinamo would certainly endear him to the Steaua faithful.

With the exception of the eighth-minute goal by Kapetanos, the first half was a drab encounter between two teams devoid of quality in the final third of the pitch. Players were committed, tackles were fierce and the referee did well to stop the game from descending into chaos. Bruce Lee introduced the world to the art of fighting without fighting. I had just witnessed two teams playing football without playing football.

During the half-time interval I wandered round to the Steaua section to try and meet up with the lads again. It was quite a warm autumn evening and over 700 Steaua supporters had made the short journey across Bucharest for the game. The security fencing housing the visitors' section was adorned with a frenzy of banners bearing the names and crests of the many Ultra groups representing Steaua. As I scanned the terracing for a familiar face I saw around twenty bare-chested Steaua skinheads in the left corner of the visitors' section. I had to laugh; was there a Geordie connection I didn't know about?

Steaua's invasion of Dinamo

Steaua Ultras on tour

The Steaua 'Geordie' contingent!

I spotted Lex and Robert and beckoned them forward. They were pleased with proceedings thus far and were making plans for after the game. Brian and I were invited to a party with Lex and a group of his friends at a club in central Bucharest. Alternatively, we had the invitation of a late drink with Robert and his pals. I told them I would discuss their respective offers with Brian and call them after the match.

The players made their way out for the second half and as there was nothing between the two teams during the first period, I decided to view proceedings from the half-way line. To my surprise it was the home team who were forced to weather some concerted pressure during the opening exchanges and on this evidence I thought it best to take up residence at the rear of the Dinamo goal.

Chance after chance went begging in a shockingly one-sided second half but a resilient Dinamo defence somehow managed to keep the visitors at bay. Unexpectedly, the fans to the rear of me in the north stand became more vociferous and I saw them light several small fires within the confines of the terracing. Upon closer inspection I saw the Ultras setting fire to banners draped over the perimeter fencing. They were probably stolen from Steaua fans earlier in the day.

The stadium's firemen were close at hand and used high-pressure hoses to extinguish any threat to safety and maybe have a little fun in the process by knocking a few of the guilty parties off their feet. The fire-starters on the terracing, although becoming increasingly frustrated, remained undeterred and were quite happy to play cat and mouse with Red Adair and his crew.

I'm a Fire Starter – Red Adair in action

With the clock ticking towards the last few minutes Steaua had neglectfully failed to turn their dominance into more goals and the home side made them pay. In the eighty-fourth minute, Dinamo's number 20, Andrei Cristea, popped up on the right and crashed home a belated and undeserved equaliser, sparking delirious scenes amongst home fans. Few draws will be celebrated as wildly as this one and true to form I witnessed the goal from the opposite end of the stadium. Typical! The south stand lit up red flares and looked for confrontation with guest supporters by throwing them into the visitors' section again. Tempers were very frayed but the heavy police presence managed to keep rival fans apart. A now completely rejuvenated Dinamo side launched attack after attack at the Steaua goal and the final whistle couldn't come quickly enough for Munteanu's heavy-legged side.

Gooooooaaaaaaalllllllllll
– The south stand
celebrate the equaliser

After a very nervy several minutes' injury time the referee did indeed blow to signal the end of the game. Immediately after the final whistle, players from both teams ran to their respective supporters to thank them for their support before leaving the field. A number of Steaua players removed their shirts and threw them to the crowd, a gesture greatly appreciated by the travelling Steaua Ultras. Premiership players should take note; small gestures mean the world to loyal supporters!

Dinamo supporters in the south stand stayed behind for a while to berate their rivals in the away section. I spotted three or four blokes wearing yellow high-viz press vests. They were strategically positioned around the running track in front of the south stand. They were using hand-held camcorders to video the Dinamo fans, who by now were making a real nuisance of themselves almost ten minutes after the game had ended.

The Bucharest police commissioner definitely needs to review undercover techniques and strategies. High visibility press bibs and hand-held camcorders are not that subtle!

Lex and the boys were due to be kept inside the stadium for the next thirty minutes so I said my goodbyes and gave Brian a call to arrange our departure. We met behind the dugout and left almost immediately to find a taxi. The area outside the stadium was surprisingly clear and we managed to flag down a cab in an instant. It was getting on for 11.30 p.m. by the time we reached our hotel so it was a quick swill, change of clothes and back out again.

We got another taxi back into the centre and asked our driver to take us to a restaurant. He dropped us off at a small family-run bistro. That would be a closed family-run bistro. Not only was it closed but our driver had abandoned us to pick up his next victim and we were left with a long walk back to the centre.

It had been a long day and our lack of sleep was catching up with us. Neither of us was in the party mood so we decided to get a quick bite to eat at a nearby late-night cafe and then go back to the hotel bar for a couple of pints. I sent Lex a text thanking him for looking after us and declined his party invitation.

With Western European stadia almost completely sanitised and overrun by Roy Keane's famous prawn sandwich brigade, Eastern Europe is one of the last bastions of working-class football. Famous for their cauldrons of hate and intimidation, the giants of the Eastern bloc are slowly but surely succumbing to the megalomaniacs in suits and the corporate skulduggery that is spreading through the game like a cancer. The Ultras at Steaua have a unique persistence and indomitability about them and they are determined to prevent that from happening at their club, but the repressive regime running the game have other ideas. Plenty of sabre rattling lies ahead but one thing is for sure: the Ultras won't go down without a fight!

Relentless

The Gradski Derby

Game: FK Zeljeznicar 2 – 0 FK Sarajevo
Venue: Grbavica Stadion
Date: 9 May 2009
Attendance: 11,000

Ado looked edgy as he stared nervously at two suspicious-looking guys on a motorbike outside my hotel. 'Is there a problem?' I asked him. 'Maybe,' he replied cautiously. 'I don't trust these people, so it is best that we keep to the main street where it is busy.'

Tensions run high in the lead-up to the derby and familiar faces from Sarajevo and Zeljeznicar often clash in the twenty-four hours prior to the game. Ado is a familiar face at the Grbavica and plays an active role with the notoriously partisan Maniacs (TM87) preparing for match day.

'They could be Sarajevo boys who know my face and want to attack us. Maybe, maybe not,' said Ado. He then frowned, shrugged his shoulders, told me to forget it and reassured me that there was no problem as he turned tour guide for the afternoon.

We had a couple of hours to kill before Brian's arrival so it was nice to stroll around the city-centre sights in the hot Sarajevo sun. This multi-ethnic city lies in a valley, completely surrounded by tall hills and snow-capped mountains, and the views are spectacular.

The hillside was home to deadly Serb snipers who unleashed hell upon the Sarajevans during the infamous 1,395-day siege of Sarajevo. It is the longest siege of any capital city in the history of modern conflict. Not since World War Two has any military regime embarked upon a bloody campaign of remorseless brutality directed towards the inhabitants of a European capital city. The devastation was epic. By the end of the siege 10,615 people had been killed – of which 1,601 were children.

The city centre is a myriad of multicultural diversity, something Sarajevans are very proud of. The old town, with its quaint old cobbled streets, minarets soaring skywards and oriental-style shops, accurately reflects the legacy left behind from the Ottoman Empire. With a mosque, Orthodox church, Catholic church and synagogue all within 500 metres of each other, the existence of this unique unity of religious contrasts inspired the nickname 'The Jerusalem of Europe'.

We had arranged to meet Brian at the memorial to Archduke Franz Ferdinand, adjacent to the bridge opposite the museum on Obala Kulina Bana. This was the spot where on 28 June 1914, the heir to the Austrian Empire, Franz Ferdinand, was assassinated on a visit to Sarajevo. The Archduke and his wife were shot dead by Gavrilo Princip, a member of the Black Hand Gang who wanted to rid Bosnia of Austrian rule. It was a murder that would go down in history as the catalyst for starting World War One. Less than two months after the double murder, the Great War began and the rest is history.

As luck would have it we bumped into Brian on our way to the bridge, so after a brief introduction, Ado took us up to the Grbavica Stadium, home of his beloved Zeljeznicar. The Grbavica district lies on the outskirts of the city centre and this part of town bore the brunt of relentless Serbian assaults. Upon leaving the city-centre, war-damaged buildings that were consistent with large-scale military conflict became more prevalent, a heartbreaking reminder of the consequences of a brutal civil war. This frontline neighbourhood suffered major damage and its ravaged façade still remains scarred from three years of mortar shells and gunfire.

'This is our stadium,' said Ado, full of pride as he pointed to the innocuous-looking oval-shaped structure that blended into the background opposite us. It was the Grbavica Stadium, home to FK Zeljeznicar, known locally quite simply as Zeljo. Zeljeznicar (meaning railway worker) was founded in 1921 by a group of railroad workers and the club became second home to the city's football-mad working-class population.

Since it was a financially poor club, they used to organise dance nights and used the profits to buy training equipment. They started out playing most of their games against local teams mostly supported by the wealthier classes. But it wasn't until after World War Two that Zeljo finally gained the recognition they strived for.

Despite being unfairly suppressed by high society and the government elite, against all the odds the club managed to survive and went on to win the 1945 Bosnian qualification group. It was a feat that earned Zeljeznicar the right to be Bosnia's sole representatives in the much stronger and more respected Yugoslav league, much to the dismay of local politicians who despised the club and its working-class roots.

The 1971–72 season saw Zeljo rid themselves of their 'nearly man' image by winning their one and only Yugoslav title. The climax to the championship-winning season was at the JNA Stadium in Belgrade and on the team's return to its home town, Sarajevo partied long into the night.

In 1981 Zeleznicar reached the Yugoslav Cup final played at the Marakana Stadium in Belgrade. Over 60,000 spectators saw Zeljo lose a tight game 2–3 to fellow Bosnian team Velez Mostar. But they reached the height of their success under legendary Zeljo coach and former player Ivica Osim, who successfully guided the team through their memorable 1984–85 UEFA Cup campaign.

Some great results saw Zeljo through to a two-legged semi-final against Videoton from Hungary. They narrowly missed out on a final berth against European giants Real Madrid after a heartbreaking, dramatic late goal two minutes from time in the second leg edged Videoton into the final. FK Zeljeznicar attracted support from all over the former Yugoslavia that evening, such was the popularity of this small working-class outfit, and although the result was one of the most tragic in the club's history, it was a very proud night for their supporters and all those connected with the club.

Back in the early days, the Communist regime forced clubs to play under the ownership of sports associations. Known as SD (*sportsko drustvo* meaning sports society) Zeljeznicar, they were funded by the affluent Yugoslav government and also specialised in many other sports and games such as basketball, handball, chess and table-tennis.

Today, Zeljeznicar Football Club is still officially classed as a sports association and still undertakes a duty to incorporate other sports under the Zeljeznicar umbrella, but since the end of the Communist era they have become totally self-funded like the rest of the teams in the Bosnian Premijer Liga. It's a nervous time for Zeljo at the moment and the situation at their cross-city rivals is no different. Neither club gets any help from the city and the lack of success means wealthy sponsors are a precious commodity and very difficult to attract. Poor ticket sales bring in very little revenue, especially at 3.50 euros a pop, so the bulk of the club's finances come from selling players and private investment. The manager generally bears the brunt of the poor financial situation and this season he was left with a paltry 750,000-euro transfer budget for the whole of the 2008–09 campaign.

At one point the financial position of Zeljo was so grave that the club's bank account was suspended for two months. But on a more positive note, the board was hoping to float Zeljeznicar on the stock market, a controversial move, but one that was seen as a way of increasing much-needed revenue that would have a knock-on effect in all areas. Rumours were also rife that the city was keen to help safeguard the future of both sporting institutions. Although no official statement had been announced, it was believed negotiations were at an advanced stage about the possibility of agreeing much-needed financial aid to the two ailing clubs.

Nervousness appeared to be a common theme in Bosnian football. The Bosnian FA, who oozed uneasiness from every orifice, was currently in crisis amid swirling allegations of bribery and high-level corruption. It's a long and complex yarn that began following the restructuring of the country after the war.

Following the end of the conflict, the national team muddled their way through the international calendar, slowly improving year on year. The team played their games at the Kosevo Stadium in front of up to 40,000 screaming fans, Horde Zla (HZ87) in the north stand and The Maniacs (TM87) in the south stand.

Post-war Bosnian football was originally made up of three separate federations. Bosniak Muslims, Croats and Serbs each played in their own independent football leagues. But as UEFA and FIFA only recognised the Bosniaks Federation, only Bosniak Muslim clubs were allowed to participate in European competition.

In the 1997–98 season the Bosniak and Croat Football federations agreed to merge. After several years of transition, the inaugural Bosnian

'Premijer Liga' was officially formed in 2000. Five years later, the First League of Republika Srpska (Serbs) merged with the Bosniak and Croat FAs and the unification of all three Bosnian football federations was complete.

Everything was in order until the turn of the millennium which of course coincided with the amalgamation of the Bosniak, Croat and Serb FAs. With the change in structure came the change in key positions within the newly formed football coalition. It was agreed that the foremost standings on the board would be shared equally amongst Bosniak Muslims, Croats and Serbs.

Problems began when Bosnian FA president Jusuf Pusina was pushed aside to make way for three new political appointees with no allegiance to the game to take up key positions within the organisation. Iljo Dominkovic (Croat), Sulejman Colakovic (Bosniak) and Milan Jelic – Jelic died and was replaced by Bogdan Ceko (Serb) in 2007 – were the prominent members of the newly elected three-member presidency. Then it started.

Claims of corrupt referees, match fixing, tax evasion and unsavoury affairs, like taking 'dirty' money from the Iranian FA in order to successfully agree to an international match in Tehran, were many of the allegations levelled against the FA hierarchy. All unfounded at this juncture but the general secretary, Munib Usanovic, probably just about the most unpopular person in Bosnia, is currently under investigation for tax evasion and office abuse.

Suspicions were aroused when relatively unknown Serb outfit FK Leotar Trebinje were crowned Premijer Liga champions of Bosnia in 2003. Supporters pointed an accusing finger, making claims that Leotar had bought the title. They took maximum points from home and away fixtures against every Serb team they played and earned more than ten penalties in the last five minutes of matches to secure victories.

Ado recalled one particular decision that stood out in that championship-winning season. 'In a match Leotar won against FK Sarajevo, Sarajevo forward Skoro was involved in a counter attack from the left-hand side around 40 metres from goal when the Leotar defender took him out with a two-footed challenge that was so hard, Skoro ended up five metres beyond the touch line. It was an outrageous tackle that should have earned the Leotar defender a straight red card. But the referee took it upon himself to penalise

Skoro and award a free kick to Leotar. It was one of many incredible decisions that season!'

Many clubs protested but were left totally frustrated at the lack of support from the FA. Some clubs even threatened to exit the league unless the federation acted upon their cries of foul play. It was all to no avail and so the alleged corruption continued.

Zeljeznicar themselves became embroiled in match-fixing allegations, much to the disdain of their supporters. Zeljo were 3–4 victors in an away match at Buducnost Banovici. The fans sensed the match was bought and boycotted the next home game in protest. Clearly incensed, Zeljo supporters demanded no more match fixing, even if it meant not fighting for the title!

Ado complains of an 'express team' (meaning overnight success before succumbing to everlasting mediocrity) culture within the Premijer Liga. Brotnjo, Leotar, Laktasi, Slavija and Modrica are all considered express teams by Ado and he explains why. 'They are all from small towns [5,000–40,000 population] and all have an unhealthy influence within the FA because their people hold key positions. Sarajevo and Zeljeznicar have nobody in FA congress and furthermore have a very limited income. Both teams are financed by the city and have meagre sponsorship deals with local companies.'

'Express teams on the other hand appear to have a bottomless pit of cash, albeit with a minimal shelf life. Board members are generally company owners or politicians in local government so money and influence is forthcoming on tap.'

'Modrica hold the record for being awarded most penalties in a season, many of which were given in injury time with the game all square. The ex-president of Modrica was Milan Jelic, president of Republika Srpska and right-hand man of Milorad Dodik who was prime minister of Republika Srpska. He was also the director of Modrica oil refinery, the biggest company in RS. And of course he was the president of the Serb FA! Can you see where this is heading? It comes as no surprise that since his federation's election to the FA, Modrica have managed to climb their way up the league table, eventually going on to win the title in 2008. Jelic died the same year and the team is now struggling to stay in the top flight. Coincidence? I think not!'

The Bosnian league is something of a terra incognita in the Western world. With zero European success and only a handful of players that have gone on to achieve worldwide acclaim, the Bosniaks are confined to the lower echelons of football's talent pool.

Suspicious Bosnian fans consider their Premijer Liga to be unsatisfactorily unique. The excessive amount of home wins is extraordinary. In the 2007–08 campaign, away teams averaged a 22 per cent win ratio. FK Zepce, who finished bottom of the league on seven points, failed to pick up any points on their travels. These statistics are indicative of a Football Association that is widely perceived as the most corrupt organisation in Bosnia. Every team knows they go to an away game with very little chance of securing a victory because of corrupt officials. It has become a standing joke amongst supporters and players alike according to Ado.

Although unable to make headway in their battle against corruption, the supporters continue to be a noisy nuisance. Despite an eternal rivalry between the supporters of Zeljeznicar and Sarajevo, there is a united front in the fight against the endemic deceit that manifests itself deep within a crooked cartel that are meant to be the custodians of the national sport. Both TM87 and HZ87, the lifeblood of their respective clubs, have boycotted all international matches since 2000 and will continue to do so until change is implemented and the untouchables are removed from office. They are not the only ones. The players themselves have also had enough. Hasan Salihamidzzic and Elvir Rahimic both shunned selection for the national team and other players feigned injury to avoid being called up because they were also unhappy with the federation and their antics.

In January 2008 the Bosnian FA, in an attempt to win over supporters, appointed ex-Barcelona player and fans' favourite Meho Kodro as national team coach. Another Bosnian legend, Elvir Bolic, was brought in as Kodro's assistant. They accepted their positions after a guarantee from the federation that they would be in complete charge of all footballing matters.

Less than five months after their surprise appointment both legends were sacked after refusing to take the national team to Tehran to play a 'lucrative' friendly against Iran. The fans were furious and TM87 organised a protest against the FA but those that took part were severely beaten by the Bosnian riot police.

The FA cancelled the match against Iran and organised a friendly against Azerbaijan in Zenica. But a furious and defiant Kodro and some other Bosnian legends organised a rival game to take place on the same day in Sarajevo. It was known as the 'match for saving football in Bosnia'. Many famous players and lots of national team players played in the match, leaving the Bosnian national team with a selection crisis. Finally, caretaker manager Piric was forced to select a team full of virtual unknowns who played out the game in front of fifty supporters.

Meanwhile over in Sarajevo, over 30,000 spectators turned up to watch the protest match. The fight for justice continues!

We crossed over the busy main road and headed upstairs to the newly acquired supporters' office. It was a small, sparsely furnished room built into the old shopping complex that was part of the external fabric of the stadium. Ado introduced us to the occupants, five or six guys who were busy making arrangements for Saturday's derby, the highlight of the Bosnian footballing calendar. All of them could speak English and although they made us feel really welcome, I don't think they could get their heads around why two English lads would travel half way across Europe to watch two minnows in action.

One of Ado's colleagues, Dandi, was a good friend of the president of the club and Ado asked him about the possibility of arranging accreditation for me to see the game from pitch-side. 'No problem,' said Dandi and he called the president immediately. After a brief telephone conversation, it was sorted. I had just been given permission from the club's president to see the game at very close quarters. Job done!

With my accreditation confirmed, Ado arranged for a stadium tour and a quick insight into the history of the club and its fanatical supporters, The Maniacs 1987. This was the name adopted by Zeljeznicar supporters after the old Yugoslavia team played Northern Ireland in a European Championship qualifier at the Kosevo Stadium in October 1987.

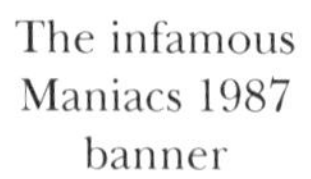
The infamous Maniacs 1987 banner

Zeljo fans turned out in their thousands for the game and spent the whole day drinking, singing and exchanging banter with the Northern Irish fans. Zeljo were in good voice and outsinging them was nigh on impossible. The Irish were impressed but this was nothing compared to the level of support that awaited them in the stadium.

Firecrackers boomed out all evening and flares lit up the night sky as 45,000 frenzied Yugoslavs turned the Kosevo Stadium into a seething furnace. The noise and intensity spitting from the stands was ear piercing, the supporters were borderline hysterical and Zeljo fans were the heartbeat inside this Sarajevan madhouse. The Yugoslavs, buoyed by such fanatical support, deservedly went on to claim a 3–0 victory. The Irish supporters had never before witnessed such frenetic support and christened the Zeljo hard-core 'Maniacs'!

We set off towards the east stand also accompanied by Zoff, a Zeljo comrade. Casual in appearance, he was tall and athletic, dressed in blue jeans, white hoodie and Nike trainers. He was a lively, friendly bloke and I liked him immediately. Zoff was well connected at the club in every way and as leader of the 300-strong Urban Corps subgroup, he was also very well respected on the terraces.

Our first port of call was to see the graffiti and murals emblazoned on the walls on waste ground opposite the east stand. The first was a black-and-white silhouette of the original leader of the Grbavica terraces, Dzevad 'Dzilda' Begic.

Hero – Dzevad 'Dzilda' Begic 1966–1992

Dzilda, as he was known, was a lifelong Zeljo fanatic who epitomised terrace subculture. He founded the infamous Joint Union movement (not active any more), famed for their fanaticism and hooligan escapades on away trips to other cities within the former Yugoslavia. Bosnian president Zeljko Komsic is probably the most famous former member of the Joint Union. Although now a prominent politician, Komsic remains a fervant supporter of the team, albeit away from the terraces that he regularly frequented for long spells during a rebellious youth.

Dzilda was amongst the first to organise a Bosnian defence in Sarajevo at the start of the war. Tragically, this terrace legend was killed in 1993 by Serb snipers whilst trying to save a young girl wounded by gunmen near the stadium shortly after the outbreak of war.

The man credited with forming Zeljo's own kop in the north stand was buried a war hero and posthumously awarded the Zlatni Lilium, Bosnia's highest military honour. The respect Dzilda commanded from Zeljeznicar's supporters is everlasting and for that reason, nobody has ever succceeded him as the leader of the terraces at the Grbavica. Zeljo's fans still pay tribute to his memory every season by singing a song they dedicated to his memory: 'Dzilda, you went away, but the sorrow stays with us. You will always be in our hearts, in the hearts of the Maniacs from the north.' At the side of the mural it quite simply says '*HEROJ*' and for that there is no translation required. Dzilda may be long gone, but fans here at the Grbavica will ensure he is never forgotten.

Next to Dzilda was a mural in memoriam to another terrace legend, 26-year-old Aner Kasapovic. Crowd disorder broke out in Zenica after a goalless draw between Celik and Zeljeznicar back in 2005. Celik hooligans rampaged through town smashing windows and attacking Zeleznicar supporters. Police used brute force to prevent Celik hooligans reaching buses carrying Zeljo fans which resulted in stone throwing and many people being injured.

Aner Kasapovic 1979–2005

Aner was caught up in this unrest and Zeljo fans accused local police of being overzealous in their actions, resulting in the death of Aner from a heart attack. The Maniacs have never forgiven the police for their part in the tragic events on that fateful day and firmly hold them responsible for his death. Over 6,000 football supporters from all over

Bosnia paid their respects to Aner at this young man's funeral. His death was an injustice felt by all Ultras in Bosnia–Herzegovina.

Dzilda and Aner R.I.P.

Moving further round the walls were littered with graffiti tags. The terrace subgroups Ragazzi Del Sud, ULFE and AP Gang had left their tags along with the famous blue smurf (Strumfovi) the adopted mascot of Zeljeznicar and a memorial to Dzilda and Aner.

Ragazzi Del Sud

ULFE – Nastrojeni (Extreme devotion)

Al-Pasino Polje (Ali Pasa's Field) – AP Gang – named after the area in which they reside

At the back of the east stand is an old black steam engine lying dormant on its own piece of track, a tribute to the railway workers who founded the club.

East stand – a permanent tribute to the railway workers

Opened in 1953 after six years of toil, the 18,000 capacity (unofficial) Grbavica Stadium remains a hybrid construction of two contrasting eras. One half is a dilapidated monument to the old Communist era and the other half is a cheap post-war makeover minus the floodlights. Despite the relatively new modification of the north and west stands, the stadium is quite clearly in an obvious state of disrepair and although UEFA allow Zeljeznicar to play domestic games at home, because the venue still incorporates standing areas, European matches are switched to Sarajevo's 38,500 all-seated Kosevo Stadium.

During the war, the Grbavica marked the front line between Serb and Bosnian forces. The pitch was littered with landmines and the first Serbian machine-gun post was established in the south stand. The west stand was completely destroyed by fire, along with all the club's silverware and artefacts from their bygone era. An integral part of the club's history was lost forever. The changing rooms, dugouts, VIP section and club offices were also razed to the ground leaving the stadium in ruins.

After the war, the stadium was slowly repaired and the old wooden west stand was completely rebuilt together with new changing rooms and club offices. In 1996, unity replaced rivalry as Sarajevo became the first team to grace the Grbavica after the war. Both groups of supporters walked in unison from the city centre to the stadium, carefully negotiating a safe passage through the mine-riddled streets. It was a momentous occasion remembered by many as the day that football united a city in mourning.

Zoff led the way to the south *curva*, also known as the holy south, home of the hard-core Maniacs 1987, the legendary fan movement responsible for creating a derby-day atmosphere that borders on insanity. He pointed to around a dozen seats missing in the top half of the *curva* and told me that the police were responsible for the damage but they blamed the supporters.

The old-school 'Holy South' stand, home to THE MANIACS 1987

Fans smuggle fireworks, flares, smoke bombs and strobes into the ground to create a prematch pyrotechnic extravaganza but police chiefs don't like it and try to prevent it by searching fans entering the stadium. Fines of up to 400 euros are issued to anybody caught with flares or anything resembling a firework or smoke pot.

Supporters soon got wise to the bully-boy police tactics, so in order to avoid detection they began to smuggle the flares and smoke bombs etc. into the ground and hide them under seats the evening before the game. But somehow the police got wind of what was going on right under their noses and a recent search of the seating area resulted in the confiscation of the curva's illegal stash. This in turn has further exacerbated the progressive decline in an increasingly volatile relationship with the police and FA who are both considered repressive regimes.

Ado informed me earlier that the police have further antagonised the Maniacs by threatening to confiscate their drums if fans ignore the ban on flares, fireworks etc. The south *curva* had a big choreography planned for the derby and had already acquired 150 Bengal flares, 200 strobes and five large smoke bombs but Ado told me that the drums are an integral part of the *curva* and the Maniacs cannot be without them. Dandi was still in discussion with the police to try and negotiate a compromise but Ado wasn't hopeful.

The Sarajevo derby is classified as a high-risk match and around 500 special forces police officers are mobilised for the game. Notoriously repressive, these heavily armed officers are considered an abusive, militaristic law-enforcement outfit whose agent-provocateur policing is often the catalyst for brutal confrontation. Their sadistic intervention in even the smallest of incidents has in the past had a destabilising effect and frequently leads to unnecessary large-scale disorder.

Unlike other Eastern European countries, although there has been an increase in football-related violence of late, football hooliganism is not considered an endemic problem in Bosnia. Bosnian law has a reputation for high tolerance regarding such matters. There are no UK-type anti-hooligan laws at sports events and police are not in receipt of any special preventative measures designed to stop potential troublemakers from attending matches.

Hooliganism is not currently deemed a hot potato that can be used for political points scoring, and so the police apply extremely violent tactics and methods whenever they choose to without fear of the consequences. Anyone currently found guilty of football violence can expect a hefty fine of up to 200 euros which equates to around 62 per cent of the average monthly wage.

Ado couldn't recall anybody from Zeljo ever serving a prison sentence for aggressive behaviour on the terraces but conceded many of TM87 had at some point been arrested for misdemeanours. The fans themselves, however, have adopted a unique approach to obtaining the release of any supporters arrested at away matches. Some 200–300 fans quite simply congregate outside the police station detaining any of their own and refuse to leave until the police agree to release the prisoner(s). They have to date a 100 per cent success rate!

The players were being put through their paces in a final training session before the derby so we walked around to the dugout to take a closer look. Ado and Zoff introduced us to the club captain, 33-year-old veteran defender Edis Mulalic, and coach Demir Hotic, the former Kaiserslautern and Bundesliga winning striker whose claim to fame was scoring 2 goals in the 3–1 victory for the German team against Barcelona in the 1991 European Cup. Sadly, Bakero's injury-time goal for Barcelona was enough to take them through on the away-goals rule.

Zeljeznicar are officially recognised as the most successful club in Bosnia–Herzegovina. Although they have won three league titles and three Bosnia–Herzegovina Cups since independence, the 1985 UEFA Cup semi-finalists are currently languishing in ninth place in the Premijer Liga.

It has been a difficult period for the club in recent years; limp performances, poor results, derisory ticket sales, lack of finances and four coaches in three seasons have all contributed to the club's downturn. The fans are not too despondent though; they have a very young team, a highly respected coach and a great club captain. 'Success is just around the corner,' beamed Ado. 'The young players will mature soon; it's just a matter of time. For now we only think about the derby. Tomorrow is very important for us.'

Zoff's mate Keki insisted we could not leave without going for a drink first, so we headed off into a nearby estate to their local watering hole. Countless bullet holes pitted the external pastel-coloured walls of the high-rise buildings that dominate this neighbourhood, providing yet another stark reminder of the past conflict.

A city still scarred by the brutal 1991–5 civil war

We sat in the sunshine outside a small bar next to the local opticians and Keki ordered up four dark beers, a coke for Ado and a couple of platefuls of cepavi, Sarajevo's most popular dish. Served on a plate with flat bread and onions it looked just like a closing-time kebab, only it was twice the size and tastier.

As we sat talking I got to learn a little more about Zoff. His English was excellent and the three and a half years spent working on cruise ships in the USA had left him with a fused Bosnian-American twang. He was quite a charismatic bloke with an infectious personality and had only recently been released from prison after serving 14 months behind bars for shooting a man he had been having problems with.

There was obviously a sinister side beyond the charming exterior. I queried the light sentence for a firearms offence. 'I had a good lawyer and I made a deal with the prosecution,' grinned Zoff. I explained that gun crime in the UK was on the increase and had he been convicted over there, he would have been looking at a minimum ten-year stint at Her Majesty's Pleasure.

'Yes, but this is Bosnia not England,' replied Zoff. 'Listen, I don't go around looking for trouble but if anybody has got a problem with me, they have a problem with my friend,' and with that he pulled out a small silver handgun (his friend). 'I don't give a f**k about the law or CCTV; if somebody has a problem, it needs to be sorted.'

'Wouldn't you be in trouble if the police stopped you with a firearm?' I asked naively.

'I already lost four guns and paid over 1,250 euro in fines but I won't be without one,' he said defiantly. 'Everybody knows me in this city. Let me tell you a story,' he continued. 'I had only been out of prison for a matter of days and called into the Guinness Bar [a city-centre pub frequented by Sarajevo Ultras] for a quiet drink. Within moments I was surrounded by up to 20 FK Sarajevo guys. "We caught up with you at last," they said, "and now we are going to kick your ass!"

'I had never seen these guys before,' said Zoff. 'Then suddenly it dawned on me. I have a younger brother who looks just like me and everyone thinks he is my twin. He must have pissed these guys off in some way, but he is my brother and he is all I have got in the world so I wouldn't let anything happen to him. One of the Sarajevo boys pulled out a telescopic cosh, so I looked these guys in the eye and smiled. They must have been thinking, is this guy nuts? We are going to kick his ass and he is laughing at us! I then pulled out "my friend" and fired two shots into the ceiling. The look on the faces of those guys as they fled the pub was priceless.

'When I came out of prison the members of the Urban Corps approached me about being leader of their group. They wanted somebody who was respected to take the group forward and I agreed. I now have the job of organising our group on the south *curva* and contribute towards making a spectacular display on match days at both home and away games.

'Choreography is very important and the best *tifo* is achieved by using banners, flags, smoke and [illegal] firework displays. We have many songs and chants and it is vital that we support the team for the whole of the game. But derby day is different for us. For a whole week before this game, nothing else matters. We think about nothing but this match; it is very important for us.'

Zoff passed me his mobile phone to show me video footage of terrace *tifosi* at some of Zeljo's previous matches. 'How about that,' he bragged, referring to a night fixture played at Sarajevo's Kosevo Stadium. The Maniacs in the south stand lit up the night sky with a defiant pyro show using red flares and I had to agree, it looked insane.

'Tomorrow, they will be crying like babies,' said Keki, the smiling assassin, and he pulled out the largest CS gas canister I had ever seen. It was obviously military issue but in these parts anything is obtainable. 'Stay clear of the north stand,' he warned as he insinuated that was where this mobile choking device would end up. 'For sure,' I replied, 'I'll stay well clear.'

To be fair, this isn't a derby that is associated with the same level of violence that normally blights the high-profile Balkan fixtures. As with most derbies, there will always be a hooligan element of some description that seeks to create disorder. However, since the end of the war, although not completely violence free, fans tend to compete to create the best choreography rather than slug it out on the streets.

This derby is representative of a societal struggle, a clash between the working class and the middle class. Loyalties will divide friends and families and so the bragging rights hold a lot of sway in the tightly-knit neighbourhoods of Sarajevo. The losers of this game will suffer a public humiliation of the highest order and the sting of defeat is a pain that will be dragged out for weeks, months or even years. To make matters worse, it is inescapable because the victors are also family, friends, neighbours and work colleagues.

Traditionally, the losing supporters of Zeljo and Sarajevo have a bit of fun by agreeing to make a forfeit, resulting in them maybe washing the car of their rival who supports the winning team. The local media have picked up on this and nearly always run with a light-hearted story about the unusual bets made between the two sets of supporters.

One such story put out to press was about two close friends who agreed to paint themselves in the colours of their rival's team should they end up on the wrong end of a derby defeat. Zeljo won that particular game, so as agreed, the losing supporter sprayed himself blue from head to toe. Unfortunately for him, he had a meeting with the headmaster of his little girl's school first thing on the Monday morning following the derby and much to his embarrassment, turned up looking like one of Father Abraham's smurfs.

The security forces are a constant thorn in the side of the Ultra groups in Bosnia and there is no love lost between the two. Zoff had referred earlier to an incident involving two undercover detectives who had infiltrated the Urban Corps group. 'I won't say how their cover was blown but needless to say when the identity of the officers in question became apparent, things became "very bad" for them!' Apparently, they each suffered a nasty fall from the coach on the way to an away game and lost the use of their legs for two months!

In recent times the police appear to be one step ahead of the Ultras residing on the south stand and once again Zoff suspects there is an informant amongst the group. 'They know all about arrangements for our terrace choreography and our travel plans to away games,' fumed Zoff. 'This can only be possible if somebody is passing on information. I am only 90 per cent sure of this guy so I won't reveal my suspicions to anybody. But let me tell you, once I am 100 per cent sure, things will be very bad for him.' I didn't doubt Zoff for a second!

Keki ordered up a final round of drinks as we discussed plans for our night out in Sarajevo. I asked Zoff to join us but Friday evening was training night for him at the local gym. He is a keen kick boxer, K1 freestyle to be precise, a perfectly legitimate sport where anything goes apart from a kick in the nether regions. Zoff had flat knuckles and had broken his nose on several occasions during the past month alone but that didn't seem to bother him. He just laughed out loud. It was business as usual for this likeable adrenalin junkie.

Time was getting on so we drank up, said our goodbyes and headed off to the hotel for a quick shower and change of clothes, before meeting up with Ado for a night out in the capital.

We met up at the bridge where Archduke Franz Ferdinand was shot and then headed off down the main pedestrianised area of Ferhadija and into the old town. Sarajevo was founded in 1461 shortly after the Ottoman occupation by Isa-Beg Isakovic, a lord from northern Greece who also founded Skopje, capital of Macedonia. He was responsible for building the core of the old town which is now home to so many great places for a cheap drink. Sarajevo makes for interesting bar-hopping and the centre is packed with laid-back bars and busy clubs where locals spill out on to the streets at the first sign of spring.

The whole city seemed to have descended upon Ferhadija, so we headed just off the beaten track to the City Pub on Despiceva. This was one of Ado's favourite bars, a cosmopolitan venue playing loud music with both indoor and outdoor seating areas.

We caught the attention of the waiter and ordered up a couple of beers and a coke for teetotaller Ado. He was a promising basketball player in his teenage years and played to a very high standard, hence his abstinence from alcohol.

Three cokes later and Ado made his apologies and headed off home for an early night before the main event at the Grbavica the following day. Brian and I had another beer, paid our tab, and then had a wander through the old town. After strolling up and down the narrow streets off Ferhadija for a while, we opted for a few beers in the Pirate Pub, an overcrowded bar decked out like the galley on a pirate ship. Young locals were being whipped up into a frenzy by a local band belting out a dodgy rendition of the old Nirvana classic 'Smells Like Teen Spirit'.

Looking around the bar I began to feel my age. I guessed I had shoes older than most of the clientele in here. Two bottles of beer later and it was kebab time and bed; we had a big day ahead of us and I didn't want to ruin it with a hangover from hell, a common occurrence that has been with me since adolescence. Besides, my age has caught up with me of late and the truth is I can't hack the late nights like I used to!

Match day was upon us. It was a stunning spring morning and with temperatures set to rise into the low 70s, I was looking forward to the day ahead. With a few hours to kill before meeting up with Ado, we decided to take a taxi up to the Kosevo Stadium, home of Zeljo's city rivals, Sarajevo.

It was quite a short but poignant journey up there as we stared out at the endless mass of white headstones that are commonplace throughout the city. Sudden, violent death was an everyday occurrence during the war years, meaning there were up to fifty funerals a day and sometimes residents would have to dig graves with their bare hands. Parks, gardens, schoolyards and alleyways, people were buried wherever they could find a space, usually late at night so that Serb snipers couldn't see the funeral and open fire on mourners.

Seeing the consequences of such a pitiless, brutal war really brought home the gravity of the situation and highlighted the suffering many innocent people endured. It is little wonder that Sarajevo is often referred to as the largest graveyard in the world.

We jumped out of the taxi on the stadium concourse and walked over to take a closer look. This municipal 35,000 capacity stadium was opened in 1952 and was reconstructed for the 1984 Winter Olympics. Formerly known as the Olimpijski Stadion (Olympic Stadium), it was renamed in 2004 and is now officially called the Asim Ferhatovic Hase Stadium after Asim Ferhatovic, the legendary FK Sarajevo player who retired in 1967. Locals, however, still often refer to it as the Kosevo.

A shot of the Kosevo taken from one of the many stadium cemeteries

Only 15 years ago this same stadium, the centrepiece of the Winter Olympics, was, like most other landmarks, shelled and mortared relentlessly by the Serbian forces, almost completely obliterating the area. Across the way we could see the former Sarajevo training ground that was turned into a makeshift graveyard to cope with the casualties from the constant barrage of attacks. Yet another silent record of those terrible years.

Walking around the stadium we saw no sign of war damage, just the usual graffiti that normally adorns the walls of football stadia in Eastern Europe.

HZ87 – Clockwork Maroon

Downton Crew

Horde Zla tag

HZ Youth

Nero Commissione

One particular piece of graffiti illustrated a football, a fist, a pint of beer and the phrase 'our life is different'. A perfect reference to the working-class terrace culture adopted by football supporters all over the world. Nothing can divide or unite so many like the beautiful game.

Supporting a football team is a vocation

The stadium, an all-seated open-air concrete bowl complete with running track, is currently shared by FK Sarajevo and the Bosnia–Herzegovina national team. Ironically, Zeljeznicar also play all their European matches at the Kosevo because their stadium, the Grbavica, is deemed unfit by UEFA. In fact, the Kosevo played host to two of the most celebrated games in Zeljeznicar's history.

The 1998 Bosnian championship play-off against bitter rivals Sarajevo will live in the memory of Zeljeznicar fans forever. Zeljo went into the match as huge underdogs in a game that Sarajevo supposedly only had to turn up to win. Finishing tenth in the first half of the season, Zeljo somehow managed to drag themselves up to a play-off position and ultimately qualify for the title decider.

Sarajevo had finished top and went into the final as overwhelming favourites. Fortunately, football doesn't work like that and invariably the underdogs somehow manage to punch above their weight in the big games.

Zeljo had lost most of their players during the war leaving them with a severely weakened and very young team. Some players were as young as 15 and 16 years old. They were even thrashed 9–1 by a team that now plays in today's fourth or fifth division.

Sarajevo dominated most of the match but never-say-die Zeljo hung on in there, even clearing two goal-bound shots off the line. Then in the eighty-ninth minute Zeljo deviated from the script. The ball was intercepted in midfield and the underdogs broke away quickly on the counter attack. Several passes later the ball fell invitingly at the feet of 16-year-old Hadis Zubanovic who scored a sensational goal that was enough to claim Zeljo's first Bosnian League championship.

It was probably one of the most important goals in Zeljeznicar's history and to this day that game is known as the 'Zubandan derby' (Zuban is short for Zubanovic and *dan* means day). And since then, Zeljo supporters renamed the Kosevo 'Zubanpolje' (*polje* meaning field).

After claiming the third of three Bosnian Championships since the formation of the new league after the war, Zeljeznicar qualified for the preliminary qualifying round of the 2002–03 UEFA Champions League competition. Another fine European run saw the Bosnian minnows dispatch Arkanes of Iceland and Lillestrom of Norway to set up a third-qualifying-round draw against Bobby Robson's Newcastle and the chance of a money-spinning shot at the prestigious group stages of Europe's premier competition.

Bosnian clubs used to go to Europe as 'whipping boys' but this fine run changed all that. Zeljo proved that Bosnian teams were capable of playing good football. They earned respect and gained self-confidence from two fine performances and looked ahead to the Newcastle game with great optimism. This glamour tie became a city's chance to re-establish itself on the sporting stage after years of horror.

Thirty-five thousand supporters crammed into the Kosevo, with hundreds more locked outside, to see a Keiron Dyer goal give Newcastle a slender first-leg advantage in front of a very hostile Zeljo home crowd. Unfortunately for the boys in blue, this was just too much of a step up in class against their English counterparts and as the pundits predicted, Zeljo were duly thrashed 4–0 in the return leg by a fine Newcastle side.

I couldn't gain access to the Kosevo but it wasn't through the lack of trying. We tried every turnstile, every door, every gate, and we even ended up in the maintenance workshop at one point, but all to no avail. With no staff around to assist us we continued our walk around the perimeter until we were on high ground enabling us to peer into this semi-modern all-seated construction. To the left of me was the famous north stand and home of Sarajevo's most fanatical supporters, Horde Zla, roughly translated meaning Hordes of Evil, but more about them later.

In October 1946, less than a year after the liberation of Sarajevo from Nazi rule, SD Torpedo was formed by members of the Yugoslav secret police, known under the acronym UDBA (Unutrašnja Državna Bezbednost). The UDBA were instrumental in team selection at the newly formed club and quite simply ordered the best players in Sarajevo to sign for them, including several of the finest players from cross-town adversaries Zeljeznicar.

Despite financial incentives and threats, one such player, Josko Domorocki, refused to agree to a transfer and was promptly jailed for his defiance. He became an overnight hero and his loyalty will never be forgotten by the Zeljo faithful. Sadly, in 1992, Domorocki was tragically killed in a car accident in Split, Croatia.

One player who did cross the divide between the two clubs was Sarajevo midfielder Albin Pelak. He signed for Zeljo back in 2006 albeit in very acrimonious circumstances. Pelak was born a fan of Sarajevo, starred in their academy, had been captain of Sarajevo as a 20-year-old, played for the national U21 team and later for the first team. He played for one season in South Korea but then came back to Sarajevo. Every time he played for them, he was without doubt their best player.

In a press interview before his first match in the national team they asked him if he would play for any other team in Bosnia. He replied, 'I will never play for Zeljo, for others maybe, but never Zeljo.' During the winter break Pelak got into a fight with his teammates and coach. Two days later he was released by the club and signed for arch rivals Zeljo on a free transfer. Within ten minutes of the news being announced, over a million texts were exchanged between supporters, a statistic released by the telecom company.

He turned out to be one of the best players at Zeljo and was welcomed by the fans, who appreciated his 100 per cent commitment. However, in his first derby against his old club, Pelak had his leg broken by one of his former teammates and he did not play again for many months. Zeljo fans cried foul play and insist his leg was broken in revenge for an act of betrayal that was deemed unforgiveable by Sarajevo supporters.

By 1947, the name was changed to S.D. Metalaca Sarajevo, before being simplified to FK Sarajevo (Fudbalski Klub Sarajevo) in 1949. The club's inaugural season in the renowned first league of Yugoslavia was a disappointing one as they bowed out at their first attempt. Not to be deterred, however, Sarajevo bounced back to gain promotion the following year and with the exception of the 1957–58 season, maintained their stay in the top flight for the duration of the league's history.

Mirsad Fazlagic, Vahidin Musemic and the heartbeat of the team Asim 'Hase' Ferhatovic were an integral part of the successful Sarajevo side that prospered during the 1957–1967 period and culminated in them winning the first of two Yugoslav First League titles. Ferhatovic gained legendary status at Sarajevo, scoring 198 goals in 422 games, and was widely regarded as the best Bosnian player ever.

His retirement in 1968 was one of the most important events in Sarajevo sport history and was glorified in a notable 1980s song by rock band Zabranjeno Pusenje, '*Dan Kad Je Otisao Hase*' (The Day That Hase Left). All the local newspapers gave him a great send-off and Sarajevo went on to rename their ground the Asim Ferhatovic Hase Stadium in his honour.

Although always on the periphery of success it wasn't until the 1980s that Sarajevo made the step up from perennial underachievers to emerging force. A new golden generation of players including Predrag Pasic and the outstanding Safet 'Pape' Susic helped rejuvenate the club and transform Sarajevo into a team capable of challenging for honours. After finishing league runners-up in 1980, Sarajevo took to the European stage by competing in the UEFA Cup in consecutive seasons.

They won their second and final Yugoslav league title in 1985 and with it came qualification for the European Cup, Europe's most prestigious competition. A disappointing 2–4 loss to little-known Finnish team FC Kuusysi saw Sarajevo exit the cup at the first hurdle and an inexplicable sharp decline in form swiftly followed.

However, the disappointing results paled into insignificance in comparison to the horror that was about to unfold. The siege of Sarajevo between April 1992 and February 1996 meant that normal everyday life was put on hold as the Bosnian capital was besieged by Serb forces.

Supporters of both clubs fought side by side during the war and were only able to resume their rivalry after the resurrection of the Bosnian League in 1997. Three Bosnian Cup successes were scant consolation for long-suffering fans as cross-town adversaries Zeljeznicar won three of the first five titles after the war. Sarajevo continued to disappoint supporters as their wretched barren period continued into the new millennium and it wasn't until 2007 that the '*Pitari*' clinched their first and only Bosnian Premier League title.

As noon approached we hailed a taxi and headed back to the centre for our rendezvous with Ado and after a quick coffee in the old town, we caught the tram together up to the Grbavica. Our first port of call was the Caffe Macchiato opposite the stadium. This trendy little café bar is the customary meeting point for Zeljo fans on match day, but the enforced derby-day alcohol ban had obviously taken its toll and the innkeeper looked set to incur a severe downturn in takings.

Fortunately the alcohol ban that threatened to put a dampener on the occasion didn't apply to the bar around the corner, and we took full advantage. The landlord was happy to ignore the booze ban and served alcohol on demand to a pub full of Maniacs. Police and security forces were happy to keep a low profile from a distance and appeared to be quite content to turn a blind eye to the legions of supporters quenching game-day thirst and exercising their vocal chords on a hot spring afternoon.

With around three hours to kick-off a steady flow of blue and white fanatics descended into the area. The sound of firecrackers boomed out from the rear of nearby flats as chanting fans cranked up the atmosphere. The highly visible but low-key police presence was now beginning to mobilise. Riot vans became more prevalent and small groups of militarised police units suddenly appeared out of nowhere. The dramatic increase in security signalled the arrival of the visiting Sarajevo supporters.

We finished our drinks and walked back up to the corner of the boulevard opposite the stadium to greet their arrival. It was here I met Jac, a good friend of Ado's. A tall, wiry, forty-something bloke, wearing a custom-made old-school Zeljeznicar t-shirt with the old club crest from their Yugoslav league days. 'Where did you get the t-shirt?' I enquired. 'It is one of twenty I had made for my friends and me,' replied Jac.

I explained that I had been looking for a decent club shop to buy souvenirs from but to no avail. He laughed before explaining to me that the club was amateur and had no business acumen. Football merchandise was almost non-existent apart from the t-shirts, caps, scarves and badges made by fans to sell to fellow supporters on the south stand for a small personal profit. The club hadn't even taken out any copyright protection on the club crest.

Jac was a passionate Zeljo supporter and clearly frustrated by his club's lack of ambition. He told me that in his younger days he used to drive to Split in Croatia to pick up large illegal consignments of Bengal flares used for terrace pyrotechnics. He risked a large fine, the confiscation of his car and even jail to make sure the south stand had the best choreography and despite the risks, he only ever covered his expenses.

There was a sudden rush of home supporters towards the police lines in front of the away section as the Sarajevo *corteo* (police escorting visiting supporters to the stadium) appeared on the horizon. Special forces, aka 'turtles' due to their protective armoury were mobilised and immediately deployed in front of the north stand to prevent rival supporters from clashing. I left Jac and managed to sneak through the segregation point to get a closer look.

Flanked by armed security forces, 3,000 guest supporters marched together forming a huge tide of maroon and white that filled the road as far back as the eye could see. Smoke bombs were discharged, distress flares lit and firecrackers thrown, and fans began to surge forward in a futile attempt to break police lines as they arrived at the north stand. They were met with a volley of missiles and a couple of half-hearted charges by overzealous Zeljo fans, whose 'hold me back' bravado and macho talk was dealt with swiftly and mercilessly by the cunning baton-wielding riot squad.

Horde Zla arriving at the Grbavica

Horde Zla, as with the Maniacs, is comprised of many different subgoups (Guiness Boys, Nero Commissione, Maroon, Vetrasi-weed guys are widely recognised as the most prominent), some of whom are more dangerous than others, and they were here in numbers for the first time in over three years and were obviously determined to put on a show. Internal rows had created serious divisions amongst supporters' groups at the Kosevo, as youth and old-school differences threatened to spiral out of control.

The younger generation had accused the older lads of being in the pockets of the club's directors. Tickets, away travel and choreography were being paid for by the club and in return the subgroups run by the older generation didn't protest against or criticise the club's hierarchy. The youth resented this, insisted they couldn't be bought and had boycotted the north stand for the last three years. But with differences resolved, the north stand was now united and for Horde Zla, it was now business as usual!

Sarajevo supporters were traditionally called *Pitari*, meaning the guy who eats pies, because of an old tradition of fans consuming … pies! In 1986, Sarajevo played Red Star Belgrade in a Yugoslav league game when an unusual and unsavoury incident was said to have occurred. Back in those days the *Pitari* used to gather in the east stand and had a formidable notoriety. Their already tainted reputation was further enhanced when legend has it that a maroon-painted snake was thrown from the east stand in the direction of the Red Star bench.

Worried officials who wanted to avoid a repeat of any similar incidents decided it was best to open up the north stand and move the *Pitari* into there. Shortly after moving into their new home, the name Horde Zla, taken from a comic book of the same name, was adopted by the *Pitari* and a new hooligan firm was born.

Horde Zla gained notoriety in the late 1980s and early '90s after being involved in some of the most serious outbreaks of football hooliganism in the former Yugoslavia. In 1991, two Partizan Belgrade supporters were stabbed in front of their own stadium after fans clashed before a league game in Belgrade. The 1988 riots in Mostar resulted in one fan being stabbed and thousands of pounds' worth of damage being done to property as rival supporters rampaged through the city before the game.

Shortly after Serbia went to war with Bosnia, most of the Horde Zla enlisted into the newly created Bosnian Army to fight against invading Serbs. Many of these brave young men lost their lives defending their beloved country in a bloody conflict that raged for over three years.

After the war, the Horde Zla reorganised and returned to the north stand. A well-publicised recruitment drive ensured they were in greater numbers and just as feisty. During the 1998 derby with Zeljeznicar, supporters invaded the pitch in retaliation for Zeljo fans attacking the Sarajevo keeper. A large-scale disturbance broke out as rival hooligans fought pitched battles, with players struggling to escape the mayhem that unfolded before them. The rubber athletics track was set on fire and over thirty serious injuries were reported as security forces struggled to restore order.

HZ graffiti on the external wall of the north stand

The Kosevo's north stand – a Horde Zla eruption

Hordes of Evil

Derby day madness within the confines of the sacred north stand

HZ lights up the Kosevo in the middle of the derby

Nowadays, although not completely eradicated, the impenitent violence that once consumed this bitter rivalry has subsided considerably. The 'wild west' days of the 1980s and '90s may be confined to the history books, but this derby is still widely recognised as one of the most passionate affairs in the Balkans and both sets of supporters contribute to a cauldron of ear-splitting noise and fervour.

With the visitors now safely escorted into the north stand, Brian and I made our way back across to the home section and joined the masses queuing for the south stand. I spotted the media entrance to my left and flashed my accreditation at the six-foot-five neanderthal on sentry duty, before navigating my way through the antiquated media area and eventually stumbling across the entrance to the pitch.

Thirty minutes away from kick-off and the noise generated by such a sparse crowd was immense. The stadium bounced up and down to a rhythmic drumbeat courtesy of The Maniacs, Zeljo's most devoted supporters. If this was a taste of things to come I feared I was going to need ear protectors. I walked across to the south stand behind the goal and spotted my friend Zoff. Bare-chested like the thousands of Maniacs around him, he was helping to display the last of the supporters' banners.

Stripped to the waist and ready for kick off

I caught his attention and he ran down to the security fence to greet me immediately. 'Hello, Shaun, how are you?' he asked. 'Hot,' I replied, 'too hot.' He grinned and then said, 'Listen, Shaun, you have any problems here, my friend, you know where I am. Come and find me and I will sort things for you.' We shook hands through the security fencing and he ran back up the dilapidated terracing to finish off the display.

I caught sight of Brian in the west stand. The south stand was a sun trap and far too hot for a ginger-haired, fair-skinned, transparent-looking Scouser. He was quite happy to take refuge in the protective shadow of the west stand for the time being.

With kick-off time almost upon us, the teams entered the field to a roar fit for a classico. With no team sheet to hand it was going to be nigh on impossible to keep track of the game but with a white hot atmosphere like this, I was more interested in the supporters than the match.

'Shall al lal lal lal lal la Zellll-jez-nicaaar, shall al lal lal lal lal la Zellll-jez-nicaaar' boomed out from the south stand as around 5,000 impassioned Maniacs laid down a marker at the start of the ninety-third Sarajevo derby. In response, firecrackers rained down on to the pitch from the visitors' section as the Sarajevo fans greeted their team with some serious terrace noise. I couldn't imagine the decibel levels getting any higher without causing physical injury. It was a madhouse, a real seething hotbed of passion.

Horde Zla greet their players' entrance to the 'bear pit'

Zeljeznicar enjoyed the better of the opening stages and looked the more likely to break the deadlock in a keenly fought contest. The blue-and-white hordes behind the goal all stripped down to the waist and started to jump up and down in unison singing along to the tune of 'Popeye the Sailor Man'. This went on for over five minutes, including several variations of jumping style, and each time they got louder. The support was totally relentless.

The carnival atmosphere continued as fans defied police orders and put on a small but acutely animated pyrotechnic show. Blue smoke canisters were ignited and flares lit up the terracing in a two-fingered salute to the authorities.

The 'holy south' erupts

Then in the thirty-fifth minute the south stand got what they came for when Zeljo livewire Bekric popped up to put the blues in front. Unfortunately for me, I was mesmerised with the support and missed the ball hitting the back of the net. Never has the term 'Maniacs' been more appropriate. The goal inspired a crescendo of noise within the Grbavica as the whole of the south stand 'avalanched' Gremio-style towards the security fence as number 14 Bekric and half the Zeljeznicar team joined them in celebration.

It was more of the same after the interval, just relentless noise. Both sets of supporters really got behind their team, both to the point of hysteria; it really was unbelievable. 'Modern football' should take note, because support like this is quite clearly missing from today's money-orientated classicos!

Fans held up a banner with the inscription '*VAS NACIN ZIVOTA, NAVIJACKA SRAMOTA*' (Your way of life, fans' disgrace). I later found out this was in reference to the Horde Zla failing to turn up to a prearranged fight they had agreed with the Zeljo Sarajevski Mangupi the evening before. The Mangupi are the casual arm of the Maniacs supporters' group, a small but dangerous youth element and always up for a row, especially with their local rivals.

'Your way of life, fans' disgrace'

Sarajevo, who went into this game as overwhelming favourites, were once again put to the sword as midfielder Pedrag Simic dictated play for Zeljo. He was a real tease, constantly tormenting the *Pitari* defence with his clever play down the right-hand side.

Suddenly, there was a huge roar that shook the stadium. Unfortunately for me I wasn't there to witness it. I foolishly chose the fifty-second minute to take a toilet break, which in turn coincided with the moment ex-Hearts of Midlothian player Beslija took it upon himself to score Zeljo's second goal of the game and once again, Simic was the architect of the attack.

The players went mental and so did the fans; it really was party time in the south stand and the noise reached an almost unbearable decibel level. The Maniacs, most stripped to the waist as they had been from the start of the match, waved their scarves in the air and taunted their rivals. 'Shall al lal lal lal lal la Zellll-jez-nicaaar, shall al lal lal lal lal la Zellll-jez-nicaaar' boomed out once again as the railway men revelled in the derby-day madness.

Shortly after the goal celebrations I received a call from Brian. He had worked his way around to the north stand into the section adjacent to the Sarajevo supporters. He told me that fans in the visitors' sector had become visibly agitated and he was sure something was about to go off. He wasn't wrong. Within two minutes of taking that call, firecrackers, smoke bombs and Bengal flares rained down on to the playing surface forcing the referee to halt the game and remove the players from the pitch.

Horde Zla force the referee to halt the game

Baton-wielding security forces were on the scene in an instant. Seats were ripped out and used as missiles as police officers came under a sustained attack from Horde Zla Ultras in the north stand.

Reinforcements arrived within moments and the initial restraint shown by security came to an abrupt end as the unforgiving Sarajevan riot police entered the north stand and laid into fans forcing them into a hasty retreat. Small pockets of supporters, faces covered to protect their identity, tried in vain to halt the police advance but their efforts were insignificant, as sheer brute force appeared to win the day. With the police now firmly in control, the referee agreed to let the match continue and the players re-entered the field of play to a rapturous reception by both sets of supporters and the game resumed.

Seats are ripped out and police intervention is necessary to restore order

Riot police restore order in the north stand

Zeljo carried on where they left off, continuing to dictate play. Their dominance was overwhelming. Sarajevo were a broken team and offered nothing to suggest they could recover from a two-goal deficit. If this was a boxing contest it would have been stopped long ago. For the boys in maroon the match was over and the referee's whistle couldn't come soon enough.

Zeljo supporters chanted, '*Cygani, cygani, cygani,*' (gypsy) in one final insult to the *Pitari* before the game ended. The final whistle was the cue for delirious celebrations and another cheeky number levelled at the '*Maleni*' (meaning the Small Ones, because Zeljo are the older of the two teams).

'*Das am pitar ja, ne bi im'o sna, ne bi spav'o ja, zbog tog Zelje.*' (If I was a *pitar,* I couldn't have a dream, I couldn't sleep, because of Zeljo.)

Bekric danced with delight and the other players raced towards the south stand with demented fervour. Fans beckoned the team towards the security fence to salute the boys in blue and the players responded by applauding the home support and throwing their tops into the south stand as they shared in the post-match euphoria.

Players celebrate Zeljo's derby day success

Meanwhile, at the opposite end of the stadium, Sarajevo players congregated in front of the north stand. Heads bowed with grimacing faces painfully visible, they paid homage to the depressed but appreciative Sarajevo fans. At least three or four of them openly shed tears. They looked utterly devastated. Several of the players tried to climb into the stand to be with their supporters but were physically restrained by overzealous stewards. This led to an angry exchange as players and stewards traded insults, head butts and punches.

Visiting supporters, angry at the treatment of their players, surged forward looking for confrontation as violence once again threatened to sour the occasion. However, an unexpectedly restrained approach by riot police took the heat out of the situation as players and stewards were separated and members of the Sarajevo team were eventually allowed to climb into the north stand where players and fans consoled each other.

Derby matches mean so much more in the lower echelons of the sport where the game hasn't yet been fully exposed to the modern football virus. Ultra mentality is accepted in these parts and the players embrace terrace culture for what it is. Players here are humble. These youngsters are living the dream and for that honour they are eternally grateful. They feel the raw pain of defeat just as much as, if not more than, their supporters and it was great to witness the emotions shown by these passionate young men.

There appears to be a healthy mutual respect here between players and fans. The players drink, eat and socialise in the very same restaurants, bars and clubs as the supporters who idolise them. There is no fear of attack or altercation as there is an unwritten rule amongst rival fans that players have immunity from the bad blood that is a by-product of football's inherently voilence-prone subculture.

I am unsure whether 'modern' professional footballers are aware of the impact they have upon the lives of ordinary working-class supporters. The fact is they do have an influence. They inspire aspiration and they have the ability to make people happy, especially on match day. The superstars of modern football should listen to the noise as they emerge from the tunnel, look around and take in the faces of the stadium's residents who hero-worship them every weekend and some more. Those are the people that really matter. Without them there would be no support, no noise, no atmosphere and nothing to play for except the thirty pieces of silver.

Here at the Grbavica, the club's rank-and-file supporters proudly boast Zeljeznicar as a working-class club for working-class people. Money is not an issue. It's the pride of wearing the blue-and-white jersey and giving their hopelessly loyal fan base something to live for. In return they get respect, devotion and ninety minutes of relentless support, week in and week out. The Beatles were right, money can't buy you love!

No one Likes Us … We Don't Care

A Derby

Game: Ujpest 2 – 1 Ferencvaros
Venue: Ferenc Szusza Stadium
Date: 3 October 2009
Attendance: 11,000

A sprawling city, Budapest is widely recognised as the crossroads between East and West. Steeped in history, Hungary was conquered by the Turks for the Ottoman Empire in 1541 before being recaptured by the Austrian Habsburgs to form part of another empire almost 150 years later. It was not until 1873 that Buda and Pest became one after almost thirty years of 'bloody' unrest. Evenly separated by the River Danube, ancient Buda is on the west side and the now more commercial Pest is on the east side.

The end of World War Two saw Hungary exchange a German occupation for a Russian one, before finally succumbing to Soviet rule and being declared a Communist state in 1949. The secret police wreaked havoc, causing misery for thousands as political repression and economic decline gripped the country. Inevitably, social unrest set in and what started as a peaceful protest by students quickly escalated and so began the 1956 uprising.

Ordinary Hungarians fought with Russian troops and the despised state police in a bloody battle for democracy. As the civil disobedience gathered momentum, Moscow ordered swift and merciless retribution. In rolled the tanks followed by the full force of the mighty Red Army. Over 30,000 people from Budapest alone lost their lives in their fight for freedom and thousands more were executed or imprisoned for their part in the uprising.

Over thirty years later, the Hungarian people finally broke free from Moscow's stranglehold as Hungary's transition from Communism to Western-style democracy gathered pace and in 1989 their dream was finally realised when the Russians agreed to a gradual withdrawal of its forces, signalling an end to the Communist era. Soviet troops finally left Hungary in 1991 and a now revitalised, cosmopolitan Budapest has one of the most thriving economies in Eastern Europe. It was therefore only right and proper that Brian and I spent a little of our time navigating our way through tourist-ville.

We'd had a relatively relaxed Friday evening drinking by Vorosmarty Square, so getting up early without a hangover was a bonus. Our early rise on match day enabled us to utilise the spare time exploring the city. With five hours to kill before our trip to the derby, we had time for some serious cultural saturation. We decided to take a taxi up to Statue Park, one of Budapest's most famous tourist attractions, situated on the outskirts of town in the 22nd district.

After the fall of Communism in 1989, many of the city's Communist statues were taken away from their original locations on the streets of Budapest and erected in this man-made memorial park. Giant statues of expressionless proletariat men and women stand together alongside Stalin, Lenin, Engels and Marx, the four iconic protagonists of Communism. Commissioned to commemorate the past, Statue Park is in equal parts inspiring, uplifting, thought provoking, eerie and quite an astounding piece of construction.

There is also a great little museum on site dedicated to Communist rule in Budapest and the 1956 uprising. No raconteur could have described a more insightful image of what life was like for the thousands of oppressed Hungarians during the Communist era. It provides a unique understanding of the secretive goings on behind the Iron Curtain.

With the obligatory sightseeing out of the way it was back to town for a traditional chicken liver lunch and then a taxi up to the Florian Albert Stadium, still known to Ferencvaros supporters by its former name, the

Ulloi. '*Ally ally ally ally ho-o-o fasszopo-o-o Ujpe-e-est, ally ally ally ally ho-o-o fasszopo-o-o Ujpe-e-est*' (Suck my c*ck Ujpest), chanted the mob of hard-core skinheads drinking outside the Szoglet bar in the warm autumn sun. The chanting animated the rest of the crowd and within moments it was reverberating around the whole area.

Hundreds of Ferencvaros skinheads had temporarily infested the hotchpotch of bars by the metro stop, located opposite the Florian Albert Stadium, home to Hungary's most successful club. The bulk of Ferencvaros Ultras always meet here for their feverishly anticipated derby-day clash with their despised arch rivals, Ujpest. Today's game was the first meeting between the two teams since Ujpest's 1–2 win at the Ulloi back in April 2006 and a three-year break meant that rival supporters were keen to resume hostilities. The 1,800 police drafted in for today's showpiece event paid testament to that.

Situated in Budapest's ninth district, the Hungarian people's club started life as Ferencvaros Torna Club, meaning Gym Club of Budapest, or FTC for short. However, nowadays they are colloquially known as Fradi, a nickname taken from the German name of the district Franzstadt.

After finishing a disappointing fifth in the 2005–06 season an investigation into financial irregularities saw Hungary's premier team removed from the National First Division (NB1). It was the first time since the league began in 1901 that Ferencvaros were not going to be involved in top-flight football and a ruling that shook Hungarian football to the core.

In what was adjudged to have been the darkest day in the club's history, Hungary's most decorated club failed to earn a Hungarian Football Association playing licence due to concerns over its financial situation. On 25 July 2006, three days before the start of the new season, Ferencvaros were officially demoted into league two by the Hungarian Football Association's arbitration panel. And although no official explanation was given by the Hungarian FA or the club, the Hungarian media reported that the demotion was enforced due to the club's tax debts and unpaid salaries to former managers and coaches.

The Ferencvaros Supporters' Association publicly called upon the club's management team to tender their resignation, blaming them and their 'years of ignominious and fruitless work' for the current 'moral and economic crisis'. The board were also accused of running its business affairs like a 1970s Communist outfit. No business acumen, poor leadership, corruption and nobody within the inner sanctum bold enough to take hold of the club by the scruff of the neck and drive it forward.

'You never had a tactical, nor a strategic plan or concept about the future of Ferencvaros,' was the official stance of a raging Ferencvaros Supporters' Association. 'You waited for a miracle, the saviour who would bring money. This is a disgrace. Not a programme, not a business or crisis management plan.' Club captain Peter Lipscei also chipped in, 'Those responsible are located one floor above the locker rooms. I know this is a brave statement to make, but they would do best for the club if they walked away quietly.'

A crowd of in excess of 400 disgruntled Ferencvaros fans staged a demonstration outside the stadium in protest at the club's enforced relegation. The peaceful protest soon degenerated into chaos as fans vented their anger at the board members. Traffic was brought to a standstill and the nearby metro station was badly damaged as supporters ran amok. Special forces were drafted in and it wasn't until late into the evening that the angry mob was dispersed and order restored.

In an attempt to placate supporters, the board turned to the law and immediately lodged an appeal to overturn the decision and vowed to seek justice in the highest court in the land if necessary. News of the appeal was greeted with dismay by high-ranking officials within the Hungarian Football Federation (MLSz) and matters further intensified when FIFA became involved. Just before the first hearing was due to be held in September 2006, football's governing body wrote to the MLSz, urging them to persuade Ferencvaros to withdraw its appeal.

If Ferencvaros insisted on continuing with proceedings, FIFA threatened to sanction Hungary by way of excluding the Magyars from all competitions. However, Ferencvaros president Miklos Inancsy held out and notified FIFA that it was his intention to press on with the appeal due to the fact that the MLSz violated FIFA's statutes by neglecting to stipulate a court of arbitration in its regulations. It was a decision that left this whole complex affair deadlocked and brought Hungarian football to the brink of collapse.

In a tit-for-tat exchange, the Hungarian Football Federation banned Ferencvaros from playing in international competitions until June 2007 and fined the club 25 million forints. The federation's explanation for such a drastic punishment was that appealing the club's demotion in a civilian court was in contradiction of UEFA and FIFA regulations, as well as its own rules. Needless to say, Ferencvaros were furious about the decision and vowed to fight on to the bitter end, even if it meant bankrupting the club in the process.

Fradi persistence, although somewhat clutching, was eventually rewarded when twelve months later, the Supreme Court ruled that the Hungarian Football Federation had acted unlawfully. The court's decision enabled Ferencvaros to sue the federation for an estimated $1,000,000 in compensation. In another twist in this acrimonious saga, FTC chief executive Krisztian Berki agreed a fragile truce with his counterpart Istvan Kisteleki at the MLSz, halting years of ill feeling between the two parties. In return for Ferencvaros dropping legal action, the Football Federation agreed to support youth training and fund the building of a prestigious state-of-the-art training facility.

A fuming FTC Supporters' Association publicly denounced Berki in a hastily released, venomous statement. They described the truce as an 'unprincipled pact betraying FTC and humiliating the club's supporters'.

Club officials, however, rejected FSzSz's (the supporters' association), calls for them to resign and in response to the MLSz's newly introduced zero-tolerance laws (enforced to combat fan disorder), risked further alienating themselves by banning their own Ultra groups from attending matches until they agreed to abide by club rules.

Whilst it was widely perceived that the directors at the club were fully responsible for the club's demise, many of the club's 'law abiding' supporters felt the notorious Ferencvaros hooligans and Ultras should shoulder some responsibility for the club's financial plight. The radical and violent right-wing following that has attached itself to the Fradi has been involved in many shameful incidents over the years. Fines and match bans have cost the club a small fortune in much-needed revenue. According to an unnamed club source, fan disturbances cost the club somewhere in the region of 100 million forints during a four-year period between 2002 and 2006.

Formed in 1899, Ferencvaros have been crowned champions twenty-eight times and won the domestic cup twenty times. They are the only Hungarian team to win a European trophy, beating Juventus 1–0 in Turin to win the 1965 Inter-Cities Fairs Cup final. A 1–0 aggregate defeat to Leeds United saw Ferencvaros finish runners-up in a two-legged 1968 Fairs Cup final and a 3–0 defeat by Dynamo Kiev gave them another runner-up spot in the 1975 Cup Winners' Cup final in Basle, Switzerland. They were also the first Hungarian team to participate in the European Champions league.

Although teetering on the brink of financial collapse, Ferencvaros, in a phoenix like rise to prominence, were expected to win promotion back to the top flight at the first attempt. This was the minimum requirement; anything other than promotion could have proven to be catastrophic and another nail in the coffin of Hungary's most prolific club.

In a hard-fought contest Ferencvaros narrowly missed out on a return to league one to minnows Nyiregyhaza, thus ensuring another financially draining season in NB2. Despite the manager's attempt to instill a siege mentality into his bedraggled squad, the team struggled to cope with life in the second division and looked like anything but a team that could win promotion back to the top flight. In a long and difficult second season, Ferencvaros were quite simply not good enough and finished third behind Kecskemet and Szolnok.

Meanwhile, there were developments off the field. Sheffield United owner Kevin McCabe's relentless pursuit of the club finally paid dividends. After five failed tenders, his offer of 11.56 million euros was accepted by the National Asset Management Company and in March 2008, Ferencvaros became the latest club to be added to his expansive portfolio. The deal also guaranteed Ferencvaros the use of its stadium for the next twenty-five years. Fans were ecstatic and saw McCabe as the club's saviour.

Loitering nervously by the entrance to the Nepliget metro station in the company of a malnourished-looking ginger skinhead with a milk-white complexion made it difficult to blend in with the home crowd. We looked different, and we dressed different. I was consumed with uneasiness, or maybe I was suffering from a diluted dose of paranoia.

We paced up and down nervously, trying not to look like two covert police officers, but the more we tried to look inconspicuous, the more conspicuous we looked. Naively dressed in undercover police attire didn't help either. With Brian in his standard police-issue Berghaus jacket, jeans and militarily-polished Clarks shoes and me in shorts, Lacoste t-shirt, trainers, sunglasses and standard police-issue rucksack, it was a schoolboy error of the highest calibre. Fashion *faux pas* didn't even come close. Most of our clothing could probably be found in the undercover apparel section of the 'football intelligence officers abroad' handbook. We were only a fleece jacket, baseball cap and earpiece short of a full rig out.

The majority of the 200–300 skins gathered here were dressed from head to toe in black clobber and wearing the obligatory Eastern European 'hoolie hoodie'. The police presence was heavy but discreet and if confrontation was to be avoided it was best for all concerned if it stayed that way, especially given the long and eventful history between the 'rozzers' and Fradi's hard-core supporters..

Security forces here are renowned for their ferocity and willingness to crack heads first and ask questions later. Only a few weeks ago in a home match against Videoton, Fradi supporters and police were involved in large-scale disturbances after police foiled an attempted attack on the visiting fans. Everybody embraces the ACAB culture in this neck of the woods.

We had made arrangements to meet one of the Ferencvaros academy players at the game. Liam was the 18-year-old son of a friend of a friend and hailed from Bury in Lancashire. The academy team had an early kick-off and Brian and I were debating where the best place for us to meet Liam would be, when we witnessed what can only be described as a gratuitous, remorseless, racial attack.

Two steroid-induced skinhead thugs approached a car that was waiting for the traffic signal to turn green. Without warning, both hoodlums launched a premeditated volley of kicks to the car before taking it in turns to attack its black occupants through the window, first with punches and then with a bottle. Stuck in waiting traffic, the driver was powerless to escape and I doubt any of them fancied getting out of the car to remonstrate. I couldn't blame them; all they could do was pray for a green signal and hit the accelerator, *rapido*!

It was a completely unprovoked racist attack that lasted less than a minute but it must have felt like a lifetime for the four unsuspecting victims. Nearby police officers neglectfully turned a blind eye whilst the rest of the crowd acted like a spot of weekend immigrant bashing was the norm. Backslapping ensued and the perpetrators milked their moment of glory for all it was worth.

Still feeling uneasy, we decided to call it a day and walked away in the hope of hailing a cab to the Ujpest area. But within moments of leaving I received a text from Liam informing me he was at the metro station. As we were literally only five minutes down the road, I called Liam to tell him we would make our way back and for him to look out for the only two lads with no tattoos, whiter-shade-of-pale complexions and not dressed in black.

As the metro station came into view I saw three young lads ahead of me, one of whom was grinning profusely. I guessed it was Liam and sure enough it was, along with a couple of his mates from the academy. Dressed from head to toe in black, Liam epitomised the Fradi dress code, unlike Starsky and Hutch here! Liam was scouted by Sheffield United at a schoolboy tournament in England. And at just 16 years of age, he was promptly packed off to Budapest to learn his trade with Sheffield United's sister club, Ferencvaros.

In a morning kick-off, Liam's team had just beaten their local academy rivals Vasas 3–0. Before leaving the changing rooms to warm up, all the academy players were instructed to spit at the Ujpest team photo the coach had pinned to the dressing-room door. Photos of the Ujpest team were also strategically placed in the nets and used for target practice by players. Hatred of their cross-town adversaries is obviously ingrained into players from an early age.

The animosity shared between the two rivals is quite simply based on nothing other than the fact that they are Hungary's two most successful clubs. It was a taster of things to come should Liam be offered his first professional contract with the club. The senior staff at the club had shared many derby-day tales with Liam but I don't think anything could have prepared him for the day ahead as a supporter for the afternoon.

I told Liam about the racial attack that we had witnessed earlier. He wasn't at all surprised. Racial abuse is commonplace in Hungarian football; it is quite simply accepted and the authorities here choose to adopt the 'see no evil, hear no evil' approach. Liam told me that three black Ferencvaros players were attacked and chased into the stadium by their own supporters only a few weeks ago and most were subjected to racial taunts and monkey chanting during matches almost every week.

Sadly, Ferencvaros has a long, unhealthy history of xenophobia and anti-Semitism. World War Two saw the rise of the far right and the deportation of hundreds of thousands of Hungarian Jews. In football, historian Tamas Krausz explains Ferencvaros had become a base for Nazism by 1939. It is well documented that anti-Semitism in Hungary reached its peak between the late 1930s and early 1940s and coincided with the winding up of Jewish club MTK in November 1940.

Club bosses at Ferencvaros, which included more than a dozen people of Jewish origin, as well as horrified officials and fans protested at MTK being snuffed out. It was in vain. As punishment, the Jewish element of Ferencvaros was ripped out of the club. In its place, Andor Jaross, the Nazi minister of the interior, became president of the Fradi and the fascization of Ferencvaros was complete. Jaross was later convicted for war crimes and executed in 1946.

The 1949 nationalisation of all Hungarian football clubs saw the start of a perceived repression against Ferencvaros. Footballing affairs only improved after the 1956 uprising, but this was only due to the weakening of other clubs rather than the strengthening of Ferencvaros. High-profile defections meant the balance of power was nearer to an even keel rather than favouring the chosen few as had been the case previously.

Unfortunately, few lessons seem to have been learned from the club's grim past. For quite some time, Fradi's boot-boy Ultra scene has enjoyed a higher profile across the globe than the football club itself. The poison of derision and racial intolerance, where angry supporters turn violently on players, appears to have become more cancerous and more sinister every season. It is like a nasty virus scheming its way through the stadium, slowly contaminating everything that it touches with hate.

The 1995 Champions League campaign, for which the club should have been lauded, will only be remembered for the abhorrent racial and anti-Semitic abuse levelled at Ajax players during their 1–5 demolition of Ferencvaros at the Ulloi. They had to endure ninety minutes of Nazi saluting and unsavoury chanting that made references to the holocaust. UEFA fined the club after protests from the Dutch FA and Ajax refused to sell any tickets to away supporters for the return group-stage game.

Even as recently as July 2009, incidentally, ten days before the start of the new season, the club's reputation was further tarnished by the Nazi extremists that masquerade as Fradi supporters. Violence flared at a pre-season exhibition game against German side Heartha Berlin. Around seventy tattooed Fradi skinheads attacked peaceful German fans before and during the game. They also taunted them with shouts of '*Seig Heil*' and '*Heil* Hitler'.

It was a match that attracted plenty of media attention due to the fact that two Hungarian legends, Peter Lipscei (Fradi) and Pal Dardai

(Heartha), were to face each other. Sadly, it was the skinhead shock troops who stole the headlines. Heartha fans told reporters how they feared for their lives as they were violently set upon in a number of completely unprovoked assaults that left several of them requiring hospital treatment. More than eighty articles were written in the German media alone about the violence at the game. One of them called the attack 'an embarrassment for Hungary, where on the streets of Budapest Nazis are marching'.

On receiving an official complaint from Heartha, the MLS distanced themselves from the incident by claiming that as the game was a privately arranged affair between the clubs and a third party, they could not be held accountable. Police officers on duty were also criticised as it came to light that during the interval, they ignored requests for help from the Heartha manager as German fans once again came under a sustained attack. Their excuse was that Ferencvaros didn't hire them to keep order within the confines of the stadium and as such they were only responsible for keeping order outside it! The plot thickens at this club with every passing season.

Back over at skinhead central, the time was around two-thirty and the mob appeared to have almost quadrupled in size. The atmosphere was raucous but not threatening and almost everyone had a drink in their hand. Singing was now widespread and everyone was in good spirits.

There was movement towards the entrance of the metro station, so we made our way downstairs where Liam's academy colleague had just enough time to get the ale in before we were swamped by the singing masses. The build-up for this derby started weeks, if not months ago and this alcohol-fuelled mob were savouring every moment. With up to 1,000 drunken supporters voicing their support, the confined space of the metro station amplified the noise to a level probably capable of causing physical injury. With respite around six stops down the line, never would such a short journey feel so long.

Like cattle, we were herded en masse down the platform and on to an empty metro train specially commissioned to take us to Ujpest. It was a complete free-for-all as we squeezed in to an already overcrowded train with no means of escape. The doors closed and we were waved off by around 200 riot police. Fans were crammed tight inside like packed sardines. Several supporters had their faces squashed against the window of the train's door, barely able to take a breath. Others struggled to reach for the nearest bar to hang on to.

Then just as I thought people were going to pass out, the carriage burst into life. The incessant chanting started and everyone on the train began to jump up and down in unison: '*Ally ally ally ally ho-o-o fasszopo-o-o Ujpe-e-est, ally ally ally ally ho-o-o fasszopo-o-o Ujpe-e-est.*' The noise was deafening and the train was rocking precariously from side to side. A bare-chested skinhead next to me was punching the ceiling so hard his knuckles were bleeding. The Jack Daniels he was drinking neat from the bottle was obviously acting as instant pain relief.

A sweaty and uncomfortable twenty minutes or so later we arrived at Ujpest and were met by the usual heavy police presence. This, however, didn't deter fans from drunkenly urinating on the platform and vandalising the metro station as they left. Outside, the area surrounding the station was in lockdown. Helicopters hovered above, whilst legions of heavily armed riot police awaited the Fradi 'riot squad'.

I lost sight of Brian as we both became embroiled in the mass crowd congestion whilst exiting the station. I veered to my right and was forced to wait until police gained control of the endless stream of Fradi skinheads that spewed on to the station concourse. It was here that I was approached by two casual-looking Fradi. In their early thirties and dressed head to toe in designer clobber, they guessed I was English and we got chatting.

I told them that I was fed up with modern football and its sterile atmospheres and preferred to travel around Europe taking in the big rivalry matches. I could have added that ticket prices were outrageous, kick-off times were a nightmare and clubs were milking their own for all they were worth but that would have been a rant! I explained that the Budapest derby had been on my radar for a few years but had not been possible due to the team's temporary exile in the second division.

'Is this the Ferencvaros hoolie mob?' I asked. 'Sort of,' one of the guys replied. 'We are a mixture of Ultras and hooligans and both can be very dangerous groups. When we play Ujpest, all Fradi are hooligans,' he said, laughing. He then pointed to a group of scary-looking guys at the front of the crowd and explained that they were the leaders of the two largest and most influential Ferencvaros Ultra groups, Green Monsters and Stormy Scamps, both of whom have a mentality bordering on insanity.

According to the same lad, around 250 Ferencvaros hooligans had made their way to an arranged meeting with rival Ujpest thugs earlier in the day. They had rendezvoused at a different metro station to the group we travelled with in order to avoid police detection. But their best-laid plans were foiled after the Ujpest mob failed to show and the Fradi firm were left to slug it out with the law enforcement team awaiting their arrival. No arrests had been made and the mob was being held by riot police away from the stadium. The highly organised violence and hostility between rival supporters is a trademark of the aggressive factions attached to both clubs.

We were held outside for around thirty minutes whilst police cleared the streets of any unsavoury characters looking to cause problems. Then, like an army marching to the front line, we began the final leg of our journey to the stadium. Ferencvaros received only 2,000 tickets for this game and demand was so great they sold out within thirty minutes of going on sale. Thousands were left disappointed and took their frustration out on anyone within striking distance, vandalising the ticket office and fighting amongst themselves.

The Fradi mob begin their journey to
the stadium under armed guard

There were also stories of desperate Ferencvaros fans buying tickets for the home sector, a personal safety risk that should carry a public health warning given the animosity between the bitter Budapest rivals.

The first thing I noticed about this sinister looking gathering was the distinct lack of club colours on show. They were nearly all rigged out in black match-day clobber. It was a dress code. A hooligan uniform; an identity. I was in real terms, freely mingling with a big firm of risk supporters who were intent on confrontation, and we didn't have to wait long before we found it. Within minutes of leaving the metro station we were ambushed by a small group of bottle-throwing Ujpest hooligans who attacked us from a narrow street on the right-hand side. It was nothing serious and lasted only a matter of seconds as riot police drew batons and chased the small Ujpest gang back down the road.

These derbies are highly charged affairs where rival hooligan gangs regularly clash before, during and after games. This match brings out the worst in the 'football terrorists' who stop at nothing in their quest to bring anarchy to the streets of Budapest. It's a war that never ends. Up to 2,000 Fradi hools have been known to take to the streets for the clash with their eternal enemy. Needless to say, Ujpest usually come off worst. Ujpest hools may win the odd street fight but it's widely accepted to be the Ferencvaros thugs who have come out on top in the lion's share of the many large scale confrontations that have cursed this bloody fixture. In the 1999 derby at Ujpest, various media reports suggested that sixty Ujpest hools armed with baseball bats and metal pipes ran from 100 weaponless Fradi who were intent on fighting in accordance with Queensberry Rules. The following year over fifty fans were injured and twelve arrested as 4,000 rival supporters went toe to toe outside the Ulloi Stadium.

Although both sets of supporters have been responsible for some of the worst scenes of football-related violence in the country, it is Ferencvaros fans with the 'no one likes us, we don't care' mentality that are the most notorious. They have form going back over twenty years and are very highly rated by the hooligan fraternity in Europe. Frank-City Hooligans, Aryan Greens, Killer Green Group, Sector 2 and Sector 16 were the old-school Ferencvaros hooligan groups who ran amok during the 1990s and into the new millennium.

In May 2003, Ferencvaros lost the title to MTK Hungary on the very last day of the season after a lacklustre 0–0 draw at home to Debrecen. MTK's tough 0–1 victory at Ujpest was enough to snatch the title from the grasp of the Green Eagles. Over 200 Fradi hooligans invaded the pitch and attacked the Debrecen players, breaking the visiting goalkeeper's nose before turning on the Debrecen coach, Lázár Szentes. He was beaten so badly that he was taken to hospital with kidney damage.

Stewards and media representatives were also beaten and even some Ferencvaros players were injured in the incident. Ferencvaros striker

Attila Tokoli was seriously attacked and vowed never to play for the team again. The Hungarian FA punished Ferencvaros with a paltry 16,000-euro fine and ordered the team to play behind closed doors until the end of the year.

The 2004 UEFA Cup tie with English FA Cup finalists Millwall took hooliganism to another level. It was Millwall's debut game in European competition and the pairing attracted plenty of media attention. Both clubs have a terrible reputation for soccer violence and the match was billed by the tabloids as the clash of the 'hooligan heavyweights'. It was an opportunity for the Ferencvaros thugs to prove themselves against Britain's finest. Media reports even suggested that some Millwall hools had come prepared for war and wore stab-proof vests for protection.

Old-school hooligans from both clubs came out of retirement for this one and they didn't disappoint. Despite high-level security measures and a considerable police presence, rival hooligans fought running battles over three nights bringing chaos to the streets of downtown Budapest. Four Millwall fans were taken to hospital with knife wounds, two of them serious. There were also reports of large hunting knives being on open sale outside the stadium. UEFA threatened to impose a life ban from European competition on Ferencvaros but eventually relented and issued the club with a fine.

The 2005 Hungarian Cup final against Sopron heaped more shame on the Green Eagles, but this time it was the behaviour of the players and coach that shamed the club. An ill-tempered affair saw three Ferencvaros players dismissed; a fourth would have caused the ref to abandon the game. Fradi coach Csaba Laszlo was allegedly heard shouting, 'Break his leg,' from the dugout in the hope that a serious injury to an opposition player would result in another dismissal and the abandonment of the cup final. Thankfully that didn't happen and Sopron went on to lift the trophy. The coach and his players further humiliated the club as they chose to ignore the medal ceremony.

As the police were busy dealing with the skirmish that had broken out to my right, I took the opportunity to slip out of the escort and make my way to the stadium ahead of the mob. I called Brian but he decided to stay with Liam and his mate so I agreed to meet up with him in the ground before kick-off.

Ujpest officials had discussed the possibility of playing today's game at the Ferenc Puscas National Stadium in order to maximise revenue. It was a move favoured by Ferencvaros and their supporters as they would have received an increased ticket allocation. Ujpest fans, however, were incensed by this proposal and threatened to boycott the game if such a move was agreed. Backed by their manager, they successfully campaigned against the proposition, arguing that Ujpest would lose home advantage because of the increased Ferencvaros support.

As I distanced myself from the visitors I bumped into Josef, an old friend of mine from Austria. Josef is the official photographer and film maker for the Rapid (Vienna) Ultras. When he is not watching Rapid, he spends his time travelling around Europe, predominantly Eastern Europe, photographing and filming the Ultra fan scene.

I had discussed the ticket situation for today's game with Josef earlier in the day. He had been to this derby at least a dozen times before and although the game was advertised as a complete sell-out, he was confident tickets would be made available for the tribune, albeit the most expensive sector in the stadium. Josef was correct but what he didn't account for was the fact that they wouldn't accept euros as payment. As a compromise, the ticket office agreed to reserve four tickets on his behalf in the hope that I had enough local currency to pay for them, which of course I did.

It was just over an hour to kick-off and the Fradi announced their arrival at the stadium by letting off firecrackers and lighting up flares. More riot police and dog handlers were drafted in as the final stages of the first half of today's security operation reached its conclusion. Each fan had to be hand searched for weapons and potential missiles before being allowed entry into the ground. And with 2,000 visiting supporters to search, it was going to take a while.

Fans arrive at the Ferenc Szusza Stadium under heavy police escort

Josef had a word with stadium security and they reluctantly agreed to provide us with access to the ticket office without having to navigate our way through overly congested streets around the perimeter of the stadium.

Founded in 1885, Ujpest are the oldest club in the country, are one of only two teams never to have been relegated from the top flight and like Ferencvaros, are named after the district (4th) they play in. The Ferenc Szusza Stadium has been home to Ujpest since its construction in 1922. It was formerly known as the Megyeri uti Stadium but was refurbished in 2001 as part of a government rebuilding plan that was meant to contribute to a successful Hungarian bid for the 2008 European Championships.

The 13,500 capacity falls way short of the 30,000 that UEFA require and needless to say the bid failed. In 2003, the stadium was renamed after Ujpest's legendary striker Ferenc Szusza, a fitting tribute to an icon of the Viola and Hungarian football.

Ujpest, or Ujpest Dozsa as they were known when they were the official team of the police back in the Communist era, have a long and colourful history and the twenty league titles and ten cups they have amassed make them Hungary's second most successful team. Only eternal rivals Ferencvaros have won more. Between 1969 and 1975, Ujpest won an unprecedented seven titles in a row and scored 500 goals in the process to set a new post-war record. At home, they proved to be almost invincible, losing only four home games in ten seasons, another post-war record.

Unfortunately for Ujpest, only two title successes in the last twenty-nine years confirms the Viola's glory days are consigned to the annals of history. Hungarian football itself is in sharp decline these days and corruption, financial irregularities, greed, lack of investment, xenophobia and yob rule have all contributed greatly to the game's demise.

The halcyon days of the 1950s when legends like Puskas, Kocsis, Albert and Bozsic graced the world stage are now a very a distant memory. Gusztav Sebes was the manager credited with creating the 'Magical Magyars', one of the finest attacking teams of all time. Their 3–6 triumph at Wembley back in 1953 was the first defeat inflicted upon England on home soil from a team outside the UK. The return match in Budapest six months later saw England annihilated 7–1 in front of 100,000 fans at the Nep Stadium.

Puskas captained this legendary side to the 1954 World Cup final against Germany in Switzerland. Sadly, the Magyars suffered World Cup heartbreak for the second time as Germany ran out 3–2 winners in a pulsating final that saw an eighty-ninth-minute Puskas equaliser controversially ruled out for offside.

Fifty-five years later, some say Hungary have never recovered from losing that World Cup final. They haven't qualified for a World Cup finals since their embarrassing exit at the group stage in 1986 and they haven't qualified for the European Championships since 1972. They were humiliated 12–1 by Yugoslavia in a two-legged play-off for the 1998 World Cup finals and their 2–1 defeat to 119th-ranked Malta in 2006 confirmed Hungary's footballing status as terminal.

At international level, players seem to lack motivation, and always facing comparisons with the iconic generation of the 1950s is further exacerbating an already grave situation. Domestically, things fare no better. The standard of football is poor with all the best players plying their trade outside Hungary and rumours of match fixing rife. There is very little TV revenue and meagre sponsorship, and mounting debt means most clubs are playing just to stay afloat. There are no quick fixes for sick footballing nations and the Hungarian FA has the unenviable task of finding a cure.

We collected our tickets and I made arrangements to meet Brian outside the tribune. He rolled up around ten minutes later. With approximately thirty minutes to kick-off, Josef made his way into the ground whilst Brian and I had a nosey in the fan shop, or lack of one. It was small, cramped and akin to an Aladdin's cave full of cheap tack. Marketing is obviously not a primary concern amongst Hungary's elite clubs.

Inside the stadium the atmosphere was hotting up. The excitable stadium announcer expertly whipped the home fans up into a frenzy as he bellowed out team line-ups with impressive enthusiasm. This game isn't going to decide who wins the title or a cup. It will, however, decide the mood of the city. It's a great occasion that fans from the country's two biggest and best-supported clubs have been yearning for, for almost three and a half years.

The added spice of British managers in charge of both teams also attracted interest from the UK media. English coach Bobby Davison was installed as manager of Ferencvaros by new owner Kevin McCabe in

2008. He masterminded the Fradi's promotion back into league one and became an instant hit with the fans; although a poor start to the season had led to murmurings of discontent on the terraces and in a previous home game he was abused by sections of the crowd singing 'Bobby go home'!

Scotsman and former Celtic player Willie McStay took charge of Ujpest this season and endeared himself to the supporters almost immediately by voicing his support for today's game to be played at the Ferenc Szusza. In contrast to Ferencvaros, Ujpest have had an excellent start to their campaign and would be looking to build on that in front of a capacity crowd.

The teams dispersed from the players' tunnel to a knee-trembling reception from both sets of supporters. The Ujpest Ultras to my right in Sector C turned the terraces into a sea of purple with pictures of former Ujpest legends riding the waves. The visitors to my left held up choreographed cards in the segregated Sector D, to display their famous club crest on a background of green and white.

Ujpest Sector

Ferencvaros Sector

'F*ck Ferencvaros, we're gonna f*ck Ferencvaros' (to the tune of 'Sing when you're winning') came the roar from three sides of the stadium as Ujpest enjoyed the early exchanges, forcing five corners in the first five minutes. The stadium shook as the pumped-up home crowd, arms linked, pogoed up and down in unison as though they were in 'the pit' at a punk rock fest for the mentally insane.

Ujpest continued to dominate proceedings but were unable to find a cutting edge in the final third. Sensing an early setback, Fradi Ultras behind the goal suddenly burst into life. Each and every supporter raised their scarf above their head before a well-choreographed eruption of noise and light. Flares were ignited, smoke bombs were set off and the rat-a-tat-tat of exploding firecrackers filled the air. The atmosphere was white hot but that is the norm for these highly charged games.

Green and white army – you'll never walk alone

There was a British physical approach to the game and the first half was in danger of being remembered for poor temperament rather than technique. A late challenge by Ujpest's Norbert Toth earned him the first yellow card of the game as the referee signalled the end of his lenient approach.

Shortly afterwards, Ferencvaros mounted a rare attack and in the words of the famous Argentinian sportscaster Andres Cantor, 'Gooooooooooooooooaaaaaaaaaaallllll.' Fradi midfielder Laszlo Fitas got the all-important touch as he poked home the ball in a goalmouth scramble. Needless to say, the lunatic fringe in Sector D went nuts. More flares lit up the terracing, more firecrackers filled the early evening air and more smoke bombs were discharged.

The lunatics have taken over the asylum – Fradi celebrate their goal

However, no sooner had the smoke settled than only two minutes later centre forward Peter Kabat headed home an Ujpest equaliser. What goes around comes around! All three stands erupted as the Viola went mental. This was as good as it gets; big rivalry games evoke a gamut of emotions from an expectant audience. In two short minutes the mood of 11,000 supporters changed from sadness and despair, to euphoric and relieved and vice versa. The half-time whistle was a welcome break for everyone from this rollercoaster of a derby.

Moments later the Viola return the compliment by celebrating their equaliser

The players came out after the interval to a pyrotechnic show in sectors B and C. Flares are an inherent part of fan culture in Europe, particularly Eastern Europe. Ujpest's Viola Bulldogs and Ultra Korps are the two biggest fan groups at the Ferenc Szusza and between them provide a strong Ultra mentality on the on the terraces. They are responsible for much of the choreography and pyrotechnics that make for the partisan atmosphere these games are famed for. To them, a good show on the terraces is just as important as the performance on the pitch.

The Hungarian FA, however, dislike the fanaticism of the Ultras and in an attempt to subdue their Ultra culture, have banned the use of pyrotechnics in Hungarian stadia. Only a few weeks ago after the game at Debrecen, Ferenvaros defender and fans' favourite Atilla Dragoner and the club physio Lipcsei were both suspended after being accused of smuggling flares into the stadium for the club's Ultra groups. And sadly, word on the street is that Dragoner may never don the green-and-white jersey of Ferencvaros again.

The second half saw Ujpest change formation. McStay obviously thought Ferencvaros were there for the taking and gambled by playing with three strikers as he sought to take all three points in his first

Budapest derby. A much improved performance saw Ujpest control the match in front of their fanatical home support. Their short passing play was a pleasure to watch after witnessing a blood-and-thunder first half.

In contrast, Ferencvaros rarely threatened in the opening period and Haber was the busier of the two keepers. Ujpest were temporarily reduced to ten men after Rajczi had to go off for treatment to a cut mouth but Ferencvaros failed to take advantage, continuing to have and then squander possession. Rajczi made a swift return to the field but play was halted for a moment after the ref spotted that he had his shirt on inside out.

Both teams made late substitutions in an effort to break the deadlock but it was Ujpest who continued to press forward. Kabat broke down the right before playing the ball back to substitute Foxi, and his perfectly weighted cross was headed into the back of the Ferencvaros net by an ecstatic Peter Rajczi to send the Ferenc Szuzsa into raptures.

Three sides of the stadium were already on their feet before the ball had even crossed the line; it was complete soccer madness in here. Everyone was hugging and kissing each other like they were greeting a long-lost family member. The hard-core Viola behind the goal were foaming at the mouth, passion etched all over their faces as they climbed the security fencing in a frenzied celebration to salute Rajczi and his ecstatic teammates. The emotion conjured up when celebrating a winning goal against your biggest rivals brings a feeling of euphoria that money can't buy.

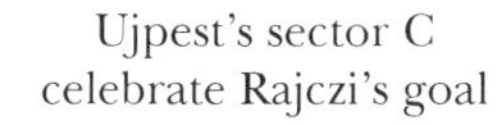

Ujpest's sector C celebrate Rajczi's goal

In contrast, 2,000 Fradistas were momentarily stunned into a stony silence of total disbelief. Then cometh the backlash. The 'mindless majority' looked all set to capture the headlines once again. The Fradi storm troopers on the left of Sector D ripped out seats and hurled them at riot police and stewards from within their fenced-off enclosure. The violence escalated after the final whistle as fans tried to break down the security fencing and had to be forced back by baton-wielding officers.

Meanwhile, Ujpest players stayed on the field for a full 15 minutes celebrating their victory with home supporters. Holding hands, the whole team took a bow in front of all three home stands before disappearing down the tunnel. The ecstatic Viola, scarves raised above their heads and many stripped to the waist, milked the moment for all it was worth and stayed behind for at least twenty minutes after the final whistle. The win had propelled them into second place in the league, ten points ahead of Ferencvaros, who could end up second from bottom should other results go against them.

Bragging rights belong to the Viola

As the disorder continued in the visitors' section more riot police were drafted in to surround the whole enclosure where they exercised considerable restraint in the face of extreme provocation. As the thugs

Riot police intervene to stop Fradi violence from escalating

realised they were making no headway they slowly but surely dispersed and immediately sought confrontation outside the stadium with a fully prepared army of riot police. The situation became so dangerous that young Liam and his academy mates were instructed to wait for Ferencvaros boss Bobby Davison, who insisted on driving them back to their lodgings.

We were just about to leave when Brian and I began talking to two Italian lads at the top of our sector. Dressed like a pair of English soccer casuals, Simon and Elvio were here for the game as guests of one of the Ujpest boys. It turned out that they were the founders of the Coolness Milano chain, a terrace-culture store specialising in old-school terrace threads. Their main store is in Milan but the Coolness Society brand is available in outlets all over Italy.

They invited us for food and drinks at a local pizzeria along with the Ujpest boys. Outside the stadium we were introduced to Zoltar and several of his mates. They were the main faces of the small but tidy MCMXC11 Ultra group. Named after the year they were formed (1992), they boasted around fifty members on a good day and had been highly influenced by the casual aficionados of the English football scene back in the 1980s.

No strangers to football hooliganism, this group, along with the hard core from the Angol Brigade and Korps firms, were part of the 500-strong Ujpest following that caused problems on their last European away-day in Bucharest. Former European Champions Steaua played host to Ujpest in a Europa League qualifier back in July of this year. Thuggish behaviour and racist chanting marred the evening. Ujpest lost the first-leg game 2–0, but it was a banner displayed by Steaua supporters that grabbed the headlines. It read: 'How long does it take a Hungarian woman to s**t? ... 9 months.' This caused outrage not only amongst Ujpest supporters but also back in Budapest as well and guaranteed a red-hot reception for visiting Steaua supporters in the return leg.

Two weeks later, as predicted, Ujpest hools brought shame on the club as they racially abused the Romanian contingent. Nazi salutes and chants of '*Seig Heil*' were aimed at the visitors. Home supporters also displayed a banner of their own in response to the defamatory Bucharest banner. It read: 'How do you know that you are a gypsy? You speak Romanian.'

During the half-time break, a baying Ujpest mob provoked Steaua supporters by hurling flares into the visitors' section, prompting them to retaliate by ripping seats out and throwing them at the Ujpest fans in the adjacent sector. Riot police were deployed and used tear gas to restore order, causing the second half to be delayed by almost twenty minutes.

The area between rival fans was also segregated to prevent further disorder. Trouble continued after the game as hooligans clashed with riot police outside whilst trying to attack the Steaua section. Police, however, did eventually manage to disperse the angry mob without the two sets of supporters meeting.

Zoltar was in the car so he pointed the rest of us in the direction of the pizzeria where he would meet up with us on our arrival. Although it was only a ten-minute walk he left with a chilling warning. 'This can be an unsafe area so beware of Fradi in cars,' he said. 'They are very dangerous, especially with the knives.' Thanks for that, I thought and without further ado the four of us marched towards the restaurant at lightning pace.

We had a good chat with the Milano boys about business and football over pizza and a couple of beers. The Coolness Society's British-inspired range focused on old-school terrace fashion. They had successfully created a great little niche for themselves and now had outlets throughout Italy and Eastern Europe. Zoltar, who was sporting a Stone Island jacket and Burberry baseball cap, was in the same line of business and also sold a range from the Coolness Milano brand in his Casual Streetwear store in central Budapest.

Football and fashion fused together almost five decades ago. Skinheadism, punk rock and the mod revivalists influenced the first football fashionistas to grace the terraces before label obsession got a grip and gave birth to the casual scene. Wearing the latest clobber at the match first took off in the UK back in the 1970s. Although never on a grand scale like in England, over time it was a trend that would be adopted by a select band of style-conscious thugs over the channel and into mainland Europe.

Budapest wasn't yet as affluent as most of the Western European countries, so the demand for designer goods on the terraces was somewhat lacking. Zoltar therefore tended to cater for a thriving skinhead culture and stocked an abundance of less expensive brands such as Fred Perry, Ben Sherman, Lonsdale, Everlast and the appropriately named Hooligan clothing brand.

As we were about to settle our bill, Zoltar took a call on his mobile. He had some bad news for us. Apparently, 200 Ferencvaros hooligans were on the way up to the pizzeria with the intent of doing some serious damage to the fifteen or so Ujpest boys drinking in there. It was therefore time to make a sharp exit so we exchanged numbers, said our goodbyes and headed off in different directions.

Brian and I chose to make a beeline for the bars in the safety of downtown Budapest. A couple of beers in the Szempla open-air bar brought an end to what was fast becoming just another day at the office!

Poor crowds, pub football, lack of elite players, xenophobia and a shocking hooligan problem was in danger of completely destroying Hungary's strong footballing identity. Jingoistic racist sentiments spewing from the stands meant that upcoming talent from the fast-emerging African nations were reluctant to ply their trade here. The terrace 'mafiosi' appeared to be almost untouchable as they engaged in illegal activities that siphoned much-needed funds from clubs barely treading water.

Players and coaches often complained of intimidation and feared for their safety from the well-organised and ruthless network of 'violence entrepreneurs' that monopolise the terraces of the Ulloi and continue to thrive because the law is weak. The violent extremism and dogmatic values that gel these like-minded individuals together make them a very dangerous animal.

If the authorities don't act quickly to rid Hungarian football of its Achilles heel, they risk losing more grass-roots supporters for whom football is life and that would be a very sad day for the beautiful game and all those who live for it!

Les Enfants Terribles

Le Classique

Game: Paris Saint-Germain 2 – 1 Olympique de Marseille
Venue: Parc des Princes
Date: 7 November 2010
Attendance: 40,234

In June 1940, a Nazi swastika flew high above the Arc de Triomphe as German soldiers goose-stepped down the Champs-Elysées, marking the beginning of a four-year occupation. Offering little or no resistance, Paris had fallen with ease to the advancing German army. In a mass exodus, almost eighty per cent of Parisians followed the French government and fled the capital city seeking refuge away from Hitler's evil Nazi regime. Sadly, it is estimated that up to 100,000 people lost their lives whilst trying to flee to freedom. Paris remained under German occupation until it was liberated by Allied forces on 24 August 1944.

Fast forward sixty-six years and the tree-lined Avenue des Champs-Elysées, once the focal point of Nazi occupation, is now a haven for tourists. It is also retail heaven for wealthy fashion junkies who 'shop till they drop' in the many exclusive designer boutiques that adorn the most famous street in Paris.

Away from the glitz and glamour of central Paris is the iconic Parc des Princes stadium, home to sleeping French giants Paris Saint-Germain (PSG), one half of French football's biggest and most volatile rivalry.

Parc des Princes stadium

The other half, Olympique de Marseille, play their home games at the Stade de Velodrome in Marseille, almost 500 miles to the South.

This north–south divide is characterised by two contrasting cities. Paris in the north is a cosmopolitan capital, enriched in history dating back 2,000 years. The numerous monuments commemorating historical events, famous landmarks and the many museums showcasing priceless artefacts make it a tourist city that really justifies the hype.

The port city of Marseille is France's second city and widely regarded as the capital of the south. The many North African and Mediterranean immigrants that have settled here have instilled their own identity into the inner-city *banlieues*, helping to create one of the most diverse and healthy cultural environments in the world.

Most supporters believe the enmity between the two teams, who had no history of rivalry, was forged in the boardroom during the early 1990s. It's a belief that was confirmed in the bestselling book *OM-PSG, PSG-OM Les Meilleurs Ennemis* (by Jean Francois Pérès and Daniel Riolo). Disgraced ex-Marseille president Bernard Tapie claimed he created the rivalry with PSG because he needed a domestic rival capable of keeping his dominant Marseille hungry for success.

With the exception of Bordeaux in the mid 1980s, Marseille had no real competition back then and were looking for another enemy. PSG was owned by Canal Plus, the broadcaster of the French championship, and they themselves were also looking to establish a French classico. The book suggests that the rivalry was encouraged by Canal Plus and preserved by the French media. Between them, they managed to conjure up the most violent and acrimonious rivalry that French football has ever seen, spiced up by a hatred that goes way beyond the realms of football alone.

Marseille has a strong identity that portrays a harsh working-class image compared to Paris, the bourgeois capital city synonymous with aristocracy and the trappings of hereditary wealth. The 1990s saw a far-right uprising in France that clearly coincided with the development of a serious hooligan problem at PSG. Right-wing militias and similar groups set up HQ on the terraces of the Parc des Princes and embarked upon a campaign of hooliganism that shook French football to the core.

In contrast, Marseille, although not without right-wing sympathisers and not averse to crowd disorder themselves, has a predominantly left-wing Ultra movement that prides itself on its multi-ethnicity. It's a rivalry made in hell and one that continues to make the headlines for both on-and off-field shenanigans each time these two warring clubs meet. True to form, both of last season's classicos again made headline news for all the wrong reasons.

The game at the Parc at the end of February 2010 was played out in terrible weather conditions as severe storms gripped the whole of France, leading President Sarkozy to declare a state of emergency in some parts of the country. I was actually on my way to the game, but the deteriorating weather conditions in Paris saw to it that Easyjet flight 7041 never got off the ground, leaving me stranded at Liverpool airport.

Marseille refused their ticket allocation for this match in protest at what they claimed were over-the-top security arrangements for their supporters. Only 14,400 turned up to see Marseille dominate proceedings and claim maximum points in a 0–3 victory. The game was held up for several minutes as riot police had to remove disgruntled PSG supporters from the playing area after Marseille's third goal sparked a pitch invasion. And the final whistle saw players leave the field to a chorus of boos and jeers as angry supporters vented their fury at such a limp display.

After the game, old internecine rivalries were renewed as home fans from the Boulogne and Auteuil stands clashed yet again, leaving one fan, 38-year-old Yann Lorence, seriously ill in hospital. Sadly, the injuries he sustained proved to be fatal and he lost his fight for survival on 18 March 2010, only a few weeks after the tragic incident. Subsequently, three PSG fans were detained in relation to Lorence's murder and the club's supporters were banned from travelling to away matches indefinitely.

This latest tragedy served only to crystallise public feeling that Paris Saint-Germain, a club with a toxic racial divide, was a club not fit for purpose. The closure of the capital's premier football club was fast becoming a very real option.

A distraught French Secretary of State for Sport, Rama Yade, condemned those responsible for the carnage that continues to attract heavy media coverage. 'The future of PSG is at stake if the club fails to rein in the hooligans,' declared Yade to the French Press (source AFP).

'The very worst thing possible happened. Passion has been transformed into sordid, senseless and murderous rage. The love of the shirt has been replaced by hatred, for each other, for sport and for life. Supporters who kill each other should be punished with the utmost severity. The very survival of the club is at stake,' fumed the Secretary of State for Sport.

The last meeting between the two at Marseille's Stade Velodrome (October 2009) was controversially postponed just before kick-off, due to an outbreak of swine flu within the PSG squad. Over 2,000 PSG fans made their way to Marseille for the season's first classico. Around 1,000 travelled on official supporters' coaches organised by the club. The other 1,000 travelled independently by bus, car and train making it very difficult for the authorities to provide adequate security arrangements for such a high-profile clash. It was a concern raised at the highest level of government but it was a concern that apparently fell upon deaf ears.

Clearly riled by the shock mid-afternoon postponement, PSG hooligans made their way to the deprived Vieux Port area of Marseille and violently clashed with local immigrants. Windows were smashed and riot police had to use tear gas to disperse the rival gangs who fought each other with an array of weapons. A crossbow, knives and baseball bats were recovered by police at the scene.

Rival gangs also clashed in and around the Marseille St Charles train station as fans returned to make their journey back home to Paris. Marseille president Jean-Claude Dassier wasn't pleased with such a late postponement and suggested the decision to call the game off was to blame for the violence. Although no serious injuries were reported, five Marseille supporters received prison sentences for their part in the disturbances.

Paris Saint-Germain FC has a short and tainted history. The dissolution of Racing Club Paris in 1966 left the City of Lights without a premier football team. Despondent football-loving Parisians, desperate for a flagship brand, pooled resources and with the help of cash donations sought to once again create a top-flight football club in the capital city.

Their dream was realised, when on 12 August 1970, after the merger of Paris FC and Stade Saint-Germain, *les Parisiens* were born. Promotion to Ligue 1 at the first attempt was swiftly followed by the heartache of relegation. But after overcoming initial teething problems and surviving a bout of infighting, PSG won their place back amongst the elite in 1974 and have been ever present to this day.

Under the presidency of fashion guru Daniel Hechter, PSG left their Stade Georges Lefevre home and became sole occupants of the newly renovated Stade Parc des Princes. It was to herald the start of a new era for the capital's newly formed premier club.

The year 1976 saw the creation of PSG's first official fan group, Les Amis du PSG. This young supporters' club was the catalyst for the creation of the now infamous Kop of Boulogne. The section of terracing behind the goal, named after the area in which it is located, was specifically reserved for the younger generation of PSG supporters, a voluble mixture of punks and skinheads, many of whom came from underprivileged neighbourhoods. Their goal was to turn the Parc into a mosh pit of noise that would roar the home side to victory.

Initially named the Boulogne Stand, fans adopted the name Kop of Boulogne after Liverpool Football Club's legendary Spion Kop, arguably the most famous football stand in the world.

PSG v Marseille 2009 – the Kop of Boulogne

As support for PSG grew so did the noise levels at the stadium. The popularity of the KOB was immense. Visiting teams had to endure a partisan cauldron of noise at the Parc and the twelfth man was born. With the support of the KOB and improved performances on the pitch, PSG finally threatened to become the dominant force in French football.

Under the guidance of Georges Peyroche, in his second stint as manager, and the captaincy of *les Parisiens* legend Dominique Bathenay, PSG announced their arrival on the French scene in dramatic fashion, lifting the Coupe de France after a pulsating encounter with Michel Platini's St. Etienne. With the scores locked at 2–2 after extra time, *les Parisiens* sealed victory in the Parc des Princes after a thrilling penalty shoot-out. They repeated the feat a year later defeating FC Nantes 3–2, giving them back-to-back Coup de France triumphs and the need for a larger trophy cabinet.

On 29 February 1984, England travelled to the Parc to play France in an international friendly. Security was tight amid fears of crowd disorder. Hooliganism was at its peak in 'Blighty' in the early 1980s and the enthusiastic hordes that followed England back then had a loathsome reputation. In contrast, France had very few problems of this nature and the authorities were confident the game would pass without serious incident.

Naive in the extreme, the heavy-handed CRS (riot police) were forced to use tear gas to quell violence on the terracing as rival supporters staged pitched battles. It marred a shock 2–0 French victory and the appalling scenes made headline news worldwide. The French thugs more than held their own that day and a number of England fans were taken to hospital with stab wounds.

Football hooliganism had now been successfully exported to France and the PSG supporters who fought toe to toe in the Parc would become the first French exponents of the infamous English subculture.

The year 1985 saw the formation of PSG's and France's most notorious fan group, the Boulogne Boys (BB85), and the Kop of Boulogne was to be their HQ. After the BB came the various groups of independents and casuals who sought to emulate the underground terrace scene that was so revered by the rebellious British youth of the late 1970s and early '80s.

Boulogne Boys – BB85

These were violent bands of skinheads, right-wing militants and casual hooligan firms with British-inspired gang names like the C.P.P. (Commando Pirate Paris), who are considered to be PSG's first main casual/hooligan collective, the Pitbull Kop (skinhead mob) Govroches, Firebirds and many more. Their sole aim was to create public disorder and they did so in abundance. When '*les enfants terribles*' were in town, chaos almost certainly ensued. By the end of the 1980s, the KOB, which by now had an indigenous white fan base, had become a full-on breeding ground for right-wing-orientated football hooligans.

Despite a newly spawned hooligan problem, PSG built on their recent cup successes and in 1986, in his first season as manager of PSG, ex-Liverpool boss Gerard Houllier delivered the league title to the capital for the first time in half a century. The team's success on the domestic front also meant European football for the first time in the club's short history, and some sterling performances against Europe's elite helped turn PSG into a household name.

PSG's renaissance coincided with the start of the Marseille revolution. Championed by Marseille's long-serving mayor Gastron Defferre, flamboyant entrepreneur Bernard Tapie was elected president and embarked on a mission to transform the flagging fortunes of one of France's oldest clubs.

Formed in 1899, Olympique de Marseille only really rose to prominence in the mid 1960s under the presidency of Marcel Leclerc. He was instrumental in recruiting some of the world's top players and the signing of Swedish winger Roger Magnusson and prolific Yugoslav striker Josep Skoblar proved to be pivotal as *les Phoceens* won successive French titles including the league and cup double in the 1971–72 season.

However, early European Cup exits to Ajax and Juventus and the acrimonious forced departure of Leclerc saw Marseille enter a long period of mediocrity. Not even the 1974 signing of Brazilian legend Jairzinho could restore Marseille as the pre-eminent force in French football. Sadly, 'the Hurricane' struggled to make an impact in France and left after only one season. By the end of the decade a debt-ridden Marseille, on the brink of extinction, were relegated to Ligue 2 and their fall from grace was complete.

Fortunately Bernard Tapie, a talented entrepreneur and former minister in Francois Mitterrand's government, had the foresight to see beyond the club's decline and sought to become king-maker. He amassed his personal fortune by transforming underperforming businesses and saw Marseille as a sleeping giant ready to be woken from its slumber after over a decade in hibernation. This ailing club was in desperate need of wholesale changes and a considerable financial injection. With the right investment, Tapie firmly believed that he could create a team capable of achieving success at the very highest level.

With Tapie's financial backing, Marseille were able to invest heavily in quality players. And within months of his presidency, 1986 World Cup stars Karl Heinz Forster, Alan Giresse and the celebrated Jean-Pierre Papin were all wearing the famous all-white strip of Marseille.

Less than three years later Marseille were crowned French champions for the first time in seventeen years after a thrilling two-horse race with Paris Saint-Germain. Frank Sauzee's late 30-yard strike was the difference between the two teams and the 1–0 home win at the Velodrome proved to be enough to secure the title. The giant was awake and fans from both teams agree that the 1988–89 title race generated the start of a rivalry like no other in France.

Over in the capital, events off the field threatened to derail PSG progression. Boardroom squabbles and an ever-increasing racial divide developing between rival supporters' groups was becoming a major cause for concern. The club, however, turned a blind eye to the increasingly nationalistic behaviour of the KOB and instead chose to redress the balance by authorising the creation of another kop in the Auteuil stand. Virage Auteuil, with an Italian Ultra mentality, gained in popularity and became home to many of the Parisian ethnic minority groups who were not welcome on the KOB.

The Auteuil Supras, formed in 1991, was the first Ultra group to establish itself on Virage Auteuil. Shortly afterward's, Lutece Falco 1991, a newly formed breakaway Ultra group from the Boulogne Boys' joined them on the same *curva*. The year 1993 saw the formation of the Tigris Mystic Ultras, the biggest fan group on the Auteuil. They helped take the *curva* to another level and their fantastically choreographed *tifo* displays helped them become one of the most respected Ultra groups in France. By the mid 1990s the Parc des Princess had two stands generating a colourful cauldron of noise to rival any stadium in the world.

PSG v Marseille 2009 – Virage Auteuil – Home to
Supras, Lutece Falco and Tigris Mystic

Tapie's almost instant success had also transformed Marseille's fan base and the team found themselves regularly playing in front of 60,000 screaming supporters in the footballing-mad south. *Les Phoceens* were now ready to enter the next phase of Tapie's transformation, a serious assault on Europe. But first, more quality signings were brought in. Chris Waddle, Didier Deschamps and Uruguayan midfield sensation Enzo Francescoli took Marseille to the brink of their first ever European Cup final. A bitterly disappointed Tapie saw his star-studded team lose out on away goals to Benfica after they failed to hold on to a 2–1 victory from the first leg at the Velodrome.

A second successive league title wasn't enough to keep Marseille-born manager Gerard Gili in a job. The ruthless Tapie demanded European success and a poor start to the 1990 campaign saw Gili relieved of his managerial duties and replaced by World Cup winner and German icon Franz Beckenbauer. The Kaiser fared no better and was duly sent packing only six months into his tenure. His successor was former Belgian national coach Raymond Goethals.

Chain-smoking Goethals, aged 70, had just steered Bordeaux into second position behind Marseille in the French championship and was the surprise choice to succeed Beckenbauer. He duly delivered Marseille's third French title in succession and guided the club to its first ever European Cup final in his first five months in charge. Bari's Stadio San Nicola hosted a drab 0–0 encounter that saw a talented Red Star Belgrade side break Marseille hearts in a penalty shoot-out to become the first Yugoslav team to lift the coveted trophy.

Despite his bitter disappointment, Tapie's confidence in Goethals' ability never wavered, even after a disappointing second-round exit to Sparta Prague in the following season's campaign. Just one year later, the Belgian maestro repaid the club's faith in him with interest and ensured legendary status and a place in the L'OM hall of fame. On 26 May 1993, Tapie's dream was realised as his Marseille team overcame a formidable Milan side that featured Marco Van Basten, Frank Rijkaard, Franco Baresi and former Marseille favourite Jean-Pierre Papin to become the winners of the inaugural European Champions League. A 44th-minute Basil Boli header was enough to give France its first and only Champions of Europe crown.

Three days later Marseille secured a 3–1 victory over eternal rivals PSG to secure a fifth consecutive French title and condemn *les Parisiens* to runners-up. It was a unique double that saw Marseille's profile raised to elite status and secured the ambitious Monsieur Tapie's position as one of the most powerful men in European football.

The euphoria of being newly crowned European Champions in Munich's Olympiastadion was still very much in full flow, when a catastrophe of epic proportions began to unfold. Only six weeks after becoming the first French European Champions and also securing a fifth successive French title, Tapie's love affair with the biggest, most successful club in France was about to hit the rocks. Marseille had become embroiled in a scandal that rocked the footballing world.

Allegations of match fixing were made against the French giants after Valenciennes player Christophe Robert claimed that Marseille midfielder Jean Jacques Eydelie and the club's general manager, Jean Pierre Bernes, had offered him and his teammates Jacques Glassmann and Jorge Burruchaga a cash incentive to throw the game. Marseille's 0–1 victory at Valenciennes' Stade Nungesser, six days before the European Cup final, all but secured them a fifth consecutive French championship and no injury worries ensured ideal preparation for the forthcoming clash with Italian giants AC Milan.

It wasn't the first time Tapie's name had been tarnished with accusations of match fixing. In 1991 it was alleged that Tapie's Marseille tried to fix matches against Caen, Brest, St. Etienne and Bordeaux. The allegations were not proven but Tapie was still suspended for twelve months for damaging sporting morale and insulting referees.

The Valenciennes scandal made headline news after French police discovered 250,000 francs buried in the garden belonging to Christophe Robert's aunt. The discovery of the alleged bribe led to the arrest of Marseille's Jean Pierre Bernes. A dozen Marseille players had their pre-season training interrupted as they were also taken in for questioning. A brief but thorough investigation led to corruption charges being levied against Eydelie and Bernes, both of whom were remanded in custody whilst awaiting trial. Weeks of club denials and protestations of innocence by Marseille supporters followed but to no avail.

Police, however, finally made a breakthrough after Jacques Eydelie broke rank and confessed to his part in the sordid affair. He made a statement confirming that he had paid a bribe to three Valenciennes players in return for an underperformance that would guarantee Marseille maximum points with minimum effort. It was a confession that was to play a major part in bringing down the most successful club in French history.

In a very public trial, Tapie, amongst others, was convicted of match fixing, subornation of witnesses, and tax fraud. He served six months in prison.

Marseille were stripped of their 1992–93 French championship success and subsequently banned from competing in the European Champions League. The FFF (French Football Federation) also condemned a bankrupt Marseille to Ligue 2 football. The downfall of the disgraced Monsieur Tapie and his high-profile team of French Galacticos was complete.

The collapse of Marseille coincided with French pay-television company Canal Plus investing heavily in PSG. Their lucrative deal with such a wealthy company ensured they were in pole position to capitalise on the demise of their bitter rivals. As runners-up to Marseille in the 1992–93 season, the FFF awarded the capital club the league title but Canal Plus refused to accept the crown for fear of reprisals from its subscribers in the south-east of France (Provence). History books now show the title for that scandal-hit season to be vacant.

Former Newcastle and Spurs star David Ginola and FIFA World Player of the Year (1995) George Weah helped PSG to consecutive Coupe de France and Ligue 1 titles as a resurgent Paris team threatened a Marseille-type domination of French football. Former PSG midfielder Luis Fernandez took the helm in 1994, the year in which PSG were officially ranked number one in the Club World Rankings and remain to this day the only French club ever to achieve the honour.

Fernandez brought back another French Cup in 1995, before successfully guiding the club to the European Cup Winners' Cup final in Brussels a year later. A 28th-minute Bruno N'gotty goal was enough to secure a 1–0 victory against Austrian side Rapid Vienna and give the capital's club their first and only European title success to date. He almost repeated the feat again twelve months later against the late, great Bobby Robson's Barcelona in Rotterdam, but the Parisians succumbed to a 37th-minute Ronaldo penalty that ensured the Cup Winners' Cup was hoisted by the Catalans.

After spending the previous three years in the shadow of *les rouges et bleus*, Marseille were keen to ignite the fierce rivalry with their old foes. Anglo-Irishman Tony Cascarino's goals were instrumental in Marseille's promotion back to Ligue 1. However, lack of finance ensured the only rivalry would be for terrace supremacy as hooligan groups from both teams clashed at every given opportunity. By the end of the 1990s, *Derby de France* was widely recognised as the most dangerous game in the country and costly large-scale security operations had to be planned to cope with marauding mobs intent on inflicting serious bodily harm on one another every time these two teams played.

French football peaked towards the end of the decade and in a tidal wave of euphoria over one million people danced the night away on the Champs-Elysées in celebration of the country's 1998 World Cup success. Two years later the French national team completed a remarkable double by being crowned European Champions after a hard fought 2–1 victory over Italy in Rotterdam. A David Trezeguet golden goal ensured France were crowned champions for the second time in sixteen years. But despite success at international level, French clubs failed to reach the dizzy heights of the Tapie-inspired era of the early 1990s when French teams were feared by the whole of Europe.

Lack of investment, poor business acumen and a spiralling hooligan problem all contributed towards dwindling crowds and disappointing performances against Europe's elite. Since the incident that led to a member of the French riot police being badly beaten in 1993 and subsequently saw PSG become the first French club to provide their own stadium security, football hooliganism has been the bane of French football and PSG fans have been chief instigators. Consequently, the club is more famous for the behaviour of its supporters than its achievements on the field.

Whilst the authorities are dealing with an endemic hooligan problem, players and officials from both clubs need to be aware of the impact their behaviour has on their supporters. Tit-for-tat derogatory comments and incessant public slanging matches played out through the media do little to promote a fan-friendly environment. Their actions in the past have brought about mayhem and bitter resentment that destroy a special occasion and fuel fan violence.

In March 2005, an enraged Marseille president Pape Diouf gave a press conference accusing PSG officials of putting his supporters' safety at risk. Marseille had initially been allocated 1,000 seats for the game at the Parc, half their legal entitlement under league rules. When they asked for an increase in their allocation Marseille were refused, with PSG officials claiming it was part of a gentleman's agreement between the two clubs and in line with the PSG allocation at the previous encounter in Marseille.

It came to light that PSG had in fact sold the tickets to their own supporters and with the seats in question being situated in the upper tier above the away section, a furious Diouf felt PSG were putting his supporters at unnecessary risk of serious injury. To inflame an already volatile situation further, word had also reached Diouf of rumours suggesting that many of the infamous PSG hooligans were the recipients of the disputed seats.

Despite Diouf's protestations, PSG maintained their stance and no further allocation was afforded to Marseille. In response, Diouf urged his supporters not to travel to the match and he insisted Marseille would send a reserve team to the prestigious Ligue 1 game.

Diouf carried out his threat and Marseille reserves came away with a point in a creditable 0–0 draw played without guest supporters. Despite no away fans, 1,200 police were mobilised for the game; there was an alcohol ban and police were given special powers to detain any supporters congregating in groups of more than fifteen people. Police made over 100 arrests and both clubs were docked one point for their actions.

According to an article on 24 November 2006 by Guardian journalist Paul Doyle, the findings in a 2005 report suggested PSG hooligans were responsible for fifty per cent of violence in French stadia. But while PSG yobs were undoubtedly the architects of the hooligan phenomenon in France, they were not alone.

The infamous South Winners (1987) – Olympique Marseille; Meinau Boys (1987) & Ultras Boys (1990) – RC Strasbourg; Brigade Sud (1985) – OGC Nice; Ultra Marines (1987) – Bordeaux; Magic Fans (1991) and Green Angels (1992) – AS St Etienne; and Ultras Bad Gones (1987), Lugdunums (2000) & Cosa Nostra (2007) – Olympique Lyonnais – were amongst many violent groups involved in terrace-related violence during two decades of right-wing-orientated mob rule on the French terraces.

However, despite football hooliganism being a widespread problem, it's always *Le Classique* that attracts the lion's share of unwanted media attention. Extreme violence is a persistent feature of this fearsome rivalry.

In 1995, nine police officers were injured and 145 fans were detained after rival groups clashed before, during and after the semi-final of the French Cup. PSG supporters also rioted after a 2–0 home defeat to their eternal rivals in October 1999 and then went on the rampage attacking the police and seeking confrontation with Marseille supporters returning to their coaches.

Violence between the two escalated to another level during the new millennium. For the game at the Velodrome in 2001 over 600 Parisian supporters made the long journey south on coaches organised by official sources.

Despite organised travel being provided, over 100 Boulogne Boys opted to travel independently by train. Disgruntled security forces considered them a risk to public order and refused them entry into the stadium. Tempers became frayed, fighting broke out and stewards, Marseille fans and police officers were all injured during violent exchanges.

Inside the stadium missiles were thrown at PSG officials and players, resulting in the game being delayed at half-time whilst the pitch was cleared of debris, including mobile phones, batteries and stones. In the return match at the Parc des Princes, an 18-year-old Marseille supporter was paralysed after being hit with a seat thrown by PSG supporters. His only transgression was that he sat too close to the home supporters.

Only weeks after the disturbances at the Velodrome in the February of 2001, disorder broke out at the Parc during the half-time interval of the PSG v Galatasaray Champions League game. Supporters tried to rip down security fencing and hurled missiles at each other. The club was fined one million Swiss francs and banned from the Parc des Princes stadium for three European games. UEFA ordered PSG to play their next three games at least 300km from Paris.

In a 2003 French Cup classico at the Parc, over 2,000 police officers were mobilised for the most policed fixture in Europe. Security forces confiscated weapons including iron bars, knives and catapults after searching Marseille supporters' coaches before the game.

And so year after year the violence continued with a Groundhog Day theme, leaving the authorities struggling to contain mob rule with a 'no one likes us, we don't care' mentality.

The successful Canal Plus era looked to be slowly grinding to a halt. Despite being one of the founder members of the all powerful G14, PSG were a club in crisis. Heavily in debt and with a fan base deemed racist and out of control, the club desperately needed a period of balance and stability.

After finally completing a gradual takeover of PSG in 2005, Canal Plus decided to sell the club just over a year later to an American/French investment consortium. The optimism generated by the takeover was, however, short-lived. The club nosedived into a downward spiral. Disappointing performances on the pitch and misjudgement in the transfer market resulted in the club flirting dangerously with relegation. With the club on the brink of flat-lining, more humiliation was about to engulf the fallen giants as another shameful chapter began to unfold.

On 24 November 2006, only five months after the club's new owners had completed their much-heralded takeover, PSG and French football sank to a new low. Plain-clothes police officer Antoine Granomort shot dead PSG supporter Julien Quemener, after PSG hooligans targeted Jewish fans at the end their 2–4 UEFA Cup home defeat to Israeli side Hapoel Tel Aviv. Hundreds of home fans ran amok after the game hurling racial abuse and anti-Semitic epithets at Jewish supporters.

Twenty-three-year-old Hapoel fan Yanniv Hazout was targeted and became separated from his friends. Granomort, who was looking after police vehicles at the time of the incident, saw Hazout was in danger and rushed to his aid. The police officer instructed the terrified supporter to take cover behind him whilst he confronted the baying mob using tear gas. But there were too many of them and within moments he was overpowered and punched to the ground. In the melee that unfolded, Granomort drew his pistol and fired a shot which caused enough panic for him and Hazout to escape and take refuge in the nearby McDonald's where they waited for reinforcements to arrive.

It was discovered shortly afterwards that the bullet that killed Julien Quemener first passed through the lung of another PSG supporter, Mounir Bouchaer. But unlike Quemener, Bouchaer lived to tell the tale. Media reports claimed both men were identified as members of notorious far-right group the Boulogne Boys.

Racism is a regular occurrence in French football, especially in Paris. Outraged by the actions of the racist mob involved in the attack on the French police officer, the French interior minister (now president) and PSG supporter Nicolas Sarkozy declared war on the yobs. 'We want no more racists in the stadium, no more Nazi salutes, no more monkey calls when a player of colour touches the ball,' screamed Sarkozy. 'There will be sections half empty; that is not important. It's better to be alone than to be in such bad company.' Sarkozy went on to promise the fast-tracking of new legislation designed to combat racist or xenophobic factions that shame football, especially his own club, PSG.

The much-publicised internal war between rival supporters' groups from the Boulogne and Auteuil sections of the Parc has quite literally torn the club apart. The increase in violent incidents involving the two *curve* has become a very real concern at the highest level of politics. Despite the club's efforts to mollify the fan groups, intermittent outbreaks of violence have continued and PSG have sadly reached pariah status with no immediate solution to stop the chaos off the pitch that has threatened the very existence of the club.

The escalation of conflict between the two warring blocs can be traced back to a home match with Rennes back in 2003. Former Boulogne Boys member Patrice recalls the incident with clarity. 'To celebrate their tenth anniversary, Tigris Mystic, the largest and most powerful Ultra group on the Auteuil stand, unfurled a banner, "*L'avenir c'est nous*" (We are the future). This small comment was deemed cocky and provocative by some of our leaders in the Boulogne stand and the only solution was confrontation.'

Clearly riled by the actions of the Auteuil contingent, the KOB extracted bloody revenge several days later at the PSG game in Auxerre. In the first of many acts of violence, around thirty independents, a casual firm loyal to the KOB, attacked a group of Ultras from Virage Auteuil, causing widespread panic in the visitors' section.

A week later PSG and Auxerre contested the French Cup final at the Stade de France in Paris. Police intervention was required as fan violence overshadowed Auxerre's 2–1 victory. Rival supporters from the Boulogne and Auteuil sections fought running battles inside the stadium heaping further embarrassment on the capital club.

Threatened by the growing importance of Tigris and their Auteuil counterparts, relations between rival fan groups deteriorated even further, and from that one innocuous incident in the home match with Rennes, the threat of violence escalated with every game.

Under pressure to instill order on the terraces, PSG president Francis Graille empowered his head of security with unlimited authority in an attempt to turn up the heat and root out the risk supporters. Incensed by the president's actions, the fans turned on Graille. Media reports claimed he was subjected to death threats and it was even alleged that he had coffins delivered to his home. The stress took its toll on the president and he backed down. His head of security was immediately relieved of his duties and normal service resumed on the terraces.

Graille was dismissed a year later and earlier this year he found himself convicted in the French courts for his part in a series of suspect transfer dealings. He was handed a hefty fine and a suspended jail sentence.

In September 2005, fighting erupted between warring PSG groups at their away fixture with newly promoted Le Mans. But on their return to Paris, media reports alleged that over 100 Tigris boys attacked a smaller group of unarmed independents with an array of weapons, leaving several hospitalised and one in a coma. Retribution was swift and unremitting as the Boulogne Boys and their cohorts sought vengeance at every opportunity.

Serious clashes between rival PSG groups were reported in away games at Auxerre, Toulouse, Strasbourg and Metz. In the French Cup game at Lens, the official Tigris Mystic coach was wrecked and all material belonging to them was stolen and destroyed. By the end of the 2005–06 season it was the Tigris Mystic Ultra group who had become embroiled in a very violent power struggle with the fascist right-wing boot boys from the Boulogne.

Based in the lower section of the Auteuil, the 400-strong Tigris mob, a mixed-race supporters' group mainly originating from the deprived Paris suburb of Seine-Saint-Denis, were considered the most vocal and politically motivated group in tribune Auteuil. It was a classic case of the multicultural extreme left versus the fascist white right.

One of the most serious clashes between the two factions occurred after the PSG game at Nantes. Fighting broke out between the two sets of supporters during the game but escalated further on the way home. Media reports claimed Tigris Ultras attacked the Boulogne Boys with baseball bats and smashed up a motorway service station in the process. A very irate PSG Chairman, Pierre Blayau, later seethed that the French club had been 'taken hostage' by the criminals responsible for such acts of shameless behaviour.

With no abatement in the mayhem between the two main protagonists, the fratricidal turf war finally took its toll. Clearly consumed by violence and under pressure from sources within, the Tigris Mystic Ultras concluded their loyal 13-year association with the club by issuing a public statement announcing their dissolution. Roughly translated, it read:

> The reason for being a group has always been the diffusion of marked values at the heart of its most active members (friendship, solidarity, pride). Motivated by a common passion, the Tigris has been able to unite its individualities, thus playing its social role. Social diversity, cultural and generational, has been, for the majority of the Tigris, a source of enrichment and of openness constituting one of our principal strengths.
>
> A lot has been written about us these last months, whether in the media or in the microcosm of the Ultras. We were neither manipulated politically nor motivated by a hegemonic desire as many have claimed. Simply motivated by the will to liberate oneself from an oppression that has become insupportable. We have failed; and today, the page turns.
>
> Tigris Mystic 1993-2006

Their involvement in the politically motivated violent exchanges with the KOB will undoubtedly overshadow their passion for PSG and their spectacular choreography that so regularly customised the Auteuil stand. It is a truly sad demise of a fan group that had such a positive influence on the French Ultra scene.

Despite the downfall of Tigris and the introduction of tough new British-type anti-hooligan laws, the violence continued and by the end of the 2006 campaign, the internal terrace feuding was raging out of control. The Parc had become a very dangerous place and the incessant infighting between rival fan groups was responsible for driving normal supporters away from the club.

In March 2007, less than a year after the dissolution of Tigris, French newspaper *L'equipe* alleged renewed clashes between Tigris and Boulogne Boys at a fourth division Red Star Paris game. Former members of Tigris also supported Red Star who are based in Seine Saint-Denis, home to many former members of the disbanded group.

The clashes between supporters reflect the perennial bout of race riots that continue to blight the poor suburbs of Paris. The 2005 riots saw over 200 vehicles burned out and shops looted as police fought running battles with disgruntled immigrant youths, who, submerged in poverty, vented their anger at a government they believed were responsible for their plight.

France, Paris in particular, is a political time bomb waiting to explode. With a 25 per cent non-white population, almost on a par with the USA, the far right are exploiting a very volatile situation and Jean-Marie Le Pen and his National Front party are gaining ground at a rate of knots. Extremists see football grounds as a prime source for recruiting new and young activists and indoctrinating them into the far-right ethos.

Not content with an ultra-violent rivalry with their southern counterparts and the conflict within, PSG yobs have waged war against all and sundry for over two decades. On the opening day of the 2009–10 season, hundreds of PSG hooligans fought in the streets around the stadium in Montpellier which led to one Paris supporter losing an eye.

Before the 2008 UEFA Cup tie with Dutch side FC Twente, hundreds of rival supporters clashed in the centre of Paris. Dozens were injured during these violent confrontations and terrified passers-by had to flee for cover.

Given the persisting incidence of PSG spectator aggression and disrespect, the French governing body (LFP) finally reached breaking point after shameful scenes at the PSG v RC Lens 2008 Coupe de la Ligue final. Shortly after half-time, a section of the stadium occupied by the Boulogne Boys briefly held up a 25-metre-long racist banner with the words '*Paedophiles, chomeurs, consanguins: bienvenue chez les ch'tis.*' (Paedophiles, unemployed, inbreeding, welcome to the north).

Ch'tis is the nickname given to northerners who have been stereotyped as drink dependent and depressive. An outraged President Sarkozy threatened to leave the match unless the offensive banner was removed immediately. Security forces were deployed to the offending sector without delay and within minutes the banner was confiscated.

Le Parisiens' cup final victory was further soured when the LFP announced the club was to be punished for the offensive banner by means of expulsion from the 2009–10 Coupe de la Ligue and a one-point deduction.

Furthermore, despite protests of innocence by the Boulogne Boys, on 17 April 2008, Prime Minister Francoise Fillon, under the direction of the Minister of the Interior, Michele Alliot-Marie, announced the dissolution of the Boulogne Boys fan group. The prime minister also added that failure to comply with the dissolution would result in heavy penalties, including jail time. The judgement was not negotiable. PSG were, however, reinstated into the 2009–10 competition after overturning the federation's decision at appeal.

The tragic death of Yann Lorence, the PSG supporter killed by rival fans from his own club, brought about extraordinary new measures to combat the dramatic increase in football-related violence in and around French stadia, especially the Parc des Princes.

In May 2010, the national commission for the prevention of football violence made national news headlines. 'This is a measure that is unprecedented in French sport,' wrote *Le Parisien,* after the commission took the unparalleled step of disbanding seven fan groups, five of whom were official supporters' associations attached to PSG: Supras, Authentiks and Grinta from the Auteuil, together with Milice Paris and Commando Loubard from the Kop of Boulogne. All five groups were accused of being instrumental in the mayhem that has plunged the much-maligned club deep into crisis. It is an accusation the fan groups from the Auteuil section vehemently deny. But despite providing video evidence supporting their protestations, the decree was upheld and the Ultras must abide by the government's decision or face serious consequences.

Many of the members of the outlawed groups, including the Boulogne Boys, have also received lengthy stadium bans and those subject to banning orders are forced to sign in at their local police station on match days in order to ensure compliance. Football for the Ultras will never be the same again.

In addition, the owners of PSG have themselves come up with radical proposals to help eradicate the sporadic outbreaks of conflict that have become an intolerable regular occurrence at the French capital's club. The purchase of new and the renewal of 13,000 existing season tickets in the KOB and Auteuil sections of the stadium has been prohibited.

Supporters now have to buy individual tickets with randomly allocated seat numbers if they want to sit in the Kop of Boulogne or Auteuil sections and no more than four supporters can be seated together in the same block in any other part of the stadium. Also, in a bid to create a family atmosphere, the club are offering free tickets to all women and half-price tickets to under-16-year-olds.

A pre-season game at home to Porto saw the new measures implemented for the first time. PSG Ultra Nic described the atmosphere as dour. 'I was really shocked at the way things turned out,' said Nic. 'Anybody who dared to stand up was ejected from the stadium and all the flags and banners of PSG were forbidden. In contrast, Porto Ultras were allowed to stand in the Auteuil section with all their stuff. It was business as usual for them.'

Nic was also present at the opening game of the 2010–11 season. PSG played host to St Etienne. 'The atmosphere was a little better but still ridiculous. The upper stands of the Boulogne and Auteuil sections were reserved for families. Fan group activities were impossible due to the new ticketing arrangements,' said a despondent Nic.

Before the St Etienne game, demonstrations against the new security measures were organised by disgruntled fan groups. Despite members of the Auteuil stand condemning the KOB for their malevolent brand of politics, supporters from all sections of the Parc united as one in a loud but peaceful protest against the new regulations.

Two hundred and forty-nine supporters were detained by the feared French CRS riot police as disillusioned fans sat down in the roadways leading to their respective sectors, in a bid to block access to the turnstiles. Police intervention was swift and without mercy as fans were forcefully removed from the area and bussed away from the stadium before being taken into police custody. But reports of violent clashes with protesters were dismissed by protesting fans as nothing more than propaganda designed to tarnish the image of the supporters in a bid to justify the oppressive new legislation. The courts imposed stadium bans on all detained supporters, a decision that is sure to exacerbate an already volatile state of affairs.

One game into the season and lifelong PSG supporter Nic raised the white flag. He, like so many others, had had enough. 'The club is sick,' he said. 'The Parc can never be the same.' He hasn't been back to the stadium since.

Despite the ongoing saga with club officials and disgruntled supporters, *les Parisiens* were in a rich vein of form. Former PSG player Antoine Kombouare has miraculously turned around this ailing club. An eight-match unbeaten run has seen his team surge up the table to within five points of the summit and a victory against their despised rivals would certainly validate their title credentials.

Les Phoceens were also in good form. After losing the opening two matches of the campaign, a now buoyant Marseille side have found their feet and after the 7–0 midweek drubbing of Zilina in the Champions League, tonight's grudge match could scarcely have been better timed.

It is almost 18 months since the return of Marseilles prodigal son Didier Deschamps. The former captain has brought renewed optimism to the rebel city where supporters celebrated their first title success in 18 years, as Deschamps dethroned 2009 French champions Bordeaux in his first season.

Ridiculed when he was playing as nothing more than a 'water carrier' by Eric Cantona, Deschamps went on to win two French league titles and at just 23 years of age he captained Marseille to their historic European Cup success. In 1994, in the wake of the Tapie scandal, the accomplished defensive midfielder jumped the sinking Marseille ship and signed for Juventus, where he accumulated another ten trophies in five memorable years, including three Scudetti and another Champions League title. He also captained France to World Cup and European Championship victories before bringing down the curtain on a glorious career with short spells at Chelsea and Valencia. Not a bad little haul for a water carrier, eh, Eric?

Shortly after retiring as a player he took up the reins at Monaco where he was an instant success. He secured the French League Cup title and guided the team to their inaugural Champions League final appearance in 2004. He left Monaco for Juventus in 2006 but resigned immediately after steering the club back to Serie A after their enforced relegation to Serie B for their part in the infamous Italian match-fixing scandal.

The man with the Midas touch will be hoping to further enhance his growing reputation and victory here would see Marseille go five points clear of the capital team with the added bonus of also having a game in hand.

It was a rainy autumn morning on my arrival in the capital city ahead of the first classico of the 2010–11 campaign. With the whole day ahead of me, I opted for an early liquid lunch, before heading into Paris to source my accreditation. Foreign journalists were refused access to the stadium for last season's fixture and there was no guarantee that I wouldn't meet with the same fate. My good friend Ted had always come up trumps in the past but even he was unsure of protocol for the first *Derby de France* since the death of Yann.

Whilst awaiting ticket news I passed a couple of hours in Corcoran's Irish pub situated in the heart of Place de Clichy. It was a multiscreen bar and live football was plentiful. I ordered a pint of the black stuff and sat down to watch the last fifteen minutes of a feisty Rome derby before watching El Nino destroy Roman's galacticos with a glorious brace.

Time was of the essence now and with barely two hours before kick-off I got the call I was waiting for. Good news. Ted had called in a favour from a French colleague and confirmed pitch-side accreditation would be waiting for me upon my arrival. Nice one. I finished another pint of the Emerald Isle's finest and headed for the metro.

The Paris metro system is fast, cheap and idiot-proof. Armed with only a metro map and my carnet, I navigated my way to the platform. Line 13 with one change at Duroc on line 10 was the logical route. ETA at the stadium around 20.00 hrs. Perfect. The metro was reasonably quiet considering France's two greatest rivals were about to do battle in less than ninety minutes.

Seven stops later and the tranquility of a quiet Sunday evening was shattered as tourists and locals appeared to morph en masse into a sea of blue-and-red shirts. Clearly inebriated, they were in good spirits, singing and chanting loudly. 'PSG PSG PSG,' they roared. Another ten minutes with this lot and I swear I would have endured permanent cochlea damage.

As the metro pulled in at Porte d'Auteuil the chanting grew louder. Their enthusiasm for singing loudly in unison was quite apparent. As the carriage doors opened a crescendo of noise greeted the awaiting CRS, who, kitted out in full riot gear, loitered on the platform with intent. Clearly not intimidated by the waiting riot squad, the departing hordes taunted the police before being herded to the exit without incident.

I broke ranks with the maddening crowd and set off in search of the media entrance. But first I had to navigate myself safely through half a dozen over-the-top security checks. Every street corner had a mini army of riot police. Every roadway had a convoy of water cannons and armoured vehicles. Security fencing had been newly erected around the perimeter of the stadium and every access point had its own posse of hired muscle.

French media reported over 2,000 police officers were on duty for tonight's marquis fixture. This is normal for a game that is anything but normal. The high-profile security arrangements still didn't deter small gangs from lurking in the shadows. I saw no end of tasty little mobs hanging about, some in football clothing but the majority in black casual attire.

There is nothing unusual about the vast majority of Parisian security forces being mobilised for the French classico. But today's game is different. The crowd will be minus a Marseille contingent for the second consecutive occasion. The French Football League barred Marseille supporters from this evening's bout over security concerns, but nine Marseille supporters' groups contested the decision and initially won their appeal.

Olivier Grimaldi, spokesperson for Marseille fans, said: 'The LFP wants to portray OM supporters as thugs, even though all of the supporters' groups have made huge efforts and acted responsibly. There have been no incidents at the Velodrome. The barbarians are at Paris-Saint Germain, not at OM.'

The fans' delight at the ruling was, however, short-lived. Less than a week later the courts overturned the appeal and ruled in favour of the LFP. There was also talk of Marseille boycotting the game in support of their fans but Marseille distanced themselves from the rumours as such a drastic action could have damaged the club's chances of Champions League football. But despite the ban, it was alleged that around sixty independent Marseille supporters were arrested whilst trying to make their own way to the game.

Having talked my way through at least half a dozen security points, fate played its part as I somehow managed to unwittingly stumble upon the media entrance. But then fate threw in a curve ball. Monsieur Jobsworth in charge of *l'accreditation* couldn't speak English. '*Avez vous le my accreditation?*' I asked in my finest northern English dialect. Jobsworth shrugged his shoulders and gave me a baleful death stare before launching into what sounded like a volley of verbal abuse. Just as I was about to tear back into him a nearby photographer played peacekeeper by volunteering to be my interpreter. My accreditation was sorted in under sixty seconds. Result. Although to be fair, I think my original request was lost in translation.

My new-found friend also became my temporary guide as he gave me a quick tour of media facilities. I had already experienced two previous PSG–Marseille encounters, once in the Parc for a league game (2009) and the other at the Stade de France for the lively 2007 Coupe de France final. Both were memorable occasions and the Ultras from both teams put on some great choreography, especially for the cup final.

Coupe de France 2007 – Marseille choreography

Coupe de France 2007 – Commando Ultra 84 and South Winners 87

Coupe de France 2007 – PSG choreography

PSG – Coupe de France winners 2007

I ventured pitch-side to soak up a touch of prematch atmosphere but couldn't help feeling perplexed. Something was missing. From past experience, twenty minutes before kick-off, the stadium would normally be rocking, a real passionate bear pit of animosity. But it wasn't. The crowd would normally be flag waving and showing their colours. But they weren't. There were no flags. The many Ultra groups would have decorated their sections with colourful banners draped over railings and hanging from balconies. But they didn't. There were no banners.

PSG v Marseille 2010 – Virage Auteuil minus Tigris, Supras and les Authentiks

PSG v Marseille 2011 – Kop of Boulogne (KOB) minus the Boulogne Boys 85

The first thing that hits you at the Parc is the wall of noise created by the home and away supporters, each vying for supremacy in their quest for terrace superiority. Noisy support is de rigueur at the Parc, but there was no noise and the Marseille supporters were conspicuous by their absence in the empty guest sector.

PSG v Marseille 2010 – empty visitors' sector in the Parc

Football matches need rivalry; it is the intensity between fan groups that turns games like this into the spectacles that make football the most unique spectator sport in the world. Supporters bring something to a game that money can't buy … passion! You sometimes have to look beyond the vitriol and racism to enjoy the game for what it really is. Only a genuine football fan can truly understand this mentality.

The atmosphere generated by these noble adversaries is unrivalled anywhere in France. And the omission of the infamous Marseille Ultra groups from this fixture for a second successive encounter will be detrimental to Deschamps' Marseille unit who are seeking a sixth successive victory.

Marseille fans are thought to be the pioneers of the Ultra movement in France. Formed in 1984, the Commando Ultra 84 (CM84) group was the first of many such fan organisations to take up residence upon the Stade Velodrome terraces. South Winners (SW87), Yankees, Dodgers, Fanatics and Marseille Trop Puissant (MTP) are the other main Ultra factions that dedicate their life to the weekend.

PSG v Marseille 2009 – CU84, SW85, MTP, Yankees, Dodgers and Fanatics Ultras

Each group has an area reserved on the terracing at the Velodrome. Virage Sud – Chevalier da la Roze, is home to Commando Ultras 1984, South Winners, Amis de l'OM and Club Central des Supporteurs.

Virage Nord, a predominantly left-wing *curva*, is situated adjacent to the guest sector and is home to Yankees, MTP, Dodgers and Fanatics supporters' clubs. In 2002, Virage Nord was officially renamed Virage Nord – Patrice de Peretti in remembrance of the late Patrice Peretti (1972–2000), *les Phoceens*' most celebrated supporter. Famously known by his nom de plume Depe, this legendary capo (leader) died suddenly on 28 July 2000 aged just 28.

He dedicated thirteen years of his young life to the white-and-blue port city outfit, seven years with South Winners and the last six years with MTP, the Ultra group he founded in 1994. MTP was started with just ten members and the goal was to transform the north stand into a cauldron of noise to rival the south stand. Depe managed to attract many young supporters from the poorer suburbs of Marseille and the MTP membership had swelled to over 3,000 by the time of his death. With the stadium boasting two stands creating a human sway of passion, Stade Velodrome became a fortress and visiting teams are often overawed by the hostile home support.

Depe was famed for orchestrating the crowd with his megaphone whilst stripped naked to the waist. Rain, shine, snow or ice, this young Marseille revolutionary would lead from the front, half naked, for the whole ninety minutes. Loved by all, it was a sad day when he passed. As a mark of respect, the club arranged a minute's silence at the following home game and in a moving and unprecedented moment, each and every player stripped naked to the waist in his memory.

Back in the 1990s, supporters' idol Tapie had a great respect for the Ultras and believed their support was key to the success of the team. He interacted with them, formed a working relationship with them and gave them a voice. He also entrusted them with season ticket sales. The club allocates season tickets to the different Ultra associations who then have exclusive rights to re-sell them to their members in the north and south stands with a supposed 15 per cent mark-up.

These industrious fan groups also produce fanzines, scarves, badges, DVDs and other Ultra merchandise for sale and use profits to buy materials for choreography, subsidise away travel and arrange social events for their members. Journalists estimate the main Ultra groups at the Velodrome amass a yearly net profit of around £500,000 between them.

However, with money comes corruption and some of the leaders of the Ultra associations have been accused of profiteering for personal gain. This has inevitably led to hostility between rival members which, although not on the grand scale of their Parisian counterparts, has at times spilled over into violence. The most serious of such confrontations occurred back in November 2003, resulting in three supporters and a club official being remanded in custody.

South Winners Ultras attacked MTP Ultras after a home game against Rennes, leaving four MTP members seriously injured. The defendants were accused of attacking rival MTP Ultras with baseball bats and pick-axe handles. Although none of the accused would confirm the catalyst for the attack, one of several incidents between the two groups, lawyers implied that it may have been an internal feud motivated by money.

Described by rival supporters as ruthless, the South Winners contingent is thought to be Marseille's most volatile and feared fan group. Formed by high school students in 1987, SW were the second Ultra group to set up HQ at the Velodrome. Primarily made up of North Africans from northern Marseille and its deprived Panier neighbourhoods, SW87 boasts a fan base of around 4,000 members.

Away from the internal wrangling, there is also the dark underbelly of hooliganism connected to the fanatical Ultra groups. Whilst PSG hooligans are considered the vanguard, Marseille also have a noxious attachment of undesirables linked to the club and it isn't just the PSG game that brings out the worst in them.

In March 2009, Dutch police seized dozens of knives, baseball bats and other weapons from Marseille thugs travelling by coach to a UEFA Cup match against Ajax in Amsterdam. In January 2010, at least thirty OM thugs fought a pitched battle with fifty Bordeaux hooligans in a prearranged meeting before the game at the Stade Chaban-Delmas. It is, however, in the grand scheme of things, only a token minority of Marseille supporters that have earned a negative reputation for violent acts.

Over at the Parc, the Marseille players entered the field to a loud, unified chorus of boos and this was only for the prematch warm up. A special reception was reserved for a former PSG favourite, the grinning Gabrielle Heinze. He was booed mercilessly with every touch.

The home crowd continued in much the same vein with a group of Marseille schoolchildren who were invited on to the pitch for a knock about just before kick-off. What should have been a memorable occasion for these young kids quickly turned into a harrowing experience as they were callously abused in front of the Auteuil stand. Their game was almost certainly cut short in order to remove them from the hostile environment they had encountered. I found that distasteful at best but this is PSG and this game brings out the worst in their supporters.

As the teams entered the pitch, the players from the home side were read out with the usual theatrical zest you come to expect from the overly eccentric stadium announcers at football matches. The home fans leapt from their seats with overwhelming enthusiasm, cheering loudly and clapping non-stop for each member of their team. The primal roar from the crowd and the deafening applause was off the scale and really justified the hype this game generates.

PSG v Marseille – two tribes go to war

In contrast, the Marseille team was announced to a roar of disapproval. Anger and revulsion was etched on the faces of the home supporters as they whistled and booed the enemy with intent.

'Marseille, Marseille, *on t'encule* (Marseille we f**k you) … Marseille, Marseille, *on t'encule* … Marseille, Marseille, *on t'encule*.' The chant was incessant and grew louder as it reverberated around the whole stadium.

The game kicked off and as Marseille gained possession the chanting immediately turned to ear-splitting boos with every Marseille touch. It really was quite an incredible and intimidating noise.

Clearly inspired by the crowd, it was PSG who enjoyed the lion's share of possession in the opening exchanges and after only nine minutes, Turkish striker Mevlut Erding sent the home fans delirious after netting a rebound from close range. Marseille shot-stopper Mandanda spilled an angled shot from cunning midfielder Nene, gifting a deserved early lead to PSG.

Ten minutes later and PSG doubled their lead when French striker Guillaume Hoarau finished with aplomb, nutmegging the Marseille keeper after getting on the end of a sublime pass from chief tormentor Nene. The crowd erupted like a volcano and taunted the Marseille team with a sustained bout of French vitriol. Then with backs to the pitch and their arms around each other, the whole of the Boulogne stand jumped up and down in unison copying the celebration made famous by Polish supporters of Lech Poznan.

The Marseille players looked shell shocked as they struggled to cope with the oral vilification raining down on them from all four sides of the Parc. A furious Deschamps paced up and down the technical area screaming instructions to his team who were clearly second best in a very one-sided classico.

However, in the face of adversity, Gonzalez threw Marseille an unlikely lifeline, scoring from the rebound after French international keeper Apoula Edel failed to hold on to Gignac's effort at the near post. The stadium fell silent for a moment and then burst into a non-stop crescendo of boos and whistles.

The goal clearly lifted Marseille but they couldn't break down a stubborn PSG defence protected by Old Father Time himself, Claude Makelele. Form is temporary but class is permanent and this 38-year-old veteran oozed class from every orifice as he broke up any sign of a Marseille revival almost single handedly.

With half-time almost upon us, Marseille continued to press for the elusive equaliser and when Gignac went down theatrically in the box the stadium held its breath, but the referee held his nerve and waved away desperate Marseille claims for a penalty. The crowd reacted furiously at Gignac's theatrics and dozens of green laser pens shone down on the player as he was receiving treatment.

'Gignac, Gignac *on t'encule* ... Gignac, Gignac *on t'encule*,' roared the fractious Auteuil hordes as the Marseille striker was helped to his feet. The physio had worked wonders with his magic sponge and after limping away gingerly from the scene of the crime, Gignac miraculously returned to full fitness within moments, much to the anger of the baying mob in the stands.

The half-time whistle blew with Marseille in the ascendency and the mood of the home side and their followers was markedly different from the opening exchanges. It was an enjoyable first period and although PSG just shaded it, both teams created enough chances to increase the score line. The excitable crowd kept the home team on their toes, but poisonous as ever, they spewed unpleasantness at their unwelcome visitors at every opportunity.

Shortly after the interval, Remy blazed his first-time shot over the bar as Marseille pressed for an early equaliser. An inexplicably lacklustre PSG had no response to the visitors' sustained early onslaught and although an equaliser looked inevitable, the home side dug deep and held firm. As the home crowd grew restless, Gabrielle Heinze suffered the wrath of the Parc, as he did in the pre-match warm up, and was once again singled out for the type of customary invective supporters reserve for ex-players who cross the divide. Undeterred, the former PSG favourite played with a smile and revelled in his role as pantomime villain. The dog's abuse levelled at him only served to enhance his game.

Despite the monopoly of possession, Marseille could find no way through a blanket PSG defence and as frustration set in tempers became frayed and Marseille picked up three yellow cards in succession. An entertaining game threatened to spill over into turmoil as opposing players resorted to persistent fouling and play acting but the referee never wavered and wasn't swayed by the actions and gestures of the aggressive home support.

As the game entered the latter stages it became stretched, PSG soaking up everything Marseille threw at them and effectively hitting them on the break. With the visitors visibly tiring, PSG grew in confidence and played some excellent retention football, passing the ball with a Barca-esque swagger to the '*olé-olé-olé*' of the crowd. It was left to a disgruntled Heinze to break up the party with an angry 80-yard aggressive punt upfield. It was quite apparent at this point that Marseille had nothing left in the tank. Their opponents knew it and the supporters knew it. Crowd noise intensified and the final few minutes were played out in a carnival atmosphere.

After spending the last couple of seasons toying with relegation, tonight's victory against current champions Marseille had elevated a rejuvenated PSG close to the summit of Le Championnat, firmly establishing the capital's club as genuine title contenders. Football makes people happy and *les Parisiens* all over the capital will be sitting in their little *arrondissements* toasting their success over the eternal enemy.

Off the field PSG continue to make strides in their efforts to make the Parc a safer place and rid the club of the hooligan element that has shamed them so often. The displays of bigotry and violence in and around the Parc support the public perception that many of the PSG hard core are little more than far-right football thugs masquerading as supporters.

French football's flagship fixture has been so disfigured by vicious fighting that security forces in the capital consider it almost unpoliceable and could not guarantee the safety of visiting supporters at tonight's game. It's a fact that PSG and Marseille bring out the worst in each other, officials and players included. But the spectacle as a whole will undoubtedly suffer if the most celebrated fixture on the French calendar has to be played without guest supporters on a permanent basis.

The role of racism and far-right groups in French football is a countrywide problem. After three decades of terrace thuggery, the French government's new and controversial legislation has hit fans hard and been met with anger and disdain by the groups who consider themselves the lifeblood of the game.

Dissolving the powerful hard-core Ultra groups has been the most controversial fundamental of the government's newly adopted zero-tolerance approach. Although it is widely believed amongst the game's hierarchy that the highly influential Ultra groups have been largely responsible for much of the violence and racism within the French game, many supporters feel they have been unjustly targeted.

Despite the violent nature and unscrupulous behaviour of some of these people, it would be an ignorant and ill-informed view to suggest they love the game any less than regular supporters who choose not to be a part of the extreme fan culture phenomenon. Many of the accusations levelled at the Ultras are considered to be politically motivated headlines scribed by lazy journalists thought to be in the pockets of upwardly mobile politicians, and there is a very strong belief amongst ordinary fans that banning the Ultras from stadia will serve only to drive this popular fan culture dangerously underground.

The mudslinging will no doubt continue; the Ultras will carry on fighting for justice and we can all look forward to another episode in a compelling political-points-scoring saga that looks set to run for quite a while yet.

Meanwhile, PSG and Olympique Marseille will remain the best of enemies and *Derby de France* will continue to be played out in a hostile and poisonous atmosphere, with or without the Ultras.

A Pictorial Tribute to the Supporters ... because Football without Fans is Nothing ... AMF

La Bombonera – Boca Juniors v River Plate

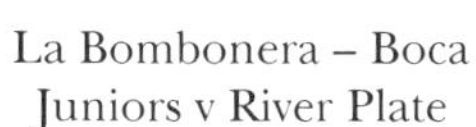

La Bombonera – Boca Juniors v River Plate

Toumba Stadium – PAOK v Olympiacos

Kaftanzoglio Stadium – Iraklis v Panathinaikos

Kaftanzoglio Stadium – Iraklis v Panathinaikos

Kleanthis Vikelidis Stadium –
Aris v PAOK

Kleanthis Vikelidis Stadium – Aris v PAOK

Fritz Walter Stadion – Kaiserslautern v Eintracht Frankfurt

Bulgarska Armiya Stadium – CSKA Sofia v Levski Sofia

Poljud Stadium – Hajduk Split v Dinamo Zagreb

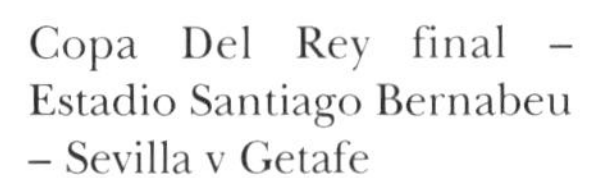

Copa Del Rey final – Estadio Santiago Bernabeu – Sevilla v Getafe

San Siro Stadium – Internazionale v AC Milan

San Siro Stadium – Internazionale v AC Milan

Georgios Karaiskakis Stadium – Olympiacos v Panathinaikos

Marakana Stadium – Crvena Zvezda v Partizan Belgrade

Partizan Stadium – Partizan Belgrade v Crvena Zvezda

'Time and time again I have drummed into my players that they are privileged to play for you.'

Bill Shankly 1913–1981

Afterword – a Brief Update

It has been five years since my first visit to the welcoming city of Belgrade and much has changed in such a short space of time. Since surrendering the league championship on home soil in May 2007 and after a season marred by internal conflict, Partizan Belgrade went on to clinch a record fifth consecutive championship (including three league and cup doubles), their twenty-fourth overall and more importantly only one title behind their fierce rivals across the park.

Since winning their last league crown in the 2006–07 season, ten Red Star Belgrade managers have tried in vain to break Partizan's dominance. But despite the lack of silverware and considerable financial difficulty, Red Star have still managed to secure a multimillion dollar sponsorship deal with MTS who are part of the state-owned Telekom Srbija group. Red Star manager Robert Prosinecki would have been hoping funds would be made available for him to bring in new players, but Partizan's continued supremacy and the board's lack of patience ensured a premature August departure for the former Pompey midfielder. He was swiftly replaced by former Red Star player Aleksandar Jankovic, who will also be hoping funds are made available to sign new players!

Fan-on-fan violence at the eternal derby has without question subsided since the introduction of tough new anti-hooligan laws. The obligatory full-scale riots that have been a persistent feature of this game appear to have been successfully contained for now. But despite the crackdown on hooliganism, the poisonous game-day atmosphere still remains at fever pitch. All the seats in the south stand at the

Marakana are now removed before every derby, thus preventing Partizan supporters using them as missiles or setting them on fire as is customary on derby day. The 2011 fixture at Red Star proved to be particularly volatile. Aleksandar Stanojevic was forced to conduct his half-time team talk in the dugout after his players were subjected to a sustained attack of missile throwing. Scores of firecrackers and lighted flares rained down on them from the north stand each time they tried to enter the sanctuary of the players' tunnel leaving them no choice but to abandon their attempts to leave the pitch and improvise.

All the seating has been removed from the Marakana's south stand

In 2010, Grobari celebrated their fortieth anniversary and in order to commemorate the occasion, the Grobari 1970 boys changed the group's name to 40+ (Forty plus). A new flag was commissioned to confirm the group's new identity. A black-and-white-striped flag with the 40+ insignia in the centre now takes pride of place on the south stand and a new era begins.

40+

In August 2011 an internal conflict between a large number of independent groups and the all-powerful Alcatraz firm threatened the very existence of Grobari. By the end of the 2011–12 season the south stand had been consumed by violence, culminating in an all-out terrace war as rival factions fought to gain control of the terraces.

Alcatraz

The alliance between Young Boys, South Family, Grobari Beograd, Koalicija and some smaller groups was responsible for creating a new group called Zabranjeni, translated as Forbidden and so called because when they first got together they were forbidden by the police (allegedly under orders from Alcatraz leaders) from entering the stadium, even though they had legitimate match tickets. Unable to support the team they love, they temporarily switched their allegiance to Partizan's women's basketball team.

Zabranjeni – segregated from the south stand in the Marakana

Members of Zabranjeni believe Alcatraz is corrupt and in partnership with the police and some high-ranking Serbian officials and are running the south stand for monetary gain. It's a scurrilous allegation which of course the leaders of Alcatraz steadfastly refute.

In October 2011, Zabranjeni member 20-year-old Ivan Perovic became the first casualty of the conflict. Ivan and his young friend were believed to have been brutally gunned down by Alcatraz affiliates in a drive-by shooting that shocked the Serbian footballing community. Both kids were taken to hospital but Ivan died from his wounds. The death of Ivan galvanised the group and over the course of the 2011–12 season Zabranjeni grew in number and became more powerful. After many protests and countless clashes with Alcatraz and the police, they were finally allowed back into the stadium and took up residence in the east stand, leaving the police with the unenviable task of segregating rival Partizan factions at both home and away games.

My good friends from 40+ maintained a dignified neutral stance throughout the whole of this sorry episode until an incident at the Serbian Cup semi-final with Red Star in April (2012) split the group. Cegi, Pidja, Lubo and Andrija remain neutral and still enter the south stand with the 40+ banner. Combe, Rajko and a handful of others formed their own group called Kontra (meaning against) and now stand with Zabranjeni on the east stand. All, however, remain the best of friends and firmly believe that at some point in the near future, the internal strife will be resolved, fan conflict will end and the 'south will rise again', bigger, stronger and more united than ever before!

By the end of the 2012 season, Zabranjeni, although still not without numbers, have been decimated by arrests and prison sentences imposed upon its members for 'ghost' offences. Alcatraz's influence on the south has shown no sign of diminishing under pressure and so the conflict continues.

Shortly before the Inter Milan v Partizan Belgrade Champions League tie in October (2012), I was reliably informed that a Serbian SWAT team carried out a series of dawn raids in order to prevent certain units of Grobari travelling to Milan. A number of arrests were made shortly afterwards resulting in the temporary imprisonment of my good friend Combe and several of his associates. My source informed me that they were being held on a number of seriously trumped-up allegations and although they had been remanded in custody pending further enquiries, all expected to be released shortly without charges being brought against them.

In a prison amnesty aimed at reducing the number of prisoners incarcerated in Serbian jails, Uros Misic, the young man convicted of brutalising the Belgrade policeman Nebojsa Trajkovic at the Hajduk Kula game in 2007, is to be released from prison (December 2012) after serving five and a half years of his ten-year sentence for attempted murder. The amnesty will also apply to those implicated in the murder of Serbian warlord Arkan.

Holland's biggest feuding rivalry has been a tame affair since the mayors of Rotterdam and Amsterdam banned away fans from each other's games due to the escalation in violent activity between the two fan groups. As a result of the ban, supporters from both clubs accused the authorities of murdering the classic or as one Feyenoord banner read, '*Klassieker Vermoord*'.

The 2010 Ajax v Feyenoord Dutch Cup final also fell foul of the ban. The final of the KNVB (Royal Netherlands Football Association) Cup competition has been played in a one-off game at Feyenoord's De Kuip since 1989, but after initially agreeing a 10,000-ticket allocation to each club, the Dutch FA changed protocol and agreed to play the final as a two-legged affair, due to the substantial cost of policing the game, an estimated 1 million euros, and increased fears of fan violence. Ajax of course went on to lift the trophy with consummate ease after inflicting a humiliating 6–1 aggregate defeat upon their eternal rivals.

Ronald De Boer, the fourth Ajax coach since my visit to the arena in 2008, led the Amsterdam club to consecutive Eredivisie titles in 2011 and 2012, their first league success since 2004. In contrast, rivals Feyenoord almost self-imploded under the burden of substantial financial difficulties. A record 10–0 defeat at PSV Eindhoven in 2010 confirmed the demise of a great Dutch footballing institution and further reinforced their status as an 'irrelevant club'.

Three months later, Feyenoord fans mourned the passing of Coen Moulijn (February 1937–January 2011), legendary winger and icon of Feyenoord Rotterdam. Thousands of supporters lined the streets to the stadium and gave their hero a royal farewell, befitting a player held in such high esteem by the club's fanatical supporters.

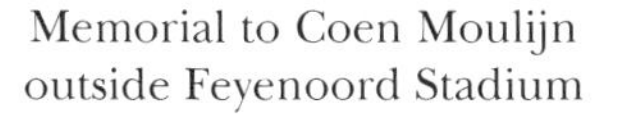

Memorial to Coen Moulijn
outside Feyenoord Stadium

By the middle of June (2011), the Rotterdam club's debts were believed to have spiralled towards the 40 million-euro mark. Results were awful and supporters found themselves issued with stadium bans for no good reason. Fans couldn't take any more and turned out in high numbers at the team's return to pre-season training, to protest about the running of the club. Further demonstrations continued throughout the summer and into the start of the 2012 league campaign, culminating in a riot outside the stadium after 2,000 supporters took part in a protest march before the De Graafschap game. Police had to draw guns and riot police used batons and tear gas to disperse the angry mob.

Despite De Boer's awakening of the famous Dutch giants, Ajax became embroiled in turmoil behind the scenes when newly appointed board member Johan Cruyff took the club to court over their clandestine appointment of Louis Van Gaal as CEO. Cruyff was appointed as king-maker with a remit to overhaul the club's structure. However, Ajax's most famous son was not consulted about Van Gaal's appointment and resigned his post in April 2012.

Over in Rotterdam, out of adversity came strength. Former Ajax coach Ronald Koeman steered the team to a second-placed finish behind their Amsterdam foe in a remarkable reversal of fortune. Less than a year after angry supporters stormed the club's HQ, the Rotterdam club's financial nightmare appears to be on the mend, the club having cut their debt and secured a more stable financial position. And for the long-suffering faithful, there appears to be a very bright light shining at the exit of a very dark tunnel!

The 2012 UEFA European Championships carried the modern football virus into Poland and preparation for the prestigious event was met with a tsunami of protests from Ultra groups throughout the country. Prior to the start of the Euros there was a crackdown on Ultra culture, culminating in the banning of pyrotechnics, smoke pots and banners, and new laws enforced which have led to unjust stadium bans and disproportionate prison sentences for fictional offences.

Ultra groups see themselves as the custodians of Polish football and the authorities' new hard-line approach towards their activities has served only to galvanise the country's Ultra movement. 'F**k Euros' and 'against modern football' graffiti became more apparent in the lead-up to the finals and domestic attendances were severely affected by supporters disillusioned with the government's repressive stance towards their culture.

On the Slaski front, Ruch achieved their best league position since winning the title in 1989. Only a point separated them from winners and Euro finals hosts Slask Wroclaw. A noteworthy ten-place improvement on the previous season and more importantly, they reclaimed bragging rights over their Slask derby rivals Gornik Zabrze. Gornik themselves, although achieving only a mid-table finish, look to have established their place in the Polish top tier again after their 2009 relegation.

Fan violence between the two best-supported teams in the Slaski region has shown no signs of abating. The derby hasn't returned to the Slaski stadium since the 2009 match when up to 300 Ruch hooligans entered the pitch and attacked stadium security forces. More recently, the game in April 2012 was marred by large-scale disorder before, during and after the match. Despite only receiving an allocation of 500 tickets for the game at the Miejski, Gornik mobilised a following of around 1,000 supporters.

The train taking them to the game was due to stop at Chorzow-Batory station but Gornik hooligans pulled the emergency cord one kilometre short of the train's destination and headed over the tracks to the main street for a prearranged confrontation with rival Ruch hooligans. Four hundred hooligans fought running battles, hurling flares, bottles and stones at each other. Media reports suggested riot police used live ammunition to break up warring factions.

At the stadium, 500 ticketless Gornik supporters tried to smash their way in but were forced back by security forces and mounted police who used tear gas and water cannons to restore order. Inside the Miejski, balaclava-clad Ruch supporters broke through security fencing and attacked the Gornik contingent with flares and other missiles as police struggled to cope with the situation.

Visiting Gornik supporters were held for up to four hours after the final whistle and were each made to pose for a photograph to help police identify those responsible for causing the disorder. After further investigation, many Gornik fans received stadium bans for their part in the troubles. There will, however, be no repeat of the anarchy in the return game at Zabrze; Ruch supporters still uphold their boycott to away games at the Ernest Pohl, out of respect for Rajmund and Remik, the two innocent Ruch supporters brutally murdered by Gornik thugs.

* * *

Perennial bridesmaids of the new millennium, Sporting have become susceptible to losing their prestigious place in the triopoly that has dominated Portuguese league football since its inception in 1938. Sporting Club de Braga have gatecrashed the Porto, Benfica and Sporting 'love-in', threatening seventy years of domination by Portugal's three most successful footballing institutions, and it's the Lisbon bridesmaids who look set to fall foul of the underdogs from 'the quarry'.

Sporting president, the low-profile and all-round good guy Jose Eduardo Bettencourt, fell on his sword and resigned (January 2011) his dream post after the *Leoes*' downturn in form was attributed to his leadership. The club haven't recovered from the acrimonious transfer of club captain and youth team prodigy Joao Moutinho to southern rivals Porto, a move that enraged Bettencourt and fellow *Sportinguistas*.

Away from the boardroom and on to the terraces, the acrimony that exists between the two Lisbon enemies has shown no sign of subsiding. Aggrieved by their team's 1–0 loss (November 2011), the lunatic fringe set fire to a section of Benfica's iconic Stadium of Light. Luckily, the fire was contained very quickly and only a small section of the stadium was damaged.

Self-proclaimed people's club Benfica ruthlessly dismissed the charismatic Quique Sanchez Flores after an unacceptable third-place 2009 finish, seven points to the rear of Sporting and eleven points adrift of champions Porto. He was swiftly replaced by Benfica's twentieth coach in as many years Jorge Jesus, who ended the club's title drought in his first league campaign, losing only two games all season and scoring seventy-eight goals. *Benfiquistas* were ecstatic and Jesus was rewarded with a very rare contract extension.

Fast-forward twelve months and the honeymoon period ended in tears for Jesus as Benfica bombed in dramatic fashion, finishing the 2010–11 league campaign as runners-up, twenty-one points at the back of champions Porto. Another second-placed finish this year has left the club president with an itchy trigger finger and although Jesus is still in charge at the time of writing, that may not be the case by the end of summer. At Benfica, to quote Bill Shankly, 'If you are first you are first. If you are second you are nothing!'

Extreme football fandom in Romania is in steep decline. Dragomir's continued persecution of Bucharest's, indeed the nation's, hard-core supporters has created an unbridgeable chasm between the LFP and the football-crazy Ultras.

In December 2011, the president of Romania, Traian Basescu, supported by the LPF's Dumitru Dragomir (Ultras refer to Dragomir as Mitica), Steaua president George 'Gigi' Becali and Dinamo co-owner Cristian Borcea, endorsed amendments to existing anti-(football) violence laws, with the sole purpose of systematically breaking the spirit of Romania's storied Ultra movement.

Some core amendments to the existing legislation:

> Crowd encroachment on to the field of play is punishable with 6–12-month incarceration and a stadium ban of up to two years. Should encroachment involve violence the prison sentence can be increased by up to a further 12 months and the stadium ban doubled.
>
> Any supporter found to be in breach of a stadium ban can be imprisoned for up to three months and heavily fined.
>
> Banned supporters have to report to a local police station during matches. Those who fail to comply can be fined up to 400 euros and hit with a community work order of between 120 and 200 hours.
>
> The attempt to possess, prepare or use pyrotechnics (signal flares, smoke pots etc.) inside a stadium is punishable with a custodial sentence of between two and five years and a 2–4 year stadium ban.

The new laws were introduced in response to repeated protests by Ultras against the 'Teflon trio' of Bucharest-based untouchables, all of whom have been dogged by recurring allegations of bribery and corruption. Dragomir, a man with a villainous past, has served two prison sentences. He was jailed for three months in 1976 for illegal gambling and in 1990 for seven months for abuse of office. The irrepressible Gigi Becali, an apparently self-confessed practising homophobic, who once cancelled a transfer because he thought the player was gay, is widely perceived as a modern-day village idiot who prides himself on controversy. In 2009, he was temporarily incarcerated while under investigation for kidnapping several people, allegedly at gunpoint, that he suspected were involved in the stealing of his prestige Mercedes car. And Becali's godson Cristian Borcea, was, along with seven other defendants, including two of Becali's cousins, recently acquitted of tax evasion, money laundering and fraud, after a three-year investigation by the National Anti-corruption Office (DNA).

In conjunction with the new law, police officers have undertaken new strategies to combat the Ultras' activities and stadium unrest. CCTV has been installed at some stadia and most clubs now only issue match tickets to fans that provide names and agree to have their photograph taken for security reasons. Undercover policing is wide-scale and stadium banning orders are issued at every opportunity.

Furious at the draconian constraints, the leaders of supporters' groups at Steaua (Gheorghe Mustata) and Dinamo (Mihnea Ionescu) have both reacted with anger and dismay. Whilst neither spokesperson disputes the need for law and order, both feel the ambiguity of the new amendments to the existing law is open to unprecedented abuse and both gave examples to ZIUA News to back up their fears. Ionescu claims that at a recent Dinamo–Rapid derby match, sixty luminous flares were lit by Dinamo supporters resulting in 482 stadium-banning orders. Mustata is ultra fearful of mass sanctions. For example, two smoke pots were ignited in the VIP section at the Steaua–Rapid game and although video evidence could not identify those responsible, 400 stadium-banning orders were issued to Steaua supporters in the vicinity of the area affected.

In Romania, Bucharest in particular, nobody cares if you are innocent. The ambiguity of law enforcement is staggering. A supporter celebrating a goal by jumping on the perimeter fence can be arrested and banned for 12 months for attempted pitch invasion. Of course, the opportunity to appeal is available but the authorities ensure the result of the appeal will only be disclosed eight months into the banning order, rendering the appeal worthless. Fans can also earn themselves a financial penalty for the most minor of misdemeanours. The size of the fine very much depends on whether the person issuing the fine likes your face or not and can range from 50 to 500 Euros.

My good friend Lex confirmed that he had himself been one of the many victims of overzealous policing and was harshly issued with a one-year stadium ban for an altercation with a gypsy who insulted his girlfriend close to the stadium. Quite incredible really, a stadium ban for a non-footballing incident, but quite typical of a regime hell bent on ridding the game of the Ultra movement!

Lex has had enough of Commie-style state repression and along with the majority of the Ultras from Peluza Sud, has undertaken a self-imposed exile from the Ghencea and will not return until Becali relinquishes ownership.

Corruption is unquestionably endemic in Romanian football, but as long as the gamekeepers are in bed with the poachers, those responsible for illegally profiteering from the national sport will continue to sleep easy in their multimillion-pound properties. Meanwhile, fans will continue to suffer unjustifiable repression as the 'Teflon' dons look to rid the game of its lifeblood … the Ultras!

In the summer of 2009 there were big changes at Zeljeznicar. With club presidential elections looming supporters were in a strong position to instigate changes. A meeting was set up between fans and potential candidates for the post, giving the supporters an opportunity to voice their opinions. After a disappointing ninth-place finish, fans demanded a change in stewardship and promised to support any of the nominees who could bring back former coach Amar Osim. The ex-Zeljo midfielder and son of Zeljesnicar legend Ivica Osim managed the railway workers between 2001 and 2003 and won two league titles, two national cups and the Bosnian Super Cup and is held in high esteem by the fanatical blue-and-white brethren.

Osim insisted he could only work under the presidency of Sabahudin Zujo, who was president between 2000 and 2003. Zujo was an unpopular choice with the fans because of the two-million-euro debt the club accumulated under his guidance but they supported him as he was the only candidate who could bring Osim back to the club. Zujo became club president and Amar Osim was appointed manager shortly afterwards.

His first game in charge was away at Celik Zenica; Zeljo won 0–1, their first away victory for two years! He has won two league titles in three years, including a league and cup double last year. Osim is a maverick coach, the Bosnian equivalent of Brian Clough. He yields a lot of respect from his players who appear to thrive on his unconventional coaching methods. His class of 2012 have broken many club records including a record-breaking run of twelve straight victories, one of the best successive win sequences in Europe. Osim is renowned for his discipline and fine attention to detail. He reportedly makes his players train at midnight or run around the pitch for an hour after the game if the team suffer a home defeat, believing it gives the players the extra incentive to succeed. Needless to say, Zeljo don't lose at home. In fact, Zeljo just don't lose.

Osim is a hands-on coach who works tirelessly behind the scenes. He has total control over all the club's footballing affairs. He basically decides who comes and who goes and is responsible for youth and academy development including the appointing of staff. Prior to his appointment, almost the entire team would be sold during the summer months but now Zeljo sell only one or two players and the money is reinvested.

In total contrast, their same-city rivals FK Sarajevo are in dire financial straits at present and really struggled to pay a debt to UEFA enabling them to compete in this season's Europa Cup. In order to help meet the deadline for payment, Sarajevo doubled the price of tickets for the last derby at the Kosevo and this, together with the visitors' ban, undoubtedly had a profound effect on the low attendance of around 12,000, some 23,000 short of capacity. Despite the ban, some 2,000 Zeljo supporters defied the authorities and managed to gain access to the west stand with relative ease.

Zeljo's illegal invasion of the Kosevo (May 2012)

The supporters' ban at the Kosevo was part of sanctions introduced due to an upsurge in spectator violence which has become an unlikely common theme in Bosnia. A blanket ban on all away supporters was adopted after Zeljo supporters became the victims of a premeditated attack by Borac fans in Banja Luka and were then involved in large-scale disturbances at a celebratory home game with Hajduk Split just two weeks later.

My good friend Ado, a much-travelled Zeljo supporter, was caught up in both incidents but found the Borac trip particularly unnerving. 'Borac's hools (The Vultures) invaded the pitch shortly after Zeljeznicar had taken the lead and proceeded to violently attack our sector with stones, bricks and flares. Some of the rocks were so big they couldn't even throw them over the three-metre-high security fence. When they ran out of missiles they headed back to their own stand and then the police attacked us without provocation.' The game was abandoned and after an FA enquiry the visitors where awarded a 0–3 victory.

Ado believes the attack was politically motivated and organised by right-wing politicians looking to whip up rising ethnic tensions. 'There was no police on duty pitch-side and gates preventing access to the pitch were not locked. Police allowed us to make our way home via the city centre without a police escort,' said a clearly agitated Ado. The lack of security meant Zeljo fans were openly attacked on every street corner and many of their vehicles were substantially vandalised. Multicultural Bosnia is safe, friendly and boasts a culturally diverse society, but football tends to bring out the worst in people. Right-wing, mainly Serb and Croat supporters' groups, supported by Machiavellian right-wing politicians, are thought to be responsible for much of the increase in terrace-related violence that has blighted the Bosnian game of late.

The home game with Croatian team Hajduk Split (October 2011) was a friendly match organised to celebrate Zeljeznicar's ninetieth anniverary. The match was sold out and the Maniacs had organised a huge celebratory choreography on the south stand. Hadjuk are a popular club and have support all over the former Yugoslavia. They have a fiercely partisan following and Hajduk's Torcida Ultras are widely regarded as one of the best and oldest Ultra movements in the world.

The first wave of Torcida, mostly based in Herzegovina, arrived early and as a precautionary security measure were escorted to the stadium approximately four hours before kick-off. With only a few police officers on duty inside the stadium, the Split fans made their way to the south stand, attacked a small group of Zeljo and destroyed the huge choreography they were preparing. Another mob of Torcida, mostly from Croatia, arrived in Sarajevo around an hour before the game. With no police escort to control them (most were deployed to restore order at the stadium) around 150 Croats went on the rampage in the city centre. Ado recalls furious Zeljo fans confronting Split supporters on the outskirts of the city. 'Most of the lads were at the Grbavica seeking revenge on the Split supporters who destroyed our choreography but some Zeljo fans clashed with the Hajduk mob running amok in the suburbs just outside the city centre. Running battles occurred and were so violent that media reports suggested Split fans had jumped from a bridge into the River Milijacka in fear of their life.' The game was cancelled amid fears of widespread rioting. Two days later the FA announced a complete ban (October 2011) on all away supporters in Bosnia.

Of course it isn't just Zeljeznicar who have been the victim of premeditated match-day violence. Shortly after my visit to the derby at the Grbavica in May 2009, Sarajevo fans suffered a similar fate in the Croat-dominated municipality of Siroki Brijeg just outside Mostar. In a league game with Siroki in October 2009, the Horde Zla (HZ) supporters' group also accused right-wing politicians of inciting a riot at the game that resulted in the death of 24-year-old Sarajevo supporter Vedran Puljic.

Over 500 Sarajevo supporters made the trip to Sikori and once they had parked their buses they were afforded no police protection for the long walk to the stadium. They were subsequently attacked by local hooligans intent on inflicting serious bodily harm on them. Shops were vandalised, property was damaged and cars set on fire as fans became embroiled in an inexplicable bloody battle that came out of nowhere. HZ claim local police stood idly by before actually linking up with Sikori thugs and local residents to administer severe beatings upon them.

Puljic was thought to have been shot with an AK-47 rifle fired by Oliver Knezovic, believed to be ex-military. But tests later revealed he was shot by a police pistol. Knezovic, who maintains his innocence, escaped custody and fled to Zagreb where he remains because there is no extradition treaty between Croatia and Bosnia–Herzegovina. A number of local police officers were reportedly detained following Knezovic's escape but nobody has yet been brought to justice for the young boy's murder. In a show of unity, over 7,000 protesters, including supporters from rivals Zeljeznicar, took to the streets of Sarajevo to demand a public inquiry into the wilful police negligence that supporters have to endure every time they travel to Herzegovina. The fight for justice continues.

In Memorium – graffiti outside the Kosevo

On a brighter note, the law finally caught up with the mobsters responsible for tarnishing the integrity of Bosnian football. Former FA leaders have been suspended and some jailed for corruption and theft. A temporary UEFA ban on the Bosnian FA was lifted after a reorganisation of the FA led by Zeljo icon Ivica Osim. The interim committee will rule the association until December (2012) when a new election will determine a single presidency for the first time in post-war top-flight football. The quality of the top league is much better now. There is more money in the game and less corruption meaning games now have to be won, not bought.

With just three years at the helm, Zeljo coach Amar Osim is the Premier League's longest-serving manager by some distance. Coaches in this division have a shelf life of approximately three months, one of the worst in European football. With the support of his president and shrewd dealings in the transfer market, he has helped to reduce the club's debt to around 300,000 euros, less than half that of their struggling rivals across the city. Former Zeljo prodigy Edin Dzeko's transfer from Wolfsburg to Manchester City brought in a much-needed 1 million-euro windfall that has helped the manager retain the team's quality players. Zeljo are no longer a selling club. With a healthy annual budget of around 2.5 million euros the club appears to be heading for the safe zone. New laws are being prepared allowing clubs to be floated on the stock exchange and Zeljeznicar are certainly the club that will benefit most. They are the only team in the Premier League that owns their own stadium, which of course is built on prime real estate. In 2011 the club opened its first fan shop at the stadium, a massive step in the right direction for the development of a club in ascendency. The future is bright, the future is blue!

Bobby Davison's turbulent eighteen months in the hot seat of Hungary's most demanding club came to an abrupt end just twenty-seven days after the 2–1 defeat at Ujpest in October 2009. Despite leading the fallen giants back into the top flight after a three-year absence, Davison had to cope with a frenzy of unpleasantness. Sinister threats from the football terrorists whose mob rule threatens the safety of everyone connected with Ferencvaros left Davison so fearful for his own wellbeing that he reportedly felt the need to drive a different route home every night.

With the escalation of stadium violence and the threat of having to close the ground, new security measures were hastily put into operation by the club's hierarchy. Shortly after Davison's departure, similar in format to the ill-fated Luton Town prototype, the club introduced the controversial 'Fradi-card'. Supporters were forced to sign up to the new ID card scheme or be refused access to the stadium and not be allowed to purchase tickets for away matches. It was a move that infuriated some of the most prominent fan groups at the Ulloi and caused such serious internal wranglings within the Stormy Scamps' ranks that the division amongst the members was enough to end their 11-year association with the club.

After the death of one group came the birth of another. Former Stormy Scamps Ultras along with disgruntled members from other organised fan groups, namely the Cannibals and 7SIDE, formed the E.E.E. (Ero Egyseg Egyetertes), who signed up to the new ID card scheme and now take their place as one of the strongest Ultra factions at the Ulloi.

Convicted football thugs now face stiffer penalties after new legislation was approved by the Hungarian parliament. The stringent new laws took effect from September 2011 as a result of extreme crowd violence before, during and after the Green Eagles 0–6 defeat to their cross-city adversaries at the Szusza Ferenc Stadium in September 2010. The game was stopped several times and it needed an army of riot police to prevent a large-scale pitch invasion by the Fradi lunatic fringe. The occasion was further marred by news reports of a 17-year-old Ujpest supporter being taken to hospital with stab wounds after being subjected to a vicious knife attack by rival fans. Police arrested twenty-two supporters for their part in the derby-day madness. Hungarian Minister of the Interior Sandor Pinter claimed previous laws were not effective in the fight against a violent subculture that was affecting the future of the game. The new provisions are extremely restrictive and penalties include:

> Prison sentences of up to three years for group violence, carrying weapons and repeat offending.

> Up to two years' incarceration for a pitch invasion and missile throwing.

Supporters can also be prosecuted for vandalism and violence whilst travelling to and from stadia which can result in stadium bans or imprisonment. On match day fans will only be allowed into football stadia on condition that they show personal ID when requested and agree to be filmed on security cameras.

Football violence has reached its zenith in Budapest and after years of dithering, the authorities have finally adopted a long-overdue zero-tolerance approach. The right-wing militia who have held the terraces to ransom for two decades have suddenly become vulnerable. The Ultras now have a chance to rid their groups of infection and concentrate on the extremities of their sacred fan culture but must do so under the Achilles heel of repression. Football is life for contrasting reasons in Hungarian football. The hooligans have a thirst for violence and the Ultras have a hunger for passion. Despite the erratic behaviour of both parties and contrary to popular belief, both have a deep-seated love for their clubs.

October 2011 saw the passing of Ferencvaros legend Florian Albert. The 1967 Ballon d'Or winner failed to recover from heart surgery and was laid to rest in a moving public funeral that was broadcast live to the nation. Later in the evening, Fradi fans paid homage to the local hero at their home game with Paksi SE. Before the match the floodlights were turned off in the grand old stadium named after him and a near-capacity crowd lit candles and sparklers. The team wore custom-made black shirts in his honour and the fans displayed a huge banner revealing the words 'God shall be with you Emperor'. Unfortunately, the players couldn't deliver the perfect end to a sad day as they played out a 0–0 draw in a drab and emotionally drained encounter.

Dutchman Recardo Moniz was appointed as the new Fradi manager in August 2012 and becomes the fifth manager that the perennial underachievers have appointed in the three years since my trip to the derby with Ujpest. In June 2012, Belgian coach Jos Daerden became the Viola's fourth manager since Willie McStay's resignation in April 2010. Both face a mammoth job to restore the two giants of Hungarian football back to their former glories. It's a daunting task and the weight of expectation at both Budapest clubs will no doubt once again prove to be a heavy burden.

Only seven months after my trip to the Parc in November 2010, PSG was rapidly transformed from a debt-addled business model dining out on the highs of past glories into one of the world's wealthiest football clubs. QIA (Qatar Investment Authority) assumed ownership of the capital club in the summer of 2011 and sanctioned a 100 million-euro spending spree in their first season of ownership. The team had been making steady progress under the guidance of Antoine Kombouare but the new owners wanted a leading and trusted figurehead to propel the PSG brand into the cash-crazy commercialised world of modern football. Former Chelsea boss Carlo Ancelotti was profiled as the coach to lead the club forward and was duly appointed PSG's twenty-fourth manager in December 2011.

Argentine midfield sensation Javier Pastore, at a cost of 42 million euros, was the season's marquee signing. His thirteen league goals helped PSG qualify for this year's Champions League for the first time in nine years and helped mask the heartbreak of losing out to Montpellier in a thrilling title race that was only decided on the last day of the season.

With new French hooligan laws firmly established, the stadium violence that used to tarnish the club's image on a weekly basis has all but been eradicated, giving the Parc a clean bill of health and a sturdy platform the new owners can build upon. But whilst banning orders and restrictive enforcements have taken their toll on the domestic scene, the mob rule that has shamed *les Parisiens* on so many occasions in the past has continued to wreak havoc away from the jurisdiction of French law. With no legislative powers in place to prevent risk supporters travelling abroad, the club's army of casuals and right-wing degenerates are free to ply their trade away from French officialdom. In last September's (2011) Europa League match in Bilbao, hundreds of PSG hooligans ran amok in the city centre causing major problems for Spanish police. Restaurants and pubs were damaged as fans fought running battles with riot police before the game with Athletico.

With incomprehensible wealth behind the club and a new global image to enhance, the Arab investors will want all potentially damaging hooligan issues eliminated before commencement of their 2012 money-spinning Champions League campaign.

Although fan-on-fan violence is clearly in decline, the threat of major confrontation still haunts the country's biggest footballing spectacle. The last classico of the 2011–12 campaign succumbed to the same fate as the previous season. In a statement published by the French government's *Journal Officiel* and reported by *L'Equipe*, it was confirmed that Marseille supporters would again be banned from making the trip to the capital for their game with Ligue 1 rivals Paris Saint-Germain. The statement read:

> On April 8, 2012, from midnight to midnight, moving individually or collectively, by any means, any person claiming to support Olympique de Marseille or behaving as such is prohibited between the municipalities of the department of Bouches-du-Rhone and the city of Paris.

The government claimed a 'high risk of violence on the modes of transport or the routes taken by supporters of the club Olympique de Marseille to get to Paris' was the primary motivation for the order.

France's eternal grudge match shows no sign of mellowing and the stadium ban on visiting supporters, sadly, looks set to continue for the foreseeable future.

Shortly after collecting his record-breaking third Coupe de Ligue in succession, Marseille icon Didier Deschamps stepped down as coach of *les Phoceens* (June 2012) and was replaced by fellow Frenchman Elie Baup. In stark contrast to their uber-rich Parisian rivals, Marseille are on the brink of financial meltdown and like many of Europe's other fallen giants, look set for an uncertain future. Despite the chasm in wealth, Marseille sat proudly at the summit of Ligue 1 after winning their opening six matches.

Ancelotti spent big again during the summer, adding Ezequiel Lavezzi (30 million euros), Thiago Silva (42 million euros) and Zlatan Ibrahimovic (23 million euros) to his expensively assembled team of galacticos (212.6 million euros). But despite the glut of talent, PSG struggled to find form, drawing three of their opening six games. Consistency improved as the season progressed but they are not alone. At the halfway stage of the season only goal difference separates PSG in first place and their eternal rivals Marseille in third place. In one of the most exciting league campaigns in decades, the script looks set to be chopped and changed as the season unfolds. *Les Phoceens* are hanging on in there, proving that determination can sometimes overcome the power of the euro.

PSG's new-found wealth has seen them shamefully shake off the working-class roots that served them so well during the club's rise to prominence. Ticket prices, although still relatively cheap in comparison to other more affluent parts of Europe, have risen almost 50 per cent since the QIA takeover. It's a steady increase that has contributed greatly to the demise of the street urchin and signalled the influx of the 'in crowd' from the bourgeois Parisian *banlieues* who contribute very little in the way of atmosphere but are aesthetically sound for the image of the new brand.

Worldwide exposure is critical to the success of the modern football phenomenon. It's therefore no coincidence that the scheduling of live football matches has undergone seismic changes since the Arab takeover at PSG. Qatari-based Beinsport have recently won the contract to schedule all live TV games in France. Ligue 1 will show one live game on a Friday evening and three live games at different times on a Sunday. Ligue 2 will show one live game on a Friday evening, one game on Saturday afternoon and another game on Monday evening. French supporters are furious with the Arab interference in their fixture list and have protested vehemently against it since the contract was signed, but this is the modern football concept where kick-off times are aligned to meet demand in other parts of the world, not to satisfy the needs of the fans.

Money dictates every aspect of modern football. PSG will get richer and at some point in the very near future will dominate French football leaving the rest playing catch up. Whilst money will undoubtedly bring success, it won't buy love and PSG, like other wealthy clubs, will reach pariah status. But this time not because of their fanatical supporters but because of their inordinate wealth!

Football used to be cyclic, a national sport in most countries where winners could just as easily become losers and vice versa. Then along came satellite television, followed swiftly by the game's new power brokers, a combination of American business tycoons, Russian oligarchs and billionaire Sheiks that have transformed football into the most potent of modern-day business vehicles. These uber-wealthy foreign owners have the financial muscle to play God with our national sport, cheating the system to ensure an elite minority of clubs share the unbridled wealth of the game between themselves, ultimately creating an unbridgeable chasm that grows with every increased broadcasting and sponsorship deal. Success is now predictable, not cyclic, and the pressure on clubs to succeed has become immeasurable. The sixteen clubs in this book have dispensed with the services of sixty-nine managers between them in little more than five years. The game is sick, infected by the modern football virus beyond repair and with no measure to contain it.

Six years after me pontificating about the German model and how we should be looking to adopt a similar structure in our game, the same plight that coincided with the inception of the English Premier League looks set to be patiently phased in, in the Fatherland. The people responsible for the corporate mutation of our sacred fan culture in the UK look set to slowly instigate a process that will destroy German fan culture, as the importance of a turn in profit takes precedence over the values and traditions of the rank-and-file supporter.

There is no doubt that German football has already been affected by the modern football virus; it clearly has. The scheduling of live games in particular has been a contentious issue and Bundesliga chiefs have come in for heavy criticism from angry supporters' associations incensed at satellite TV's increased domination of the fixture list. But supporters in Germany, particularly the Ultras, have a voice and are strongly represented by official fan movements who have been instrumental in slowing down the introduction of the modern football template. That was until a couple of isolated incidents involving Dynamo Dresden's massive (10,000) travelling hordes away at Dortmund (October 2011) and Hannover (Oct 2012) in the German cup. The German media, chiefly *Bild-Zeitung*, which is considered to be the German equivalent of *The Sun*, took it upon itself to embellish the confrontations and place the Ultras in the public spotlight. These incidents, coupled with several non-violent pitch invasions described by the press as 'a new level of violence' or 'aspects of civil war', have been the catalyst for a media frenzy against German football supporters, especially the Ultras and their extreme fan culture.

As a result of the politically motivated, media-driven negativity geared towards the Ultra movement and the alleged increase in 'ghost' violence in and around German stadia, police chiefs and politicians called upon the Bundesliga hierarchy to put their house in order. Under intense pressure to institute remedial measures the DFL (Deutcshe Fußball Liga), supported by the DFB (Deutcsher Fußball-Bund), proposed radical new solutions to combat the alleged fan violence.

The initial draught, called '*Sicheres Stadionerlebnis*' (Safe Football Experience), was rejected by the majority of Germany's thirty-six top-flight clubs who claimed the new safety measures were far too radical to deal with minimal fan disorder.

Some of the controversial proposals included:

- Substantially reducing ticket allocation to visiting supporters for perceived high-risk games
- Tents erected outside stadia to enable security personnel, supported by police officers, to carry out a full-body searches targeting the detection of pyrotechnic materials
- A reduction in standing areas at all top-flight stadia
- Personalised ticket allocation
- Increased use of CCTV surveillance

So the DFL, who found themselves under intense media scrutiny for lack of dialogue with supporters' associations during the draughting of the security paper, went back to the drawing board and came back with a watered-down version of the original proposals. During the editing of the original draught, again without fan dialogue, dismayed supporters' groups organised protests against the new document to conclude on the new day of reckoning, 12/12/12.

The 12:12 protests, '*Keine Stimmung Ohne Stimme*' (No Atmosphere Without a Voice), were organised to take place in every top-tier stadium at the last three games prior to the outcome of the new ballot. For the first twelve minutes and twelve seconds of each match the game was played in complete silence. Proclaiming the protests were a success after backing from players who found the experience of playing in stadiums devoid of atmosphere unacceptable, fans were optimistic that the clubs would support them in their protests and reject the revised security paper. Sadly their optimism was short-lived. In Frankfurt on 12 December 2012, the DFL announced that their newly proposed legislation had been accepted in its entirety by a vast majority of the thirty-six Bundesliga clubs and would be implemented at the earliest opportunity.

The acceptance of such restrictive measures has created a huge chasm between Bundesliga chiefs and the fan groups who feel betrayed by the DFL's overly aggressive stance. The Ultras have been instrumental in the fight against the introduction of the despised 'English' modern football experience and feel the new proposals will prove to be a significant step towards a change in crowd dynamic, the sanitisation of German stadia and a hefty increase in ticket prices. And so the cycle begins again and the Germans' unique match-day experience will at some point succumb to the same fate as the once lauded UK fan scene. The flame still burns for now but the reality is that the fat cats will plunder the Fatherland's storied football clubs and German football will make the transition from working-class sport to blue-chip business model. Capitalist repression will ensure the Ultras and their sacred terrace culture will be forced out of the stadia and a new generation of middle-class supporters will be manufactured to take their place. Welcome to the world of modern football where greed is good and prawn sandwiches are all the rage!

THE TRUTH – Wednesday 12 September 2012 was a momentous day for the families of the ninety-six men, women and children who needlessly lost their lives at Hillsborough in Britain's biggest sporting tragedy. The long-overdue enquiry into the 1989 Hillsborough disaster completely exonerated Liverpool fans of any blame.

Some of the key findings:

- 116 of the 164 statements were doctored to remove or amend comments unfavourable to South Yorkshire Police.
- 41 victims may have been saved had the response from emergency services been better.
- Blood samples were taken from all the deceased in order to determine alcohol levels.
- Police officers ran criminal records checks on the dead.
- No evidence was found to support police accusations of drunkenness and aggression amongst Liverpool supporters.
- Crowd safety was compromised at every level.

With the truth now in the public domain and the unforgivably corrupt South Yorkshire Police rightly condemned at the highest level for their attempted cover-up, justice edges ever closer. Tick tock … Tick tock …

The sun will always shine on the righteous

RIP the 96 … for whom football *was* life. God Bless.

Bibliography

Sources, Useful Reading and Acknowledgements

Websites

www.afp.com, www.ajax-bg.com, www.ajaxtalk.nl, www.ajax-usa.com, www.at5.nl, www.bbc.co.uk,

www.bbcnews.co.uk, www.belgrade-news.com, www.bigsoccer.com, www.budapesttimes.hu,

www.budapestsun.com, www.cafyd.com, www.champpenal.revues.org, www.cnn.com,

www.collectif1899, www.delije.net, www.europeanultras.com, www.feyenoord.nl,

www.feyenoordstuff.webs.com, www.fifa.com, www.footballblog.co.uk, www.footballderbies.com,

www.football-history.net, www.foxsports.com, www.france24.com, www.fzr.ro, www.goal.com,

www.goal22.com, www.greenspun.com, www.grobari1970.org, www.gsp.ro, www.guardian.co.uk,

www.ifhof.com, www.independent.co.uk, www.jdsport.com, www.laprovence.com, www.leparisien.fr,

www.lequipe.fr, www.mancelegenda.blogspot.com, www.marsellais-du-monde.org,

www.midfielddynamo.com, www.mtp1994.e-monsite.com, www.nytimes.com, www.offside.com, www.om.net, www.om-passion.com, www.planetbenfica.net, www.planum.net,

www.premierleague.com, www.philosofooty.afootballreport.com, www.polishsoca.com,

www.przegladsportowy.pl, www.reuters.com, www.seattletimes.com, www.sirc.org,

www.soccer24-7.com, www.soccerphile.com, www.soccerlens.com, www.soccernet.espn.go.com,

www.soccernews.com, www.srpskatribina.net, www.starbacks.ca, www.sudouest.fr, www.sw87.com,

www.telegraph.co.uk, www.teletekst.nos.nl, www.thebohs.com, www.thesundaytimes.co.uk,

www.thisislondon.co.uk, www.timesonline.com, www.tomathon.com, www.tsn.ca, www.uefa.com,

www.uk.reuters.com, www.ultrasspirit.com, www.ultras-tifo.net, www.ultrasworldwide.net,

www.unprofessionalfoul.com, www.usatoday.com, www.worldsoccerreader.com, www.wsc.co.uk,

www.xtratime.org, www.ziuanews.ro

Newspapers and Magazines

Belgrade Insight, Budapest Times, Daily Mail, Daily Mirror, Four Four Two, Journal Sporting, London Evening Standard, PUP Magazine, The Guardian, The Observer, The Independent, World Soccer, When Saturday Comes

Media/Journalists/Authors

Yomi Akenyemi, Robin Bairner, Nick Bidwell, Howard Booth, Rick Broadbent, James Buchanan, Stefan Coerts, David Conn, Peterjon Cresswell, Bruce Crumley, Johann Cruyff, Lawrence D'Ancona, Jules Deeder, Tobias Dietrich, Paul Doyle, Sorin Dumitrescu, Tom Dunmore, Dave Fowler, Marcus Gee, Oliver Holt, Sean Ingle, Neil Jones, Damian Kavanagh, Jane Kirby, Branislav Kovac, Tamas Krausz, Simon Kuper, John Lichfield, Gabrielle Marcotti, Paul Marshall, Neil McCarthy, David Miller, Zoran Milosavljevic, John Nicholson, Ted Nugent, Ozgur Dirim Ozkan, Ozren Podnar, Menno Pot, Jeff Powell, Jerome Pugmire, Brian

Reade, Francois Revilla, Giles Richards, Eliot Rothwell, Shourin Roy, Henry Samuel, Owen Slot, Michael Sokolove, Leo Spall, Daniel Sunter, Radu Timofte, Patrick Wasilewski, Kim Willshew, Jonathan Wilson, Henry Winter, Paul Wood, Marton Vajda, Babbette Van Haaren, Adri Vermaat, John Verrall

TV, Radio and Press Associations

Amsterdam (AFP), BBC *Late Kick Off* Show, Belgrade AP, Belgrade's B92 Radio, France (AFP), First Sport Media Publications, Hungarian News Agency (MTI), Paris (AP), PA News, Romania (AP), The Associated Press, View From The Terrace, Xinhua.

Photos

Shaun Duffy

Acknowledgements

FRIENDS, FAMILY & CONTRIBUTORS – Adrian Beiu, Michael Brotherston, Brian Cannon, Phillip Cooper, Karl Cummins, David Cunliffe, Jurgen Custers, Callum Duffy, Julie Duffy, Elvio (Milano), Bartok Gellert, Dave Gibson (Media Accreditation), Josef Gruber (Rapid Vienna), Lee Harrison, Poitr Jaworski (To My Kibice), LFC Rd End, LFC Urchins, Andreas Magnet, Brian Raymond, Anthony Rivers, Mark Shepherd, Simone (Milano), David Sykes, Mark Travis, Miroslav Vasilev (CSKA Sofia), Hanoracul Verde, Wigan GS, Michael Williams.

PARTIZAN – Goran A, Andrija V, Dejan B, Cegi, Combe, Davor, Jovan Ivanovic, Lubo, Aleksandar M, Zare, Pidja, Rafa, Rajko, Igor Todorovic, Mihajlo Vucinic, Zoran

AJAX – Marko, JJ

RUCH – David Hanak, Peter 'Konkret', Pawel Ossowski

BENFICA – Benfiquista, Glorioso

SPORTING – Jose, Paulo Coelho Pereira

STEAUA – 'Scouse' Robert, Alexandru S
ZELJEZNICAR – Dandi, Dino, Adnan Isajbegovic, Keki

FERENCVAROS – Nemeth Miklos

UJPEST – Zoltar

PSG – Nicolas Portero, Stephane R.